Security, Socialisation and Affect in Indian Families

Sociological research on Indian families has largely focused on questions of household form and structure, to the exclusion of not only the more nebulous dimensions of family life and relationships but also the discursive and imagined aspects of our familial worlds such as may be accessed through an analysis of film, literature and the electronic media. Moreover, when sociological inquiry has sought to go beyond the demographic and census aspects of the household, it has trained its eye on the heterosexual family centred on the conjugal couple, frequently at the expense of those relational patterns and diversities that fall outside the familiar circuits of desire within the family. The present volume brings together ten essays from a range of disciplines including law, literature, anthropology, sociology, and queer studies, to engage with hitherto neglected and emergent aspects of Indian family life.

This book was published as a special issue of *South Asia: Journal of South Asian Studies*.

Ira Raja is Assistant Professor in English at the University of Delhi, India, and Honorary Research Associate, *Thesis Eleven* Centre for Cultural Sociology, La Trobe University, Australia. She has edited *Grey Areas: An Anthology of Contemporary Indian Fiction on Ageing* (2010), with Kay Souter, *An Endless Winter's Night: Mother-Daughter Stories from India* (2010), and with John Thieme, *The Table is Laid: The Oxford Anthology of South Asian Food Writing* (2007). Her work has appeared in journals such as *South Asian History and Culture*, *Narrative*, *Thesis Eleven* and *The Journal of Commonwealth Literature*, among others.

Security, Socialisation and Affect in Indian Families

Unfamiliar Ground

Edited by
Ira Raja

LONDON AND NEW YORK

First published 2014 by Routledge

2 Park Square, Milton Park, Abingdon, Oxfordshire OX14 4RN
711 Third Avenue, New York, NY 10017

Routledge is an imprint of the Taylor & Francis Group, an informa business

First issued in paperback 2018

Copyright © 2014 South Asian Studies Association of Australia

All rights reserved. No part of this book may be reprinted or reproduced or utilised in any form or by any electronic, mechanical, or other means, now known or hereafter invented, including photocopying and recording, or in any information storage or retrieval system, without permission in writing from the publishers.

Notice:
Product or corporate names may be trademarks or registered trademarks, and are used only for identification and explanation without intent to infringe.

British Library Cataloguing in Publication Data
A catalogue record for this book is available from the British Library

ISBN13: 978-0-415-62201-1 (hbk)
ISBN13: 978-1-138-38301-2 (pbk)

Typeset in Times New Roman
by Taylor & Francis Books

Publisher's Note
The publisher accepts responsibility for any inconsistencies that may have arisen during the conversion of this book from journal articles to book chapters, namely the possible inclusion of journal terminology.

Disclaimer
Every effort has been made to contact copyright holders for their permission to reprint material in this book. The publishers would be grateful to hear from any copyright holder who is not here acknowledged and will undertake to rectify any errors or omissions in future editions of this book.

Contents

Citation Information   vii
Notes on Contributors   ix

1. Introduction
   Ira Raja   1

2. Chosen Families and Self-Transformations in Dhan Gopal Mukerji's Books for Children, 1920s–1930s
   Rimli Bhattacharya   7

3. The Romance of Siblinghood in Bombay Cinema
   Ruth Vanita   23

4. Aliens, Aliases, Surrogates and Familiars: The Family in Jhumpa Lahiri's Short Stories
   Deepika Bahri   35

5. Contested Representations of Remittances and the Transnational Family
   Supriya Singh and Anuja Cabraal   48

6. In/dependence, Intergenerational Uncertainty, and the Ambivalent State: Perceptions of Old Age Security in India
   Sarah Lamb   63

7. Contractarianism and the Ethic of Care in Indian Fiction
   Ira Raja   77

8. Feminist Mothering? Some Reflections on Sexuality and Risk from Urban India
   Shilpa Phadke   90

9. My Brother's Keeper: Regulation of the Brother–Sister Relationship in the Religious Personal Laws of India
   Archana Parashar and Vijaya Nagarajan   105

10. Desirable or Dysfunctional? Family in Recent Indian English-Language Fiction
    Paul Sharrad   121

CONTENTS

11. White and Indian? Intermarriage and Narrative Authority
 in South Asian American Fiction
 Shameem Black 132

 Index 147

Citation Information

The chapters in this book were originally published in *South Asia: Journal of South Asian Studies*, volume 36, issue 1 (March 2013). When citing this material, please use the original page numbering for each article, as follows:

Chapter 1
Introduction
Ira Raja
South Asia: Journal of South Asian Studies, volume 36, issue 1 (March 2013) pp. 3-8

Chapter 2
Chosen Families and Self-Transformations in Dhan Gopal Mukerji's Books for Children, 1920s–1930s
Rimli Bhattacharya
South Asia: Journal of South Asian Studies, volume 36, issue 1 (March 2013) pp. 9-24

Chapter 3
The Romance of Siblinghood in Bombay Cinema
Ruth Vanita
South Asia: Journal of South Asian Studies, volume 36, issue 1 (March 2013) pp. 25-36

Chapter 4
Aliens, Aliases, Surrogates and Familiars: The Family in Jhumpa Lahiri's Short Stories
Deepika Bahri
South Asia: Journal of South Asian Studies, volume 36, issue 1 (March 2013) pp. 37-49

Chapter 5
Contested Representations of Remittances and the Transnational Family
Supriya Singh and Anuja Cabraal
South Asia: Journal of South Asian Studies, volume 36, issue 1 (March 2013) pp. 50-64

Chapter 6
In/dependence, Intergenerational Uncertainty, and the Ambivalent State: Perceptions of Old Age Security in India
Sarah Lamb
South Asia: Journal of South Asian Studies, volume 36, issue 1 (March 2013) pp. 65-78

Chapter 7
Contractarianism and the Ethic of Care in Indian Fiction
Ira Raja
South Asia: Journal of South Asian Studies, volume 36, issue 1 (March 2013) pp. 79-91

Chapter 8
Feminist Mothering? Some Reflections on Sexuality and Risk from Urban India
Shilpa Phadke
South Asia: Journal of South Asian Studies, volume 36, issue 1 (March 2013) pp. 92-106

Chapter 9
My Brother's Keeper: Regulation of the Brother–Sister Relationship in the Religious Personal Laws of India
Archana Parashar and Vijaya Nagarajan
South Asia: Journal of South Asian Studies, volume 36, issue 1 (March 2013) pp. 107-122

Chapter 10
Desirable or Dysfunctional? Family in Recent Indian English-Language Fiction
Paul Sharrad
South Asia: Journal of South Asian Studies, volume 36, issue 1 (March 2013) pp. 123-133

Chapter 11
White and Indian? Intermarriage and Narrative Authority in South Asian American Fiction
Shameem Black
South Asia: Journal of South Asian Studies, volume 36, issue 1 (March 2013) pp. 134-148

Notes on Contributors

Deepika Bahri is Associate Professor in the English department at Emory University. She is the author of *Native Intelligence: Aesthetics, Politics, and Postcolonial Literature*. She is also editor of three collections of essays, *Between the Lines: South Asians and Postcoloniality*; *Realms of Rhetoric: Inquiries into the Prospects of Rhetoric Education*; and *Empire and Racial Hybridity*, a special issue of the journal, *South Asian Review*. HIV/AIDS in developing countries is a secondary research interest.

Rimli Bhattacharya studied Comparative Literature at Jadavpur and Brown Universities. She has published on gender and performance, visual culture, primary education and children's literature. Her corpus of translations of fiction and memoirs from Bangla to English includes *Binodini Dasi: My Story & My Life as an Actress*. Her ongoing research on Dhan Gopal Mukerji has been presented at various fora, and is now being finalized as a book-length study. A monograph on performance contexts and Rabindranath Tagore tentatively entitled *The Dancing Poet* is forthcoming. She currently teaches at the Department of English, University of Delhi.

Shameem Black is a Research Fellow in the School of Cultural Inquiry at the Australian National University. She is the author of *Fiction Across Borders: Imagining the Lives of Others in Late Twentieth-Century Novels* (Columbia University Press, 2010). Her work on contemporary literature and globalization has appeared in *Public Culture, Social Text, Modern Fiction Studies*, and other journals. Her current research concerns the role of fiction in contemporary contexts of transitional justice and humanitarian crisis.

Anuja Cabraal is an anthropologist and sociologist. Her PhD is on microfinance in Australia from RMIT University. She is currently a researcher with the Smart Services Cooperative Research Centre at the Graduate School of Business and Law, RMIT University, Melbourne, Australia.

Sarah Lamb is Professor of Anthropology and co-chair of the South Asian Studies Program at Brandeis University in Massachusetts, USA. Her primary ethnographic research has been carried out in West Bengal, India and among Indian immigrants in the San Francisco and Boston areas of the United States. She is the author of *White Saris and Sweet Mangoes: Aging, Gender and Body in Northeast India* (2000) and *Aging and the Indian Diaspora: Cosmopolitan Families in India and*

Abroad (2009), and co-editor (with Diane Mines) of *Everyday Life in South Asia* (2002 and 2010).

Vijaya Nagarajan is a Senior Lecturer at Macquarie University, Sydney. Her research is in the area of regulation, gender and legal geography. She is currently examining the interface of regulation and gender, and the diverse dimensions of economic regulation including corporate governance and sustainability as well as competition law and the public interest. She has completed a number of consultancies and publications in these areas. Recent publications include 'Regulating for Women on Corporate Boards: Polycentric Governance in Australia', 'Obstacles to Growth: Gender, Discrimination and Development in Tonga' and 'Co-opting for Governance: Use of the Conditions Power by the ACCC'.

Archana Parashar is Associate Professor of Law at Macquarie University, Sydney. Her research interests focus on the potential of law to achieve social justice, and include areas of critical legal theory, feminist legal theory, family law and anti-discrimination laws. Her published work includes books and articles on the topics of gender justice for women in personal law, the relevance of legal pluralism for gender justice as well as the importance of legal education in creating ethical citizens. She is the author of *Women and Family Law Reform in India* (Sage, 1992) and has co-edited (with Amita Dhanda) *Engendering Law: Essays in Honour of Lotika Sarkar* (Eastern Law Books, 1999); *Redefining Family Law in India* (Routledge, 2008); and *Decolonisation of Legal Knowledge* (Routledge, 2009).

Shilpa Phadke is Assistant Professor at the Centre for Media and Cultural Studies, Tata Institute of Social Sciences, Mumbai. She has been educated at the Xavier's College, Mumbai, SNDT University, The Tata Institute of Social Sciences, Mumbai and the University of Cambridge, UK. She has taught undergraduate sociology and anthropology at St Xavier's College, Mumbai. As a pedagogue, she has designed and coordinated several discussion groups, a lecture series and workshops. Shilpa Phadke has published academically in journals and edited book volumes as well as in newspapers and popular magazines. Her co-authored book: *Why Loiter? Women and Risk on Mumbai Streets* was published by Penguin, 2011.

Ira Raja is Assistant Professor in English at the University of Delhi, India, and Honorary Research Associate, *Thesis Eleven* Centre for Cultural Sociology, La Trobe University, Australia. She has edited *Grey Areas: An Anthology of Contemporary Indian Fiction on Aging* (2010), with Kay Souter, *An Endless Winter's Night: Mother-Daughter Stories from India* (2010), and with John Thieme, *The Table is Laid: The Oxford Anthology of South Asian Food Writing* (2007). Her work has appeared in journals such as *South Asian History and Culture*, *Narrative*, *Thesis Eleven*, and *The Journal of Commonwealth Literature*, among others.

Paul Sharrad teaches Postcolonial Writing at the University of Wollongong, Australia, with special interests in India and the Pacific. He has books on Raja Rao, Albert Wendt, and Postcolonial literary history and Indian English fiction, and has published also on Australian, Caribbean and Southeast Asian writing. He was editor of the *CRNLE Reviews Journal* and *New Literatures Review* and is currently editor for the New Literatures section of *The Year's Work in English Studies*.

NOTES ON CONTRIBUTORS

Supriya Singh is Professor of Business and Law at RMIT University, Melbourne, where she heads the Community Sustainability Program of the Global Cities Institute. She is also a senior project leader in the Smart Services Cooperative Research Centre at RMIT Business; and Deputy Head, Research, Graduate School of Business and Law, RMIT. Supriya Singh's research on money and the Indian diaspora builds on her work on money, marriage and banking in Australia, *Marriage Money: The Social Shaping of Money in Marriage and Banking* (Allen & Unwin, 1997).

Ruth Vanita teaches at the University of Montana and was formerly Reader in the English Department, Delhi University. A well-known critic, translator and poet, she is the author of several books, including *Sappho and the Virgin Mary: same-sex Love and the English Literary Imagination*, and the co-edited *Same-Sex Love in India:a Literary History*. Her latest book is *Gender, Sex and the City: Urdu Rekhti Poetry in India, 1780-1870* (2012). She is currently working on a book on courtesans in Bombay cinema.

Introduction

IRA RAJA

Sociological research on Indian families has largely focused on questions of household form and structure, to the exclusion of not only the more nebulous dimensions of family life and relationships[1] but also the discursive and imagined aspects of the familial worlds we inhabit. As Kalpana Kannabiran observes, compared to the abundance of empirical field studies on family-household systems, little research has been done on the construction of the idea of the family in film, literature, television, and the new media.[2] Moreover, in general when sociological inquiry has sought to go beyond the demographic and census aspects of the household, it has trained its eye on the heterosexual family built around the conjugal couple.[3] Conjugality is only one aspect of the rich texture of Indian family life. And yet the entire discourse of modernity appears to hinge on a model of conjugality based on equality and affection as distinguished from the oppressive conjugality of 'traditional' families.[4] As Indrani Chatterjee asks: 'What significance did the overwhelming focus on affect and conjugality during the nineteenth century have for a contemporary obfuscation of friendship and patronage, for the representation and rigors of service relationships, for the obliteration of stratification within the family and the household? How have these erasures, in turn, conditioned contemporary scholarship?'[5] To add to Chatterjee's list of questions: how do we explain sociological inquiry's marginalisation of those relational patterns and diversities that fall outside the familiar circuits of desire within the family? What, in the words of Kannabiran, might be the politics behind this exclusion?[6]

The idea for this special volume of essays on Indian families originated with a one-day workshop, 'Family Ties: Security, Socialization and Affect in Indian Families' held on 11 September 2009 at La Trobe University, Melbourne. The workshop was co-organised by Ira Raja, Kay Souter and Trevor Hogan, on behalf of the *Thesis Eleven* Centre for Cultural Sociology. It was made possible through the generous support of the Australia-India Council (Australian Department of Foreign Affairs and Trade), the Faculty of Humanities and Social Sciences, La Trobe University, and the Institute of Postcolonial Studies, Melbourne.

[1] Patricia Uberoi, 'The Family in India: Beyond the Nuclear versus Joint Debate', in Veena Das (ed.), *The Oxford Companion to Sociology and Social Anthropology* (Delhi: Oxford University Press, 2003), p.1073.

[2] Kalpana Kannabiran, 'Three Dimensional Family: Remapping a Multidisciplinary Approach to Family Studies', in *Economic and Political Weekly* (21 Oct. 2006), p.4430.

[3] A.M. Shah, *The Family in India: Critical Essays* (New Delhi: Orient Longman, 1998); and Kannabiran, 'Three Dimensional Family', p.4431.

[4] Kannabiran, 'Three Dimensional Family', p.4431.

[5] Indrani Chatterjee, 'Introduction', in Indrani Chatterjee (ed.), *Unfamiliar Relations: Family and History in South Asia* (Delhi: Permanent Black, 2004), pp.4–5.

[6] Kannabiran, 'Three Dimensional Family', p.4427.

Family is rightly identified as the place where gender roles are first learnt and reproduced,[7] but what do we know of gender role socialisation other than the rites of puberty and marriage of girls aimed at inculcating norms of feminine subservience? How have the conventions of gender role socialisation changed for young girls from urban middle-class families whose childhood is increasingly becoming closer to Western norms and values? Relatedly, what might be some of the dilemmas faced by mothers who welcome the liberating validation of new gender roles which privilege sexuality as a valued expression of female subjectivity, but who are deeply suspicious of the regime of consumer choices (and its hopelessly limited understanding of individual agency) which is partly responsible for the availability of these new roles in the first place?

In India it is families which are primarily responsible for providing welfare and ensuring individuals against vulnerability and destitution. But our understanding of the everyday choices and struggles involved in fulfilling those roles remains quite limited. How do Indian families, we might ask, deal with the task of caring for the older generation in the context of increasing life spans coupled with a singular absence, not to mention suspicion, of state support?[8]

The ideology of the joint family continues to influence resource distribution within a family even when most of its members spend some or the greater part of their lives in nuclear households.[9] What does this tell us about the relationship between materiality and affect? Are affective relationships, such as those between brothers and sisters, sustained despite or because of one party surrendering its material interests in the name of the other? How different is this from an active mobilisation of material assets as the means of maintaining affective links, as in the case of transnational families?

The present collection of articles on various aspects of the Indian family engages with many of the questions raised above. The volume opens with Rimli Bhattacharya's essay, 'Chosen Families and Self-Transformations in Dhan Gopal Mukerji's Books for Children, 1920s–1930s'. These were first published in English for a 'non-Indian audience' in the United States of America. Bhattacharya focuses on Mukerji's deployment of the imagined family as an implicit response to the emerging trajectories of nationalist consciousness in India. However unlike the utopian, idealised family central to the politics of nationalism, the family in Mukerji's fiction is not available as a pre-existing site of uncompromised selfhood offering Indians a subject position from which to address and resist their colonial masters.[10] Mukerji's writings foreground as his protagonist an adolescent boy whose socialisation involves a turning outwards and away from the biological family and the 'home', towards non-kin figures such as the guru, and birds, beasts and other living creatures from the natural world. If inclusiveness is one aspect of this reconstructed family, the other is its privileging of certain norms such as sacrifice, kindness, courage and determination, which became central to the discipline of the Gandhian *satyagrahi* whose concept of service as devotion insinuated a critical alternative to the imperial notion of service inscribed in Rudyard Kipling's 'The White Man's Burden'. While Mukerji's re-imagined family at once challenges imperial, colonial, and modernist discourses, Bhattacharya's analysis also draws attention to the paradoxes of his

---

[7] Catherine Belsey, 'Denaturalizing the Family: History at the Level of the Signifier,' in *European Journal of Cultural Studies*, Vol.4, no.3 (2001), p.290.
[8] See Sarah Lamb, 'In/dependence, Intergenerational Uncertainty, and the Ambivalent State: Perceptions of Old Age Security in India', in this issue.
[9] Uberoi, 'The Family in India', p.1073.
[10] Dipesh Chakrabarty, 'Postcoloniality and the Artifice of History: Who Speaks for "Indian" Pasts?' in *Representations*, Vol.37 (1992), p.17.

project: how is one to reconcile the violence of war with the violence of self-sacrifice? What does it mean to propose the universalisation of 'Brahmanhood' as a means of overcoming the divisions of caste? How might we explain the privileging of a model of feminine devotion with the textual elision of female presence?

Prominent among Mukerji's many literary debts is the one he owes to the ancient epics of India for the value they placed on the ability of their various wandering protagonists to form a chosen family. Ruth Vanita's essay, 'The Romance of Siblinghood in Bombay Cinema', picks up this thread of a pre-modern kinship ideal in which a magnanimous embracing of the world-as-one-family is pitted against a narrow-minded distinction between relatives and strangers. Much like the world of Mukerji's fiction, Bombay cinema endows non-sexual relationships, such as those between friends and siblings, with an emotional intensity equal to that of sexual relationships. In thus resisting the tendency of heterosexual coupledom to monopolise the meaning of inter-personal intimacy, Bombay cinema also appears to challenge the idea that the monogamous conjugal family unit of the contemporary Western type is necessarily the most 'advanced' type of family kinship organisation, one which is not only functionally suited to the demands of modern industrial society, but whose institutionalisation of individual freedom to choose signals a social and political ideal which is constructed as morally superior to the patriarchal joint family characteristic of South Asia.[11] As Vanita notes, choosing sibling, friend or community over a spouse alone is often cast in Bombay cinema as the embracing of a more varied and complex ideal of emotional interdependence and family relations. This is underscored in Bombay cinema's ongoing tendency to glorify the chosen family as much as the biological one. In the emotional economy of films such as *Bombai ka Babu* (1960), *Naam* (1986) and *Kabhi Khushi Kabhie Gham* (2001), to choose family (in its widest sense) over the romantic couple is not always an act of retrogressive self-sacrifice but one aimed at securing an individual's emotional well-being. The true lover is one who understands this, and therefore does not force the beloved to make a mutually exclusive choice. Perhaps, the most significant theme of Bombay cinema is the reality of the so-called fictive family. Love, more than biology, defines who is family, and villains are characterised by their failure to perceive the truth of this distinction.

The subcontinental penchant for establishing familial relationships with non-kin however should not be seen to imply a lack of awareness of the limits of family or its functional structure. Indeed, family relationships are identified with remarkable precision in India. Deepika Bahri notes how extending the familial bounds can be read as a defensive move to disarm and contain the threat that the stranger could potentially pose to the family. In this way the very gesture of symbolically assimilating the outsider as part of the familial unit becomes a way of distinguishing family from non-family. In 'Aliens, Aliases, Surrogates and Familiars: The Family in Jhumpa Lahiri's Short Stories', Bahri foregrounds an opposition between the familiar and the unfamiliar as characteristic of the affective experience of transnational migration in selected short stories by Jhumpa Lahiri about post-1965 Indian immigrants to the United States. In Lahiri's stories the immigrant's isolation and alienation provoke deep-rooted anxieties that have largely been contained in those more 'settled' in the real, 'true' America. Likewise, when immigrant characters in these stories encounter the 'otherness' of mainstream American lives, they are frequently met with the shock of recognition. Bahri's essay thus challenges conventional readings of the family as the site of a reassuring continuity in an alien environment to show how, beyond the threshold, it is not the stranger but the family that is revealed to be not always familiar.

---

[11] Uberoi, 'The Family in India', pp.1065–7.

Not only does migration overturn conventional understandings of the family in the diaspora, it also changes the mode of relating to the family that is left behind. In their essay 'Contested Representations of Remittances and the Transnational Family', Supriya Singh and Anuja Cabraal examine the changing meanings that attach to the idea of money in mediating relations in the transnational Indian family across generations and life stages. Money in India flows not just from parents to children but also from children to parents. It may be offered as a ritual gift to mark life stages such as birth, marriage and death, or it may be given in response to a financial need as an outward expression of filial relationships. Remittances sent home signify a migrant's overt expression of belonging to and caring for the transnational family. However as the relationship with the transnational family changes, the meaning of money changes with it: when pitted against the acts of physical caregiving provided by other family members, usually siblings in the home country, the value of the money sent may not be the same as the value of the money received. This discrepancy may be understood in terms of the failure of money to sufficiently signify intimacy and care. But when links between the transnational family attenuate, and the mode of maintaining affective relations changes from remittances to gifts, conventional understanding of gifts as being more intimate than money is overturned to show how it is money that now counts as the currency of closeness.

If Singh and Cabraal view matters from the migrant's perspective, Sarah Lamb's essay, 'In/dependence, Intergenerational Uncertainty, and the Ambivalent State: Perceptions of Old Age Security in India', turns to the recipients of remittances, in particular older parents. In her study of old age homes in Kolkata, Lamb notes that although institutional care is on the rise, co-residence across generations remains by far the most common living arrangement for India's elderly. In the population demographic that has been relatively more accepting of old age homes, the financially-solvent parents of children who have relocated to the West are the most common, albeit that their reasons for accepting institutional care are found to be quite different than those of older people in the West. Many residents, for instance, muse that it is not natural for human beings to live alone, and that life in an old age home is potentially less alienating than what for them would have been the alternative option of living by themselves. But acceptance of institutional living even on these culturally qualified grounds is not commonly found. For most residents, living in an old age home is typically associated with shame, shock, and a painful sense of having been abandoned by family. Lamb's essay thus offers a contrast to international development discourses which frequently depict the availability of state and market-based programs for old age security as signs of progress. Evidently, in India, an autonomous existence secured through the paid services of an institution is not necessarily preferable to the messy business of human interdependence in the traditional family, just as the confines of an old age home are finally more attractive compared to an independent but lonely life outside institutional care.

But what might constitute the lived experience of human interdependence for older people who do live with the family on a day-to-day basis? After all, a major function of the family is to nurture and care for those who are unable to care for themselves. Indian sociologists have only recently started to take note of how families cope with the stresses of caregiving. In 'Contractarianism and the Ethic of Care in Indian Fiction', I take this line of inquiry into the literary domain by examining a series of stories by notable Indian women writers, which show adult daughters caring for their seriously ill or dying mothers. Not quite the perfect subject of a bourgeois patriarchal family, daughters in this fiction are mostly depicted as unmarried, divorced or childless—social positions which equip them with the 'freedom' and the resources to care for their mothers. Conversely, in stories where the daughter is well-adjusted as wife and mother, her caregiving relationship to her own mother is shown to end in grief. My essay foregrounds the contested nature of care in India, particularly for daughters in the patrilineal

North where the sharp opposition between a woman's role as wife and her role as sister/daughter can make it difficult for her to assume a caregiving role in relation to her own parents. But what truly intensifies the contested nature of care in these stories is their pitting of the woman's role as wife not against her role as a patrilineal kinswoman, but against her role as her mother's daughter—the one dyadic relationship that goes unmentioned among the issues that have dominated cross-cultural research on the family in India.

Mothers and daughters are also the focus of Shilpa Phadke's essay 'Feminist Mothering? Some Reflections on Sexuality and Risk from Urban India'. While the sociology and anthropology of childhood in India are new and virtually non-existent fields of inquiry,[12] one aspect which has been studied is the socialisation of the girl child, especially the variety of social mechanisms through which she is made to internalise a feminine gender identity. Still, the rich ethnography of the 'traditional' sector of Indian society in this area of study remains unmatched by comparable work on the urban and more 'modern' sector.[13] With Phadke's essay we turn to a re-imagination of childhood for the middle classes under the new consumerism of a globalising economy which views childhood and adolescence as distinctive life stages to be plied with their own sets of consumer goods and services.[14] Through a close analysis of the daily decisions taken over clothing, fashion, consumption, sexualisation, sexuality education, and sexual choices, Phadke explores the dilemmas of mothers whose attempts to think through the competing desirable goals of freedom and safety for their daughters frequently run into the vexed question of how to reconcile a radical anti-capitalist feminist politics with a cultural context in which the exercise of a limited and limiting consumer choice often passes for feminist practice.

An important mechanism of sex role socialisation in Indian families is the sex-differentiated allocation of family resources.[15] In the North Indian patrilineal kinship system, in particular, a young girl is quickly made aware that her stay in her parental home is meant to be brief and that once she is married into another family, except in the case of extreme adversity, her responsibilities and entitlements lie with that family alone.[16] In 'My Brother's Keeper: Regulation of the Brother–Sister Relationship in the Religious Personal Laws of India', Archana Parashar and Vijaya Nagarajan examine how 'kinship ideologies' or ideas about how the family is constituted and how it functions inform the extent to which the laws of succession determine the distribution of resources within the family.[17] Focusing on the specific aspect of religious personal laws dealing with the inheritance rights of brothers and sisters, the essay examines how concepts that underwrite the discourse around these laws create the spaces for the law to maintain gender hierarchies. In Hindu (and even Indian) society, they argue, a sister is more likely to sacrifice her right to property in her father's estate than disrupt social expectations of how she should behave towards her brothers. Such decisions are as much an effect of being steeped in kinship ideology as they are of a social reality in which a married woman needs to be able to count on the ongoing support of her brothers lest her marriage falls apart. Unless legal scholars take into account women's

---

[12] Vasanthi Raman, 'The Diverse Life-Worlds of Indian Childhood', in Margrit Pernau, Imtiaz Ahmad and Helmut Reifeld (eds), *Family and Gender: Changing Values in Germany and India* (New Delhi: Sage, 2003), p.87.

[13] Uberoi, 'The Family in India', pp.1081–2.

[14] *Ibid.*, p.1082.

[15] *Ibid.*, pp.1082–3.

[16] Imtiaz Ahmad, 'Between the Ideal and the Real: Gender Relations within the Indian Joint Family', in Margrit Pernau, Imtiaz Ahmad and Helmut Reifeld (eds), *Family and Gender: Changing Values in Germany and India* (New Delhi: Sage, 2003), p.42.

[17] Uberoi, 'The Family in India', p.1077.

particular locations and the constitutive realities of their lives, the authors conclude, the grant of legislative and constitutional rights to Indian (Hindu) women will continue to fail the test of promoting gender parity.

Parashar and Nagarajan's foregrounding of gender asymmetries in the allocation of family resources questions populist conceptions of the ideal family as one where benevolence is the governing principle in family relations.[18] Thus Paul Sharrad's broad overview of Indian fiction, 'Desirable or Dysfunctional? Family in Recent Indian English-Language Fiction', draws attention to the many contemporary novels which show families to be dysfunctional sites of violence, incest, extramarital affairs and divorce, issues that have not been explored at any length by sociological research into the family in India, which, as Patricia Uberoi notes, has focused much more on 'kinship *norms* than on pathology, deviance, and breakdown'.[19] Sharrad's essay also returns us to the other theme with which we opened this volume, namely the chosen family: in the novels of young professional experience, characterised by better levels of education, urbanisation, and expatriation, the biological family is replaced as the chief means of socialisation while recuperating the chosen or surrogate family as the new site of meaning and comfort.

Families in fiction are as much a measure of continuity as they are an index of change. And this applies not just to the thematic inscription of families in fiction but also to the epistemological questions that arise in its wake. Shameem Black's essay, 'White and Indian? Intermarriage and Narrative Authority in South Asian American Fiction', analyses a new and hitherto neglected genre *within* Asian American writing, to propose an interesting and necessary set of questions for consideration in Asian American Studies: 'how narratives of multiracial families might create new spaces for narrative authority within Asian American writing'.[20] Through a revaluation of Orientalist concerns against the optic of family sociality, Black forges a new understanding of the politics of identity within a family structure (rather than a national one). In her insightful analysis of Robbie Clipper Sethi's *The Bride Wore Red*, Black presents the phenomenon of white Americans looking to be accepted into a minority American group of South Asian descent, thereby challenging the sociological assumption that assimilation is a movement from minority to majority. The narrative authority of white speakers here is articulated through modes of uncertainty and alienation rather than through the confident assumptions of social power that characterised Orientalist accounts. The family in Black's analysis is not a place for the seamless replication of identity, but a place for its potential transformation. Stories of white women inscribed within the family worlds of South Asia and its diaspora, Black argues, invite us to review our understanding of who counts as 'Indian' and how they may speak. Rather than simply pushing for an expansion of the canon of Asian American literature, Black calls for an understanding of these new narrative voices as a challenge to the underlying assumptions of literary studies which fail to see the value of stories that perceived outsiders may have to tell about minority communities.

The present volume of essays attempts to address the need for a more broad-based and interdisciplinary reconstruction of the field of family studies in India. Drawn from a range of disciplines including sociology, anthropology, literature, law and cinema, the ten essays in this volume privilege repressed aspects of sociological scholarship in ways that not only extend and deepen our understanding of the field of Indian family studies, but also pick up the challenge of redefining its disciplinary edge.

---

[18] *Ibid.*, p.1084.
[19] *Ibid.*, p.1061.
[20] Shameem Black, 'White and Indian? Intermarriage and Narrative Authority in South Asian American Fiction', in this issue.

Chosen Families and Self-Transformations in Dhan Gopal Mukerji's Books for Children, 1920s–1930s

RIMLI BHATTACHARYA

In the Indian subcontinent, the understanding of 'the family' in numerous narrative traditions has always extended into relationships with non-humans, with a pivotal emphasis on the guru-shishya (preceptor-disciple) relationship. This paper focuses on the highly popular English-language 'juvenile fiction' of Dhan Gopal Mukerji to suggest how he reconfigured these narrative traditions for a primarily non-Indian audience in the 1920s–30s. The paper considers Mukerji's young protagonists—invariably male, whether human or animal—in relation to the web of familial and outside social relationships through which the 'quest motif' is played out for a transnational readership. The epic form pervades his 'jungle books' through the figures of the animal protagonists, the search for a leader/guide/guru, and a re-imagining of caste, ethnicity and gender. Of particular interest is the composite mother figure. Dhan Gopal's oeuvre for children maps out a socialisation that is 'free' of the apparatus of the colonial home or of other disciplining institutional sites. Paradoxically, the search to be 'free from fear' can only be played in the alternative topos *of the jungle, where violence is inescapable. How, if at all, may these narrative tropes be mapped onto contemporary history?*

In the Indian subcontinent, the understanding of 'the family' in numerous narrative traditions has always extended into relationships with non-humans (as in the *Panchatantra*, *Hitupadesa* and most notably, the *Jatakas*), with a pivotal emphasis on the *guru-shishya* (preceptor-disciple) relationship (as seen in the epics, the *Mahabharata* and *Ramayana*). In recent times historians have rightly questioned any overarching normative frame of the family, which often erases the multiple forms of familial relations available in different cultures at specific historical moments. Contemporary writers, artists and filmmakers—as wide-ranging as Ritwik Ghatak, Salman Rushdie, Kumar Shahani and Vivan Sundaram—have narrativised the family in their own medium through the lens of myth and archetype, while playing with multiple subjectivities in specific historical moments/contingencies.

I consider here an early example of how a little-studied but much-published Indian author, living in the United States of America and writing in English, drew on some of these narrative traditions yet reconfigured them for a primarily non-Indian audience during the interwar years, 1920s–30s. Dhan Gopal Mukerji (1890–1936), who migrated to the USA in the early twentieth century, was as much engaged in finding a new audience as he was in rewriting

---

My thanks to Devaki Bhaya, Ira Raja, Kumar Shahani, the late Dhan Gopal Mukerji Jr. and Marianne Mukerji for their support at different times. I thank also the anonymous reviewers of this paper for their critical queries.

Kipling's Indian jungle.[1] Hailed for his 'superb epics of jungle life', Mukerji's *oeuvre* in English, the bulk of which was aimed specifically at children, was published by E.P. Dutton & Co. in the USA and translated into various European languages *as well as* into Bangla. He was the winner of the Newbery Medal for children's fiction in 1928. For reasons of space I have not dealt here with his considerable corpus of English-language publications which include his autobiography (*Caste and Outcaste*, 1923), travelogues (*My Brother's Face*, 1925, and *Visit India with Me*, 1929), and his response to Katherine Mayo's *Mother India* (1927). In these books, some of which emerged from his visits 'home', Mukerji tried consciously to record the many changes taking place in contemporary India. By contrast, Mukerji himself, and most certainly his publishers, saw his juvenile fiction as a genre distinct from his other work. His foreword to *Bunny, Hound and Clown* (1931), and several of his interviews, make clear that he meant these entertaining stories to be 'tales of wisdom'.[2] The introduction to his last novel, *Fierce-Face: The Story of a Tiger* (1936), written in the year of his death by suicide, is written as if he had his back to the wall. Acknowledging modern modes of apprehending and processing—the speed and 'angularity' of the 'camera-bred eye' as he calls it—he affirms having 'still' retained his 'mystical beliefs' in the 'Hindu belief that Man, nature, and animal life are but facets of the Divine'.[3] My reading of 'the family' in Mukerji's children's fiction follows from the tensions and contradictions of this particular project—of highlighting 'modern modes of apprehension' while affirming a non-hierarchical continuum of all living creatures (not exclusive to 'Hindu belief', I may add). The language of fiction—its sensory and affective qualities; the self-conscious forging of a 'poetic idiom'—is integral to his narrative.

Mukerji's protagonists in his 'jungle books' include boy, bird and/or animals. In some instances (*Chief of the Herd*, 1929, and *Fierce-Face*), where the locus is clearly the animal kingdom, socialisation is mapped out like a coming-of-age—through initiation, the tests and tribulations of childhood and adolescence, mating and motherhood. The presence of new offspring and their movement towards self-realisation is suggestive of a cycle of regeneration, rather than closure. Further, in exploring the virtues and the dynamic trajectory of leadership in the context of the *herd*, a later novel like *Chief of the Herd* explicitly moves beyond the nuclear family into a notion of extended families and the larger community. More frequently, where human protagonists are concerned (*Jungle Beasts and Men*, 1923, *Gay-Neck: The Story of a Pigeon*, 1927, and *Ghond the Hunter*, 1928), socialisation involves an initial movement *away* from the biological family and the 'home'. The family is effectively reconfigured through the *possibilities* of co-operation to make a community (even where killing is necessary), rather than already available as a microcosm of any overarching idea of the nation. I argue that Mukerji is extending the idea of the family, not simply by increasing numbers (as the herd might suggest) or in being more inclusive (birds, beasts and humans figuring together), but in focusing on interdependence and showing (particularly in scenes of drought or flood) modes of co-operation, This aspect, along with the absence of *any single* authority figure in the fiction, may be read as a librartory, if utopic, move.

An epic-like structure privileges the trope of wandering/wondering, involving the search for and the companionship of 'guru-like' figures. The guru or guide may be a tribal hunter, a

---

[1] In his autobiographical *Caste and Outcast*, Mukerji refers to Kipling as 'a brilliant painter of Indian life', emphasising thereby his own 'insider' status: 'I use the word painter advisedly, for everything that the eye alone takes in, that Mr. Kipling not only sees but takes in. No one however, except a Hindu, to whom the religion of his country is more real than all material aspects put together, can understand Indian life from within'. D.G. Mukerji, *Caste and Outcast* (New York: E.P. Dutton & Co., 1923), pp.3–4.

[2] D.G. Mukerji, *Bunny, Hound and Clown* (New York: E.P. Dutton & Co., 1931).

[3] D.G. Mukerji, Dorothy Lathrop (illus.), *Fierce-Face: The Story of a Tiger* (New York: E.P. Dutton & Co., 1936).

mother, or occasionally an identifiable spiritual head such as a priest or lama. The guide may also be an animal, as in the early novel *Kari the Elephant* (1922), or the bird in *Gay-Neck*. In all instances knowledge is *experienced* (rather than learnt in institutionalised spaces) with either one or a combination of such figures, with the boy protagonist 'acting' outside the domestic in the world of 'nature'. Here nature interpenetrates and often generates a new sense of community. Socialisation, as in learning skills appropriate to Brahmins and Kshatriyas, as well as honing abstract and overarching qualities of overcoming fear, take place in locations that range from the Himalayan foothills, river banks and the Sunderban delta, to the battlefields of World War I in France.[4]

By the nineteenth century there was already a well-worn path for generic animal stories in children's fiction that included a dash of natural history. *The Horn Book*, which regularly reviewed Mukerji's work, even had a category entitled 'animal stories'. However the particular mode of socialisation privileged in Mukerji's fiction is in response to multiple contexts of representation, which have both historical and civilisational dimensions. If he writes in the aftermath of war-scarred Europe with its sense of a 'crisis of civilisation', he writes equally in response to the emerging trajectories of nationalist consciousness in colonial India. In terms of literary genealogies, Mukerji's jungle books should also be counterposed against the long tradition of dime novels and the genre of the 'western', which John Williams has characterised as a transplantation of the New England Calvinist 'elemental conflict' between 'Good' and 'Evil' onto a 'Western' landscape.[5]

This Janus-faced act of representation taking place in Mukerji's children's fiction is specific to his location in the USA and the act of writing in English. His first imperative is to 'inform' his readers about a certain version of India—in part shaped by the constraints imposed by his publisher—which we may refer to as 'the Hindu jungle'. (I use this appellation with sympathetic irony.) His readership was mainly in the USA, but included—through multiple translations—readers in European languages such as French, German and Czech, as well as Bengali readers in colonial India. This links to the second strand of enactment: what part of the 'old' pre-colonial India does Mukerji privilege in his representation of the jungle? To what extent does his jungle become a repository of timeless Eastern values? What would be the nature of the affective in the relationships between bird, beast and human? Does this envision a space outside the imperial-colonial, or actually posit a post-colonial *imaginaire*?

These questions can be explored through the figure of the mother (biological or foster) who has a strong if marginal presence in these books otherwise bereft of female characters. Mukerji's figuration of the mother is not quite a reiteration of the trope of the motherland dear to various discourses of nationalism and post-colonialism. Rather, his mother (bird, beast, human), appearing in critical moments as a teacher/guide, is a composite figure of knowledge, strength, heroism and self-sacrifice. Drawing on the rationalist underpinnings of the discourse of natural history, she is also a strategist in her teaching of survival skills. There is even something of the nurturing mother in the figure of the *male* hunter or priest. The already-complex lineages of this mother figure thus take on new signification.

The epic form pervades the 'jungle books' through the figures of the animal protagonists, the search for a leader/guide/guru, the guru's tests, and involves a re-imagining of caste,

---

[4] Mukerji and his wife decided to move to France in the aftermath of the Asian Exclusion Act of 1924. Much of *Gay-Neck* was written there. Conversation with author's son, D.G. Mukherji Jr., Hilton Head Island, USA, 1 May 2008.
[5] John Williams, 'The "Western": Definition of the Myth', in *The Nation* (18 Nov. 1961), p.401.

ethnicity and gender. The jungle, as the non-domestic, non-urban (not settled), non-institutional space, affords a site for experimenting with interpenetrative discourses of kinship, hierarchy and social relations. This paper also focuses on Mukerji's young protagonists—invariably male, whether human or animal—in relation to the web of familial and outside social relationships through which the 'quest motif' is played out for a transnational readership.

Today one does not read Mukerji with the innocence of his original readers in early twentieth-century North America, or even of the Bengali child in India, to whom some of the books spoke in 'original Bangla' in the 1930s and 1940s. (Two novels superbly translated 'back' into Bangla, *Gay-Neck* as *Chitragreeb* and *Chief of the Herd* as *Juthopati*, may have something to do with this perception.[6]) On re-reading them as an adult and as a literary critic, post-'Orientalism', it is curious how one is still somewhat impelled to 'let the story speak', even in those instances (*Jungle Beasts and Men*) which parade all possible stereotypes of 'the East': tigers, elephants, snakes, snake-charmers and magicians!

Rites of Passage

The nameless boy protagonist is woven in and out of Mukerji's juvenile fiction. As an adolescent first person narrator he is located both inside and outside. Caste is crucial to this construction, for 'the Brahmin lineage' that is underscored explicitly and implicitly encourages his period of wandering, whereas in other contemporary children's fiction, it is being abandoned, getting lost, the death of a parent/parents, kidnapping, or the classic case of running away from home that enables this period of freedom. The boy is free from the constraints of domesticity (the care and restraining/disciplining authority of guardian figures) and, for the middle-class child, from that ultimate space of surveillance and regulation, the school.

Instead Mukerji employs stretches of willed 'wandering' entailing temporary spells of not having a regular home. Wandering also offers freedom from the usual regulations of caste. Paradoxically, however, it is the particular caste *and gender* location that allows for stages and phases of openness and permeability *as part of* the obligations or 'the dharma' of the caste. For instance, wandering 'as a mendicant' is a necessary rite of passage for a Brahmin boy: it is a 'pilgrimage' without a pre-determined end. Wandering allows Mukerji to present the first person narrator as the naive beholder, and simultaneously as one who has already internalised the essential guidelines for living and experienced life through the code of conduct enjoined on him *as a Brahmin boy*. At a very explicit level, the code is expressed in a certain 'detachment' from the very experience that he is going through. The adolescent experiencing self is remarkably poised, discriminating and rarely confused. There may be instances of mistaken judgment and periods of uncertainty and anxiety, but more often than not the guide or guru actually shares these states of mind. In *Gay-Neck*, there is such a strong overlapping of subjectivities by the eponymous pigeon, the boy narrator and the tribal hunter Ghond, that it is impossible to consider them as separate characters. Ghond and Gay-Neck metamorphose into World War I scouts in the second part of the novel; even here, when the boy is physically absent, the recounting of these episodes by the bird-narrator creates for the reader an intertwined experiential self.

---

[6] Suresh Chandra Banerji translated *Gay-Neck* as *Chitragreeb*, and *Chief of the Herd* as *Juthopati*. The original dates of publication are not given in the available reprints of the two novels (Calcutta: M.C. Sarkar and Sons, BS 1396/1989).

This seems a rather unconventional representation of the view of adolescence that had entered the disciplinary domains of anthropology and psychoanalysis by the early twentieth century. I will suggest however that Mukerji is partly drawing on models from the *Ramayana* and the *Mahabharata*, where the young princes are removed from the shelter of their royal courts and taken on 'a tour' of the larger world. This rite of passage, culminating in marriage, is both a broadening of their vision, of 'knowing' their future kingdom, of acquiring and testing magical weapons and, of course, of their prowess. In between, there is the slaying of the odd demon or two. Commenting on the formulaic initiation of the hero in the *Ramayana*, Robert Antoine notes:

> Rama's insatiable thirst for knowledge is matched by Visvamitra's inexhaustible store of mythical lore. The question-answer method gives to the compiler an almost indefinite scope for collecting legends of all kinds, several of which must have had their independent existence as epic songs.[7]

What does this extreme curiosity (*param kautuhalam*) on the part of the hero indicate? We may draw several conclusions: that the hero cannot act blindly; that every action has a context and a history; and that even names (of places and people) have histories and reasons, and the way to understand the self is through an understanding of one's environment, the now in relation to the many pasts. Thus, when the hero has to act (often to kill), the ground is prepared for the listener-reader through the innumerable contexts already suggested or created. Although the *Mahabharata* shares many of the features of the *Ramayana*, the *Mahabharata* privileges ambivalence, whereas the *Ramayana* upholds the 'literality of the word'.[8]

In *Gay-Neck*, the narrator and his companion, Radja, the son of a priest, wander with Ghond through villages, cities, vast un-peopled spaces, across and past all manner of topography (mountains, rivers, jungles); and are free to seek refuge with whoever grants them hospitality. However this does not imply a passive taking in of sights and sounds, of thrilling adventures which foreground a quick choreography of encounter, confrontation and combat, and which end with the death of one of the participants. Although Mukerji's fiction *does* include these characteristics of adventure fiction, there is a radical reorientation. I read the underlying text as being an *active* quest for a guru (or several gurus)—mentor figures from whom the boys will learn about the ways of the world and about themselves. But the putative disciples have first to test the potential mentor. Scepticism, interrogation, demands of proof of hearsay and the story on the surface, as it were, therefore inform the attitude of the narrator and his friend. This continual mental jousting is punctuated (often predictably, even tediously) by so-called 'adventure sequences' as understood in much nineteenth- and twentieth-century fiction for adults as well as for 'young people'.

It appears, then, that Mukerji had or chose to work within the accepted genre of adventure fiction while consciously deciding to set his work apart by drawing on the epic hero's rite of passage. He also modelled his work on the grand epics, particularly the *Mahabharata*, by inserting 'pauses' for reflection which are linked finally to the Brahmanical ethic. Meditation, both as an event as well as the word itself, is privileged throughout all his adventure stories. All action is preceded and informed by meditation, as are the consequences. It is suggested that white men—whether high-up 'English officials' or

---

[7] Robert Antoine SJ, *Rama and the Bards* (Calcutta: Writer's Workshop, 1975), p.37.
[8] *Ibid.*, p.80.

'Russian Princes'—fail precisely because they 'act wrongly'. Although they have superior technology and resources, and are the 'masters' of the land over which they rule, they are prone to knee-jerk reactions rather than reflection; therefore they are not masters of themselves. They cannot be true 'Brahmins'!

Is the democratic intent of such narratives aimed at conceptualising a possible 'Brahminhood' for *all* citizen subjects, particularly for the young Western reader in the 'New World', whose understanding of family was becoming increasingly homogenised? But is it also, more distantly (and yet more intimately perhaps), aimed at the nation that is struggling to be born in 'remote' British India? Post-colonial and subaltern histories have invested deeply in marginal and obscure struggles or contradictions in the master narratives of nationalism *within* the Indian subcontinent. As the biographer of the revolutionary Virendranath Chattopadhyaya (1880–1937) reminds us, 'the struggle for India's freedom was not confined to India alone, but extended beyond its borders, roughly from the first decade of the last century'.[9] Dhan Gopal's elder brother, Jadu Gopal Mukherjee (1886–1976), with whom he had close ties, was deeply involved in revolutionary militarism in the Anusilan movement in Bengal (although he later turned to Gandhian ideals of service). Mukerji's early years in California brought him into contact with anarchists, socialists and several members of the Ghadar Party whose diasporic network has been well documented.[10] Gordon Chang's comprehensive 'Introduction' to the reprint of Mukerji's autobiography gives us an entry into the immigration histories on the West Coast of the USA, as well as Mukerji's own political trajectory.[11] From this complex vantage point, how would one read his repeated forays outside of the known 'social'—the structures of the colonial bourgeois normative family, and certainly outside of the urban—in his juvenile writings?

By way of a preliminary mapping, we may identify several tracks. The movement away from home and the biological family allows one to temper oneself in a grander theatre—the entire subcontinent, part of a new secular-sacred intimate knowledge of the land, water and sky. I shall come back to this later. Violence resides not only in the external world, but equally in the very mode in which one faces that world. Experience through observation is privileged; it involves training the senses and the mind. One may then act through reflection and 'heal oneself' of the violence of any extreme negative feeling—whether of abject fear or hatred. The power to thus heal by appealing 'to the subconscious' is indexed as a supreme attribute in parenting. This resonates with Mukerji's autobiography where he mentions his mother's 'strange healing power' (pp.13–14). Equally critical is 'cleansing and purification' (from fear) *before* the boy narrator/bird goes to sleep for a 'night of fruitful rest'—a part of one's waking consciousness (*Gay-Neck*, p.100; *Ghond the Hunter*, pp.58–9).

Just as the seeking protagonist is a composite figure of many 'characters', cutting through the hierarchies of the human at the summit of creation, so too is the figure of guru/guide. The absence of any *one* source of authority would appear to preclude making 'the leader' a cult figure. The mother figure as the guru/guide embodies strength, knowledge and compassion, and is also 'practical' in terms of teaching survival ethics. At the same time, one notes that she

---

[9] Nirode K. Barooah, *Chatto, the Life and Times of an Indian Anti-Imperialist in Europe* (Delhi: Oxford University Press, 2004), p.i.

[10] See Maia Ramnath, 'Two Revolutions: The Ghadar Movement and India's Radical Diaspora, 1913–1918', in *Radical History Review*, Vol.92 (Spring 2005), pp.7–30.

[11] Gordon H. Chang, 'Introduction', in G.H. Chang, Purnima Mankekar and Akhil Gupta (eds), *D.G. Mukerji's Caste and Outcast* (Stanford: Stanford University Press, rev. ed., 2002), pp.1–40. Chang's comments on the irony of the unhappiness of Mukerji's own family life (pp.33–4) were echoed during my conversations with Dhan Gopal Mukerji Jr. in 2008.

inevitably 'disappears' from the narrative once her mentoring role is over. The self-realisation of the protagonist, and his socialisation into adulthood, where he is 'free' to take on responsibilities, are all important.

Given that the twentieth century marks the beginning of legitimate mass politics the world over, Mukerji's 'retreat' into the individual, into forms of action that are meditative, and his constant interrogation of the presence and power of violence, demand further exploration. His work proposes a way of life that *might have* carried a strong secular, even anti-racist dimension, through a countering of the 'frontier spirit' or the 'pioneer ideal'—the ideal of *conquering* nature and the savages who dwell therein. The awareness of, and in that sense, 'conquest' of the inner self through a symbolic enactment of a highly-individuated and 'respectful' response to the natural world would consciously propose an alternative model, more so in the USA with its strong Calvinist and evangelical traditions. Secondly, along with the mind, the body too is disciplined, but differently from the traditions of muscular Christianity.[12] Mukerji's disciplining of the body appears to be distinct from the reconfigured traditions of asceticism mobilised in late colonial India for the cause of the nation. Mukerji's texts have no recognisable 'cause', national or otherwise; the sensory and the sensual are privileged, even celebrated.

The Quest

Nature functions in Mukerji's writings as a kind of laboratory in which the environment is *internalised* through firsthand experience, scientific observation, analysis and facts, until it ceases to be mere information. In short, the narrative allows for lessons in natural history (privileging empirical observation, rational explanations, predictable patterns and so on) for young readers; but they are woven into the mental and actual journey of the protagonists, appearing simultaneously awkward and seamless. Mukerji's wandering protagonists might seem to follow a direct line from romantic individualism which drew on early Orientalist thought from the West.[13] Several new and old discourses are interwoven to bring out the distinctive history of Mukerji's locations. I shall describe some of them here, elaborating with references to select novels.

In *Jungle Beasts and Men*, Mukerji offers an episodic frame: the first person adolescent narrator and his friend Radjah set off on their 'mendicant travels' passing through country and town. Much of the narrative reflects the Bengali intelligentsia's penchant for heroic Rajput sagas from the mid nineteenth century onwards. But there is a sudden paradigm shift in Chapter VII, 'The Himalayas and the River Bank'. It is distinctive in its sketch of the Indian Robin Hood, who is moved to *choose* his dharma out of compassion for the poor, the hungry and the sick. The initial impetus is a disaster that wipes out his family and leaves the orphan 'river pirate' a wanderer. His initiation by 'a wise man' transforms him into a giver (*data*) or servitor of the oppressed, one who can bypass British government regulations. He is active precisely because he is on the margins of the colonial state and free of familial ties. This romantic story of self-construction then becomes part of the narrative of the adolescents' wanderings. The tale within a tale teases the reader to move out of the

---

[12] Peter van der Veer has persuasively argued that the 'imperialist construction of muscular Christianity was answered by an Indian nationalist construction of muscular Hinduism'. See his *Imperial Encounters: Religion and Modernity in India and Britain* (Delhi: Permanent Black, rpr. 2006), p.94.

[13] Among others, see for example studies of Byron, Shelley and other Romantics in Alan Richardson and Sonia Hofkosh (eds), *Romanticism, Race and Imperial Culture, 1780–1834* (Bloomington and Indianapolis: Indiana University Press, 1996).

immediate present of the immediate 'action'—a device as old at least as the *Mahabharata*. Another function of this frame is to emphasise that experience must necessarily be unique even when the pattern may appear repetitive (the personal or community disaster, the period of alienation or sorrow, the encounter with a wise man, the arrival at a new way of life). The pirate's life-story reveals that he is a philosopher-doer: 'He who lives without fear or hate is the only free man', or 'Think of God as something inside of you and not to be found by wandering around India from shrine to shrine'.[14] And so the possibility of the quest that is purely external is nicely deconstructed.

A Midnight Vigil

Mukerji's exploration of the ethics of caste also brings back the community and the possibility of 'extended' families. The family rarely comprises only a monogamous couple. Instead it is invoked primarily in terms of caste as occupational identity, with the priest as the 'natural' teacher. Mukerji's priest appears as an idealised combination of the loner and the doer, the thinker and the leader. The priest as teacher seldom instructs merely through words, although words in the form of recited chants or mantras are critical to the narrative.

In the most self-consciously 'ethnographic' text, *Ghond the Hunter*,[15] we have multiple guru figures cutting through axes of gender, caste and ethnicity. The priest is both young Ghond's teacher and the leader of the community as a whole. Remarkably, this old priest shares the curiosity of the young boy, the to-be-accomplished-hunter, who is not quite the noble savage. And Kuri (*khuri* is the Bangla word for aunt), the foster mother of the protagonist, is also a guru. It is Kuri who initiates Ghond into the way of the Kshatriya. Possibly the most powerful evocation of the guru is the figure of the tribal hunter to whom the book is dedicated: 'To the memory of Pradhan, the Santal, the original of Ghond'. (There appears to be an interpellation of various tribal communities here, Santhals and Gonds.) The scene presaging the drought is one instance of this 'ensemble'—the priest who joins the protagonist and Kuri at midnight to watch the unusual sight of a variety of animals coming to drink at the river. If it is hard to categorise what exactly links the future hunter, the old widowed aunt and the priest in this midnight vigil (pp.76–80), it is certainly not the single telos of god and country—the dominant trajectory of nationalism in the twentieth century! As mentioned earlier, the idea of a central source of authority, or one location of learning, one set of dicta, is here dispersed. Arguably, there is no serious contradiction between the codes practised and taught by Kuri, Ghond and the priest; their spheres of action overlap. This might have made the protagonist's mental journey more fraught. The celebration of biological as well as non-biological ties, of the village community along with its apparent 'other' in the jungle, marks a tortuous attempt to envision a community both idealised and fragmented, since the adult Ghond will always be a loner.[16]

A new dimension is found in *Chief of the Herd*, where the elephant is repeatedly called the 'citizen of the forest'.[17] 'Herd', 'drove', 'flock' and 'tribe' are used interchangeably for a group of elephants. While the elephant herd is seen as distinct and aristocratic, and decisively

---

[14] D.G. Mukerji, *Jungle Beasts and Men* (1923) (Delhi: Rupa & Co., rpr. 2003), p.158. See also Mukerji, *Caste and Outcast*, p.17.

[15] D.G. Mukerji, Boris Artzybasheff (illus.), *Ghond the Hunter* (1928) (Delhi: Rupa & Co., rpr. 2003).

[16] The desire to create a perfect composite of all castes is evident in the words given to Kuri on pp.30–31. But this is undercut by the ambivalence of Chapter XIII, which ends with the *chamar* (cobbler) being hounded out of the village on suspicion of being a 'were-tiger'.

[17] D.G. Mukerji, Mahlon Blaine (illus.), *Chief of the Herd* (1929) (New York: E.P. Dutton & Co. Inc., rpr. 1952), p.32.

violent towards other predators if necessary, it also has a responsibility towards all living creatures in times of danger. 'Co-operation' is critical, for example, during the drought in the jungle (p.96). Within the herd, the young ones are taught to 'conquer' air and water, learning the essentials of survival, as in Chapter XII. In this network of inter-dependence, the *making* of a citizen is critical in the otherwise paradigmatic narrative of the 'life-cycle' from birth to childhood, adolescence, courtship, mating and death.

However, the parent–child dyad is as significant as that of the subject-citizen because it is constitutive of the idealised role of the leader: 'To be the leader is to think of the herd as one's children'. Even if one's own offspring is specially loved (consider the moment when Bahadur, 'our only son', is encircled by a pack of wolves, and the mother rushes to the rescue [p.99]), he is seen 'not as the son but as any member of the herd' (p.123). At all times, the leader's mission of 'protection' is extended to all members of the herd. The inevitable logic of this belief is realised at the end of the novel when the chief's wife Radha and their daughter both perish in the flood. (The only novel with a female juvenile, the daughter is never mentioned by name.) Sirdar, the husband/father, cannot afford to think only of them because he has to look after the entire herd. The continual balance between these intertwined modes of parenting becomes a marker of Sirdar's identity as husband/father *and* leader. The narrative presents this as a positive balancing act between his discreet pride in the individual accomplishments of his child, and his attention to the welfare of every member of the community. At all times, though, the personal bond and the affective is privileged; a leader simply cannot be a selfish or dehumanised creature.

Further caveats on the definition of the leader's role do not allow for a straightforward reading of patriarchal or masculinist discourse: 'Mother taught me [that] authority must be humble' (pp.28–9), says Bahadur. The mother's teachings then are not only about survival, but encompass the traditional role of the guru as one who gives wise counsel, and not in a generic fashion. That is, the guru and disciple have an individualised relationship.

Very often, both parents have to die in order for the child to realise himself. By and large, however, 'mother love' is defined by its extreme nature: self-sacrifice to nurture and ensure the survival of the young, not for an abstract notion of honour (*Chief of the Herd*, p.147). Mukerji's last novel almost revels in 'the loving fury of motherhood' (*Fierce-Face*, pp.16–18). At the same time, female sexuality and the desire for a mate are glimpsed in many texts with bird or animal protagonists (for example, *Chief of the Herd*, p.62, *Fierce-Face*, p.74).

The trope of sacrifice in enacting (being and becoming) the perfect wife, or host, or parent, may be traced to disparate narrative traditions. If the dominant image is of the female as *sati*, there are other cultural models, equally powerful—the very embodiment of generosity, as in King Harishchandra, or in King Sibi from the *Jatakas* who gives the hawk his pound of flesh in order to protect the dove who has come to him for refuge. We might juxtapose the survival narrative, which also privileges heroic endurance in the face of adversity—the staple of adventure fiction in the Western canon—with the notion of suffering endured out of compassion for all—a Buddhist refrain. Enduring pain in silence (or with a smile) is common to both narrative traditions. However, Mukerji's texts imply that while endurance in the 'survival narrative' may be only for personal glory, his models of sacrifice embody a prescribed normative role.

The motif of self-sacrifice and voluntary suffering is repeated in 'Pigeons of Paradise', one of the stories in *Hindu Fables for Little Children* (1929)—a book Mukerji dedicated 'to the memory of my mother'.[18] The mother as the ruthless teacher, who is willing to sacrifice her

---

[18] D.G. Mukerji, 'Pigeons of Paradise', in his *Hindu Fables for Little Children* (New York: E.P. Dutton & Co., 1929).

own life, appears notably in *Gay-Neck*. As an alternative version of heroism, she embodies self-sacrifice, as opposed to conquest as possession. I am tempted to read into this construct of 'selfless love' the shadow of at least two intertwined discourses—of the woman as 'voluntary' *sati*; *and* also of the contemporary (usually male) revolutionary/terrorist who is ready to make the supreme sacrifice of self-destruction for her/his love of country. By transposing these two distinct yet historically-interlinked discourses into the mother as guru and sacrificer, Mukerji perhaps seeks to avoid the extreme valorisation of either discourse. This particular composite of the tough teacher and selfless giver then clears the stage, so to speak, for the offspring to take centre stage and embark on *his* (for it is inevitably male) path of self-realisation. Repeatedly therefore, the lesson of survival is articulated as one beyond material needs. Nevertheless considerable attention is given to practices of observation, reconnoitering, sensing and testing the environment, enduring the harshness of extreme climatic conditions, and dangers from beasts (the natural history bits, as it were). Self-control in the face of danger, in extreme moments of passion, and 'mastering' one's self through seeking 'freedom from fear', appear to be the chief of these lessons.

The male preceptor figure (such as Ghond) also exposes the boy to threats and perils yet is always concerned for his physical security, protecting him from pain and death. With Ghond, too, the final objective (both for himself and for his protégés) is to progress to a state that is free of fear. The student (boy, bird or elephant) has to be able to kill if necessary, and to then wash off (quite literally) the taint of blood and all the negative emotions that may have accompanied the act of violence. In *Gay-Neck*, the very structure of the novel resists any fixing of Ghond as the hero or guru. As has been perceptively noted by Mukerji's biographer, there is a slippage of identities between Ghond the hunter, the anonymous first person narrator (the boy) and Gay-Neck the pigeon.[19] Towards the end of the novel, it is Ghond who has to undergo a further trial (by slaying the marauding buffalo) in order to reclaim his Kshatriya self as well as to reach equilibrium in the very act of slaying (shades of the *Bhagvad Gita* perhaps?) At the level of the plot, however, the lama in his Himalayan retreat might well claim the clinching role of guru. The lama is simultaneously detached from, and involved in, the travelling life of the protagonist, his friend, the pigeon and the hunter, just as he is deeply concerned with the world war being fought thousands of miles away.

I have elsewhere historicised a reading of *Gay-Neck* in the context of two related boy scout movements taking place almost simultaneously in the USA and the UK, tracing their transnational connections through imperial figures such as Robert Baden-Powell, Rudyard Kipling and others.[20] Baden-Powell's Scout Movement emphasised hierarchy, obedience and teamwork as opposed to the heroics of rugged individualism. Mukerji places equal emphasis on training in almost all his fiction: Part One of *Gay-Neck* may be read as a prelude to Part Two, or World War I. The pigeon's training involves his mastery of flight, and his discovery of the qualities of leadership, courage and self-sacrifice. But the overall pedagogy Mukerji proposes is quite different from the pedagogy of movements such as the boy scouts. Mukerji's focus is on the emotional bond between parent and child which may demand the sacrifice of life itself, the impulse becoming 'a habit' (p.55). Gay-Neck's mother does not hesitate to sacrifice her life in order to save her child from the hawk, even though the sacrifice was

---

[19] Prithwindranath Mukhopadhyay, *Dhanagopal Mukhopadhyay* (in Bangla) (Calcutta: Paschim Bangla Akademi, 2003), pp.32–3.
[20] Rimli Bhattacharya, 'Transnational Scouting and Dhan Gopal Mukerji's *Gay-Neck: The Story of a Pigeon*, 1927', paper presented at the Department of English, University of Delhi, September 2008.

'unnecessary' (p.34). The bond between the boy narrator and his pet pigeon is equally intense, the more so because the boy is a surrogate parent. Moreover, it is one between two forms of life usually hierarchised according to different levels of physical and intellectual development. For Mukerji, it is the common soul that binds bird and boy together; 'home' can be anywhere. *Gay-Neck* foregrounds the bond between the teacher/guru which, in this case, includes Ghond and the boy who is his *shishya*. Part One is largely about the wanderings of the boy, the bird and the hunter, so that the 'peripatetic training' and the 'lessons learnt' are subsumed in an ever-changing landscape, with frequent cuts to the regions of the sky—Gay-Neck's world of flight, with its attendant emotions of joy and fear. 'Team spirit'—so central to public schools, the armed forces and scouting—also surfaces in this narrative, but it is not through organised militarism. Learning is therefore a continuous process, nurtured through the wanderings of three quite different beings, with pauses for recuperation in the lamasery.

To sum up, the distinctiveness of Mukerji's approach to socialisation arises from at least two sources: the epic narratives of the subcontinent (largely the *Mahabharata*); and the ongoing tensions and contradictions between various strands of nationalism in contemporary India. Thus, the imperative in conceptualising the role of mentor and the nurturing of leadership, and the growth of the protagonist, is not only in response to hegemonic discourses of imperialism, but equally from an evolving Gandhian praxis for the discipline of the *satyagrahi*: sacrifice, firmness, courage and gentleness, melding to form the true servitor or *sevak*. We might say that *seva* (devotional service) is conceptualised in contrast to the imperial notion of service inscribed in Kipling's 'White Man's Burden'.

The nature of the struggle for freedom was complicated by the militancy of the revolutionary nationalists, which had a particularly strong impact on notions of self-hood, and the discipline of the body in Bengal. Mukerji was necessarily troubled by the contours of the emerging social landscape of a colonised people seeking to articulate freedom from their own oppressive traditions. I bring in this dimension to suggest that his 'jungle books', written for young readers in the USA and elsewhere, may be read as a site for resolving some of the inevitable contradictions of this project. He attempts a resolution by privileging subjectivities over a delineation of action manifested as a series of incidents, and by making the narrative itself reflect the overlapping chronotopes of his protagonist. To read Mukerji's *oeuvre* entirely in the shadow of Orientalist binaries, such as of the material and the spiritual, would erase the multiple and contradictory historical trajectories of his India.

Language, Experience and Knowledge

As in *Gay-Neck*, some chapters in *Chief of the Herd* are written in the voice of Sirdar, for 'the real secrets of his experience' can only be told by him in 'hati (elephant) language' (pp.28–9). Besides the obvious difference in experiential reality this perspective affords, it allows Mukerji to offer glimpses of the intensely personal links between mother and child (pp.120–1). In his 1920 article 'Tagore's India', Mukerji made an interesting observation about Tagore's 1913 collection of verse, *Crescent Moon*:

> In fact, no Hindu child can tell the western reader that he really has played with his father. Fatherhood not only implies forgoing the levity of play with one's child, but also imposes upon the father the restraint of emotion; a man may feel love for his child but he should not express it.[21]

---

[21] D.G. Mukerji, 'Tagore's India', in *Asia*, Vol.XX, no.8 (1920), pp.798–80 (accessed by kind courtesy of Gordon Chang, Stanford University).

This observation about the 'Hindu child's' relationship with the father might be valid for the middle-class Victorian father as well! Alluding to the tenderness in Kipling's poem 'Shiv and the Grasshopper',[22] Mukherji adds: 'Except for Mr. Kipling no westerner has written about a Hindu woman and her child any poem that approaches the *Crescent Moon*'. Mukerji's children's fiction maps the search for an idiom that can move between the ideal training for the adolescent protagonist and the freedom of 'play' as part of this training.

I now come back to the ways in which 'knowledge' is aligned with a new historical impulse. In *Chief of the Herd*, the extended family or community is defined by interweaving the odd ones, those who 'belong' only intermittently. Ajit, the 'centurion' (p.123) 'oldest elephant' (p.116) and the repository of 'elephant wisdom', takes on the mantle of a guru. But his failing physical powers need the support of young Bahadur. Sirdar often defers to the older elephant because of his greater experience, for a 'true leader' follows a superior (p.139). The *Mahabharata* is explicitly invoked at the 'ancient's death'. The term used is *mahaprasthan*— translated as 'the grand journey' (p.148), which marks the 'Santi-parva' of the epic.[23] A modern writer's gloss on this 'final journey' adds a new dimension—love for one's land:

> The *mahaprasthan* plan was conceived by Yudhisthir and he also inaugurates it. He was the one who first discarded his kingly clothes and dressed himself in bark. Draupadi and his four brothers then followed suit. Just before leaving home they cast 'fire into water'—that is, they extinguish the constantly burning sacred fire. Yudhisthir abandons his much-cherished householder's state. But his breaking-up of home cannot be regarded as *sannyas* or even *vanaprastha* in the sense these terms appear in *Manu-samhita*. This *mahaprasthan* also bears no trace of the lonely wandering as a beggar that had seemed desirable to him after the battle was over (*Santi*, 9).
>
> From the west to the east, from the east to the south, then back along the western shores—*the way he circumambulates the entire coastline of India would make it seem that he bids his last farewell to his motherland* before heading for a destination known to him. We do not yet know what this destination is, nor do any of his companions even ask where they are going.... (emphasis added).[24]

Wandering is thus not only a means of gaining experience and learning, but the contact with the land, water and air entails a continual process of immersing oneself in a kind of sacred-secular geography which is a precondition to loving one's land. One finds this in the writings of many Indians who were 'discovering' the 'real' India in their own way, from Vivekananda to Jawaharlal Nehru. Well after he had moved away from the exuberance of the *swadeshi* era, Rabindranath Tagore celebrated this intimacy with one's land in the course of his 1927 Southeast Asian tour. He critiques those who make speeches about the motherland but lack any contact with her. *Letters from Java* repeatedly suggests a different notion of space and place—of a geography that one has to know intimately before one can claim it as one's own,[25] notwithstanding Tagore's

---

[22] Kipling's poem is found in his story 'Toomai of the Elephants'.
[23] The *Mahabharata* is divided into 18 *parvas* or books. Book 12 is 'Santi-parva' meaning 'The Book of Peace'. After the Great Battle of Kurukshetra, the newly-crowned Yudhisthir is guilt-ridden and despairing, and hence in need of counselling in order to be 'at peace'.
[24] Buddhadev Bose, Sujit Mukherjee (trans.), *The Book of Yudhisthir. A Study of the Mahabharat from Vyas* (Hyderabad: Sangam Books, 1986).
[25] Rabindranath Tagore, 'Letter of 31 Aug. 1927' (trans. Indiradevi Chaudhurani & Supriya Roy), in Supriya Roy (ed.), *Letters from Java. Rabindranath Tagore's Tour of South-East Asia* (Calcutta: Visva-Bharati, 2010), p.73.

belief that 'our history runs through the history of the civilisation of Eastern Asia.... Let us feel that India is not confined in the Geography [sic] of India'.[26]

Commenting on Jawaharlal Nehru's last will and testament, made some ten years before his death, Rajeswari Sunder Rajan observes:

> The wish to merge into the largeness of physical India, its rivers, mountains and fields, is an expression of abjection, while at the same time it assumes an identification between the individual and the nation that amounts almost [to] a proprietary relationship.[27]

Sunder Rajan is careful to distinguish 'Nehru's attitude from colonialist paternalism', preferring to identify it as 'the inchoate feeling we call patriotism'.[28] The extreme desire to 'know' is arguably a pre-condition for secularism as well. Mukerji's 'jungle-India', reified and replayed as 'acts of contemplation' and facts of natural history, nevertheless resonates with what Sunder Rajan characterises as 'an atavistic sense of belonging to the land'.[29] Naming the land, highlighting the variations in terrain, the time of the year, and the migration of the herd, allow Mukerji to bring in natural history, biology and geography—sometimes even fragments of colonial law. (For example, the ban on the slaughter of elephants, excepting those declared rogue.) This overtly pedagogic enterprise is imbued with the subjectivity of the protagonists. Each terrain also invites a particular kind of crisis that occurs in nature—flood, drought, ice-melt and so on. These moments of hostility or destruction in the natural world are also marked by human practices such as the capture of wild elephants for a princely kingdom, or a shoot organised for visiting white men.

The 'family' in this case encompasses a range of binaries: wild/domesticated; jungle/urban spaces. When Sirdar and Kumar (later rivals in love) see Radha, she is a tamed female elephant working as a beast of burden for men (*Chief of the Herd*, p.59). Her condition is humiliating both because of the hard and mechanical nature of the work, and the ill-treatment meted out by the mahout. Nevertheless, it is Radha's *knowledge* of the ways of men, of fire, that will later save the herd. Here humans are relegated to the margins, or at best represented through defamiliarisation: they are referred to as 'bipeds' (p.60) or as 'human burden', while the domesticated elephants are beasts of burden with the potential to become 'citizens of the forest'.

The Wages of Fear?

This emphasis on the training of mind and body may also be viewed as a kind of self-transformation at the heart of the modernity project. Writing to his daughter on 6 May 1935 from the Almora District jail, Jawaharlal Nehru elaborates on 'an intellectual training' which yields 'internal freedom and fearlessness'. His 'instruction' to his 'Darling Indu' reverberates strikingly with the *intended* direction of much of Mukerji's children's fiction:[30]

---

[26] Rabindranath Tagore, 'Epigraph', in *Letters from Java*.

[27] Rajeswari Sunder Rajan, 'Gandhi, Nehru and the Ethical Imperatives of the National-Popular', in Elleke Boehmer and Rosinka Chaudhuri (eds), *The Indian Postcolonial. A Critical Reader* (Delhi: Routledge Indian, rpr. 2011), pp.238–60.

[28] *Ibid.*, p.250.

[29] *Ibid.*

[30] Though beyond the scope of this paper, one notes the fairly intense friendship and correspondence between the two which reveals equally striking differences, and not only in their respective locations.

> I think a proper intellectual training is essential to do any job efficiently. But far more important is the background of the training—the habits, ideals, ideas, objectives, the internal harmony, the capacity for cooperation, the strength to be true to what one considers to be right, the absence of fear—if one attains this internal freedom and fearlessness it is difficult for the world, harsh as it is, to suppress one....[31]

Mukerji's self-designated role may be seen, as Gordon Chang underlines in his 'Introduction', as the 'task of the interpreter'. Mukerji was only one in a long line of such interpreters—Vivekananda, Ananda Coomaraswamy, Rabindranath Tagore to name only a few—who experienced the attendant dangers of being cast or shaped as the 'authentic' representative of a certain vision of India. We have seen an instance of Mukerji setting up a triad between himself, Tagore and Kipling through a paradigm of the affective, the feminine and the playful (attempting a certain inflection of familial relations) in a 'Hindu' India. Working within the confines of E.P. Dutton's marketing of his works for either 'juvenile' or 'adult' readers, and having to maintain a 'judicious' balance between 'natural history' and 'eastern wisdom', Mukerji chose the trope of 'jungle lore' as the matrix where social relations could be reconfigured and the nature–culture question explored, quite outside the normative paradigm of the quasi-emergent 'colonial bourgeoisie'. This fraught (perhaps impossible) attempt to reconcile language, ethics and experience and take them towards new directions is already implicated in the choice of the genre—the adventure novel. As Javed Majeed notes in his study of the poet Iqbal's 'geographical re-centring':

> The cross-fertilisation between travelogues, exploration narratives and works of literature (especially novels), was exemplified by the popularity of the adventure narrative and romance quest during the period 1880–1920, at the height of British imperial power, and was significant in formulating a geo-political imagination of nineteenth-century empire.
>
> However, scholars have not paid enough attention to countervailing historical geographies produced in non-European traditions of thought in the nineteenth and twentieth centuries.[32]

I have argued that drawing on the epics does allow Mukerji the possibility of evoking a sacred-secular 'geographical consciousness'.

Similarly, he is able to eschew the embattled terrain of the family (colonial or colonised) which lends itself to spheres of the public and private, the material and the affective, 'as two separate domains of human life', with the private remaining 'eternal and unchanging'. But in avoiding this tired binary Mukerji's fiction will inevitably bear a certain loss. Mukerji's approach, thus, is necessarily different from, say, that of filmmaker Ritwik Ghatak, who 'leads us to places that are proscribed and therefore dangerous'[33]—the heart of darkness *within*

---

[31] Jawaharlal Nehru to Indira Gandhi, 6 May 1935, in Sonia Gandhi (ed.), *Freedom's Daughter: Letters Between Indira Gandhi and Jawaharlal Nehru, 1922–1939* (London: Hodder and Stoughton, 1987), pp.159–60. Nehru pokes fun at his own 'professorial' diktats in the course of this long letter.

[32] Javed Majeed, *Muhmmad Iqbal, Islam, Aesthetics and Postcolonialism* (New Delhi and London: Routledge, 2009), p.61.

[33] Sibaji Bandyopadhyay offers a lyrical and ruthless reading of the intertextualities of modernity, via the *yaksha* of Kalidasa's *Meghadutam*, Rabindanath Tagore's 'takes' on the former, and Ritwik Ghatak's 'responses' to 'Kobiguru'! See 'Dis-membering and Re-membering the Art of Ritwik Ghatak', in *Sibaji Bandyopadhyay Reader: An Anthology of Essays* (Delhi: Worldview Publications, 2012), p.239.

familial relationships. *Meghe Dhaka Tara* (1960) and *Subarnarekha* (1962) are two such striking examples from Ghatak's 'Partition trilogy'.

The absence of a collective is striking in *Gay-Neck*, though it is all-important in other works such as *Chief of the Herd*, as the title makes clear. The quest is still that of loners, the answers to be discovered in silence. Leadership and mentoring continue as dominant themes filtered through a religious ideology which would need separate discussion. The jungle and the natural world take centre stage, with the occasional appearance of villagers. While sharing the anti-city, anti-technology vision of Gandhi, Mukerji is unable or unwilling to visualise anything like a community unless it is the deeply-fissured (though *presented* as harmonious) village in *Ghond the Hunter*. The displacement of the everyday that this strategy entails is made possible both through the trope of wandering and also, perforce, by the enactment of liberation in the daily lives of birds, beasts and hunters.

Writing in the shadow of World War I, Mukerji seems to be primarily concerned with exploring an ethics of 'constructive brotherhood' that he cited as part of Buddhist ethics in his 1923 autobiography.[34] His distance from the revolutionary Ghadar Party may explain in part this absence of a collective or any utopic space. He chooses not to 'travel' with many of his fellow expatriate radicals and revolutionaries, nor is he able to be physically part of the massive changes that he records in an India struggling to articulate its possible futures.

Mukerji's *oeuvre* in English for children maps out a socialisation that is 'free' of the apparatus of the colonial home or of other disciplining institutional sites. Paradoxically, the search to be 'free from fear' can only be played out in the alternative topos of the jungle, where violence is inescapable. Is this celebratory journey of self-realisation an affirmation or a lament? It is ironic that his one book for children that would have covered *contemporary* India—a projected history of ancient and modern India—was not accepted for publication during the Depression years.[35]

One returns then to the mother, whose aura flows into other preceptor-like figures: the priest, the hunter, the foster-mother, the boy narrator who 'owns' Gay-Neck, and the bird, elephant and tiger mothers. To sum up the various readings offered in this paper, the mother is consistently valorised as wise if unlettered, or even *because* unlettered. In some ways she is outside the space of the colonial. Moreover, without quite being a deity, she takes on the attributes of several.[36] She appears as the nurturer beyond the realm of the purely domestic. She is also the tough and sometimes fierce teacher of survival strategies. The topos of the jungle is particularly enabling in this regard, as is the domain of the sky in *Gay-Neck*. Finally, this fierce devotion to protection, nurturing and teaching is coeval with suffering as an affirmative choice. I have earlier indicated that there is a merging of revolutionary terrorism with the terror of imperial power. Mukerji's narrative focus is on the continuum between self-realisation and self-sacrifice, as a choice. This is played out at various stages and by various 'characters' as willed choice, if only to ensure the survival of a future actant. This is the protagonist as the new subject-citizen in whose training 'fearlessness' is the talismanic word. The subject and subjectivity of these nameless protagonists derive from the wise, necessarily violent, nurturing/sacrificing acts of mother figures.

---

[34] Mukerji, *Caste and Outcast*, p.15.

[35] In a letter of 23 Sept. 1930, Mukerji proposes to Dutton that both 'Nehru and Mrs. Mukerji's' books on Indian history be printed 'in one volume under the title *India, Ancient and Modern* for children or *Young People's India*. Information courtesy of Dhan Gopal Mukerji Jr.'s personal collection.

[36] Mukerji actually remembers his mother's deity-like appearance during his childhood: 'At last, much to our relief, our mother appeared upon the scene and we felt secure at once, for nothing ever frightened mother'. Mukerji, *Caste and Outcast*, p.37.

Dhan Gopal Mukerji's children's fiction is marked by several distinctive traits. He offers a sensuous entry into a realm that is not 'elementally' Good or Evil. He neither erases the violence inherent in the everyday cycles of life in 'nature', nor are his tales about a conquest of nature (as in natural resources, or 'people of nature') found in the typical adventure tale. Yet these considerable gains are bounded within a site of action (or the choice of a genre and mode of writing) that perforce moves away from the contradictions of imagining a free India, from his particular location, for a transnational readership. And so, one might say of his bird, beast or human protagonist, the historical subject is 'untimely ripp'd' from his mother's womb![37]

---

[37] 'Macduff was from his mother's womb untimely ripp'd'. William Shakespeare, *Macbeth*, Act V, Scene 8.

The Romance of Siblinghood in Bombay Cinema

RUTH VANITA

Bombay cinema endows non-sexual relationships, such as friendship and siblinghood, with a passionate intensity that equals that of sexual relationships, thus resisting a complete takeover of the emotional realm by heterosexual coupledom. Choosing sibling, friend or community over a spouse need not be seen only as retrogressive self-sacrifice; it can also be seen as choosing stronger, longer-standing relationships over newer, more flimsy ones. Films such as Naam, Bombai ka Babu *and* Kabhi Khushi Kabhie Gham *explore the joys and costs of different types of romantic feeling, many of which are not sexual, but are just as powerful.*

In modern Western literature and cinema, romantic coupledom has largely displaced earlier constructions of affiliation in which spouse, sibling and friend subsisted on a fairly equivalent plane. Bombay cinema too enacts and endorses this displacement that is endemic to modernity, but, at the same time, it significantly modifies its structure. Drawing on longstanding Indian kinship practices, Bombay cinema supplements the celebration of romantic coupledom with simultaneous celebration of a pre-modern kinship ideal that gives siblings and friends as much importance as the romantic partner. This pre-modern ideal is reworked and transformed in a modern setting, but it still remains recognisably connected to earlier narrative patterns, often drawn from epics and legends.

Many film critics assume that displacement of the extended family by the romantic couple is 'socially progressive' and that reconciliation between a couple and family is a retrogressive compromise with patriarchy.[1] Conversely, I contend that the romantic narrative pattern tends to reinforce a modern type of compulsory heterosexuality, while the kinship narrative pattern allows for a more diverse and complex ideal of emotional dependence and familial relations. This is reinforced by Bombay cinema's consistent tendency to celebrate the chosen family as much as the biological one.

While I agree with Jyotika Virdi that Bombay cinema 'narrows the gap between the public and the private' by treating the family as emblematic of the nation, I do not agree that the

---

I wish to thank Shohini Ghosh, Jyotika Virdi and the two anonymous reviewers for their very helpful comments.

[1] Sangita Gopal, 'Sentimental Symptoms: The Films of Karan Johar and Bombay Cinema', in Rini Bhattacharya Mehta and Rajeshwari Pandharipande (eds), *Bollywood and Globalization: Indian Popular Cinema, Nation and Diaspora* (London: Anthem Press, 2011), pp.15–34, 20; Gopal summarises this position before making her own more complex argument.

paradigm of the family romance is confined to mother, father and son.² Such an exegesis omits not only numerous films about single fathers who adore their daughters, but also the romance of siblinghood and the many relationships (biological and, more important, non-biological) that constitute the highly complicated, even cluttered, scenario of the extended family in Bombay cinema.

In this essay, I examine the romance of the sibling relationship in Bombay cinema primarily through exegeses of *Bombai ka Babu* (1960) and *Naam* (1986). These two films are typical of Bombay cinema in the way they frame the sibling relationship, but are unusual in the excessive intensity with which they invest it. The star system, wherein the star's persona exceeds any particular film, allows the spectator to simultaneously observe two characters in a narrative as well as two stars with a life outside the film. Of *Naam*, director Mahesh Bhatt observed that the off-screen chemistry between the two actors, Sanjay Dutt and Kumar Gaurav, contributed to their on-screen chemistry.³

Likewise, *Bombai ka Babu* was controversial because it depicted an attraction between apparent siblings who had grown up separately. The emotional intensity between the siblings in these two films allows for comparison with the male–female romance. I suggest that Bombay cinema endows non-sexual relationships, such as friendship and siblinghood, with a passionate intensity that equals that of sexual relationships, thus resisting a complete takeover of the emotional realm by heterosexual coupledom.

As Bombay cinema has produced a huge and heterogeneous body of work, there are dozens of exceptions to any generalisation. I outline here general and dominant patterns that certainly do not apply to every single film ever produced. Also, these patterns have been changing rapidly in the last decade, especially under the influence of independent cinema, as in the film *Love, Sex aur Dhokha* (2010) with its realistic depiction of a brother murdering his sister in cold blood.

I also wish to emphasise that my purpose here is not to read incestuous elements into sibling love in Bombay cinema—a type of reading that dominates late twentieth-century commentary on sibling love in the Victorian novel. That type of reading is based on a post-Freudian assumption that sexual emotion is the most important and life-defining of all emotions and, therefore, any intense and central emotion must necessarily be sexual in nature. If, however, one assumes that friendship or siblinghood is the most important type of relationship, one may then view conjugal relationships as forms of friendship or siblinghood. In such a view, sexuality need not be seen as the centrally-defining or most lasting element even of conjugality.

A Lifelong Friend

Siblinghood occupies a space in Bombay cinema that overlaps with conjugality, both in terms of plot and in terms of larger, life-defining symbolism. Friendship, in its widest sense, encompasses both these relations. The erotic partner is a friend as is the sibling, while the friend functions as both sibling and partner. Union with and separation from a lover can

---

[2] Jyotika Virdi, *The Cinematic ImagiNation: Indian Popular Films as Social History* (Piscataway, NJ: Rutgers University Press, 2003), pp.87–8.

[3] Of this film and *Chal Mere Bhai* (2000), Shohini Ghosh remarks that 'the implicit homoeroticism of these films is evident not only to queer subcultures but even to sections of the mainstream press'. See Shohini Ghosh, 'Queer Pleasures for Queer People: Film, Television and Queer Sexuality in India', in Ruth Vanita (ed.), *Queering India: Same-Sex Love and Eroticism in Indian Culture and Society* (New York: Routledge, 2002), p.209.

represent one's relationship with God, home or life itself, but so can union with and separation from a sibling or a friend.

In many pre-modern kinship systems, a friend can occupy the space of a sibling, and a sibling can occupy the space of a spouse. It is this insight that informs medieval constructions of the Virgin Mary as simultaneously the mother, daughter, sister and spouse of God. Likewise, Ram is regularly worshipped along with his wife, Sita, brother, Lakshman, and friend-devotee, Hanuman. Ram considers Hanuman a brother (in the *Hanuman Chalisa*, Ram tells Hanuman, 'You are my dear one, a brother equal to Bharat'), while his brother, Lakshman, is also his best friend. Likewise, Krishna, an adopted child, is inseparably coupled with his brother, Balram, but treats his childhood friend, Sudama, as a sibling, too.

In pre-modern times, friendships appear to have been ritualised in a variety of ways: in the *Ramayana*, Ram and Sugreev (his friend and political ally) walk around a fire to pledge friendship vows to one another. In rural North India, friendship was marked as special by conferring sibling status on friends, making them *dharam bhai* or *dharam behen*, and exchanging vows or items of dress.[4] Likewise, the rituals of the festival of Raksha Bandhan confer special status on the brother–sister relationship, whether biological or chosen.

While posited in the modern world as completely different types of relationships, the ideal spouse and sibling often occupy a similar space in literary texts as well as in life—companionship, caretaking and mutual dependence. In Victorian novels, which, until recently, exerted an enormous influence on Bombay cinema and on several generations of educated Indians, single or widowed siblings often live together, like Tom and Ruth Pinch in Dickens' *Martin Chuzzlewit*. Often, too, friends live together in a relationship that is more sibling-like than spouse-like, as, for example, Betsy Trotwood and Mr. Dick in *David Copperfield*.

Equally importantly, the true soul-mate often turns out to be not the stranger who attracts because s/he is one's opposite, but rather the sibling-like familial familiar who is one's similar (often a cousin, brother-in-law or adopted sibling), for example Fanny and Edmund, not Mary and Henry, in *Mansfield Park*; Heathcliff, not Edgar, and Hareton, not Linton, in *Wuthering Heights*; Mr. Knightley, not Frank, in *Emma*; and Brandon, not Willoughby, in *Sense and Sensibility*. From the man's perspective, too, the woman with whom one shares a home-life is preferable to the one who dazzles with her beauty; thus Agnes, not Dora, is the one David Copperfield ought to marry precisely because Agnes is so sibling-like that he has addressed her as sister throughout.

From the woman's perspective, the man who can play the role of brother, protecting rather than seducing, is the one who will prove a worthy husband; thus the attractive stranger proves acceptable only after he takes on this brotherly role, as Darcy does in *Pride and Prejudice*, when he expends time, energy and money to rescue Elizabeth's runaway sister. Perhaps, the clearest example of this appears in Frances Burney's 1778 novel, *Evelina*, where the heroine, a poor young woman, is beset by seducers. The only man who treats her with respect is Lord Orville. When his sister Louisa's fiancé showers Evelina with unwanted attention, Louisa asks her brother to walk with her. Evelina cries out: 'Would to heaven...that I too had a brother!—and then I should not be exposed to such treatment'. Lord Orville immediately offers her his arm and asks her to think of him as her brother. Thereafter, he frequently addresses her as his friend and sister.[5] Thus, he distinguishes himself from would-be seducers and proves himself worthy of being her husband.

---

[4] Thus, the early nineteenth-century poets, Insha and Rangin, became brothers by exchanging turbans. See Ruth Vanita, *Gender, Sex and the City: Urdu Rekhti Poetry 1780–1870* (New Delhi: Orient BlackSwan, 2012).

[5] Frances Burney, *Evelina* (London: Oxford University Press, 1970), pp.314–5.

A third feature common to major pre-modern Indian texts, Victorian novels and Bombay cinema, is the formation of an extended family through the adoption of friends as kin, especially as siblings. Virtue is demonstrated through the ability to form and sustain such affiliations.

In modern European and American literature and cinema, the spouse tends to eclipse the sibling in symbolic importance, but this transition was completed only in the twentieth century. Throughout the nineteenth century, siblings, from Dorothy in Wordsworth's poems to the sisters in Christina Rossetti's 'Goblin Market' and Louisa M. Alcott's *Little Women*, figure centrally as second selves.

The gulf between pre-modern and modern valuations of siblings and spouses is amusingly evident in modern commentators' deep discomfort with Antigone's famous statement that she would not have sacrificed her life to bury a husband or a son because these could be replaced, while a brother was irreplaceable. Modern translators either omit or agonise over these lines, while most Indians are unlikely to be disturbed by their obvious truth. The song, '*Mere bhaiya, mere chanda*' (*Kaajal*, 1965), expresses similar sentiments about a brother's value: 'My brother, my moon, my priceless jewel, I would not take anything in exchange for you'. In the recent film, *Sarhad Paar* (2007), a woman kills her lover to save her brother.[6] The film alludes to the Punjabi legend of Mirza-Sahiban, wherein the heroine makes a similar choice.

Likewise, the ultimate romantic trope, that of joint suicide, which both lovers and same-sex friends engage in, also appears in the sibling context, as in *Mere Mehboob* (1963) when a sister attempts to join her brother in taking poison but he knocks the poison out of her hand. In this film, there are two idealised brother–sister families, one in which the sister is like a mother and the other in which the brother is like a father. The motherly sister is a courtesan and the relationship is kept secret to protect the brother's reputation; when it is finally revealed, he reacts the way lovers do when a clandestine relationship becomes public, saying that he is now the luckiest man on earth (even though the revelation results in the breaking of his engagement to his beloved).

There are significant differences between brother–brother and brother–sister relationships in Bombay movies. In brother–brother plots, rivalry and antagonism are frequently rife, with one brother going astray. Although truly evil brothers are rare, a brother may even end up killing his brother, either inadvertently or driven by duty (*Deewaar*, 1975). Brother–sister relationships are far more idealised, with conflict being depicted only rarely. Husbands, fathers and boyfriends are much more likely to be shown as cruel, violent and perfidious than are brothers. Interestingly, though, the maternal uncle is often a wicked figure, which probably derives from the murderous Kansa. However, his cruelty is directed more towards his niece or nephew than his sister, and is often blamed on his wife. *Umrao Jaan* (1981, 2006) was unusually realistic in refusing to sentimentalise the hard-hearted brother. Sister–sister relationships and sisterly relationships between women friends are less prominent, although there are enough of these, too, to warrant a separate study.

Sibling-driven plots may revolve around separation at birth (*Seeta aur Geeta*, 1972; *Ram aur Shyam*, 1967; *Amar Akbar Anthony*, 1977); siblings in love with the same person (*Aah*, 1953; *Dillagi*, 1999; *Chal Mere Bhai*, 2000; *Dil Hai Tumhara*, 2002); siblings on opposite sides of the law (*Ganga-Jumna*, 1961; *Deewaar*, 1975); legitimate and illegitimate children (*Trishul*, 1978; *Main Tulsi Tere Aangan Ki*, 1978); sacrifice for a sibling, including sacrifice of one's life (*Aisa Pyar Kahan*, 1986; *Silsila*, 1981; *Resham ki Dori*, 1974), which may be

---

[6] Thanks to Shohini Ghosh for bringing this film to my attention.

compounded by that sibling's disability (*Chhoti Bahen*, 1959; *Majboor*, 1974) or may involve rescuing a sibling from a dangerous situation (*Hare Rama Hare Krishna*, 1971; *Naam*).

In addition to movies in which these scenarios constitute the main focus of the plot, there are numerous others in which they are a subplot, especially towards the end of the film, when the hero sets out to rescue siblings and others from the villain. Most of these situations (for example, being in love with the same person, rescuing from danger, making sacrifices) occur with regard to friends as frequently as to siblings, which suggests the overlap between these two types of relationship.

Chosen Kin Binds the World

Adoption, formal or informal, is one mode through which the overlap operates. The friend becomes an adopted sibling, and the adopted sibling is part of a larger kin network that includes friends. This chosen kin network, including adopted siblings, generally incorporates people of different religions and sometimes different nationalities (as in *Mangal Pandey*, 2005) to suggest the inclusiveness of the Indian ethos, or even of South Asia or of humanity in general.

Adoptive siblings may be created by parents, as in *Muqaddar ka Sikandar* (1978), where a Muslim woman, who works as a domestic servant, adopts the protagonist, a nameless street child. She gives him her dead son's name, Sikandar. This name, the Indian version of Alexander, itself suggests the fusion of cultures. She dies soon after, leaving him to care for her daughter, Mehru, now his younger sister. Immediately after his adoption, he goes to the temple to thank God for giving him a mother, a sister and a name. Later, he works to support Mehru, who ties a *rakhi*[7] on him, and, still later, he arranges her marriage to a young Muslim. An even more interesting type of adoptive siblinghood is that which is created not by parents, but by the protagonists themselves. In a typical Bombay movie pattern, the adult Sikandar befriends a Hindu named Vishal. Soon after, the two friends' families are represented as merged, with Sikandar addressing Vishal's mother as Ma and Vishal treating Mehru as his sister. The film's conclusion, in typical fashion, highlights this merging, when Vishal rescues Mehru from ruffians and Sikandar survives just long enough to see her married.

This pattern is ubiquitous in Bombay movies with the protagonist's worth being demonstrated in his or her ability to form non-biological kin networks. Thus in *Tawaif* (1985), the courtesan's suitability as a wife is demonstrated when she fits seamlessly into the hero's adopted family in the *chawl*,[8] which consists of a motherly landlady, sisterly neighbours, a friendly cop, colleagues (both Muslim and Hindu) and their families. They all address her as *bhabhi* (sister-in-law) or *bahu* (daughter-in-law), admire her virtues and intervene collectively to restore her to respectability.

The value placed on the ability to form a chosen family has a long history in Indian literature. As the twelfth-century *Hitopadesha* famously puts it: '"This is my own relative and that a stranger" is the calculation of the narrow-minded; for magnanimous hearts, the whole world is a family'. Bombay cinema tends to associate such magnanimity with the less affluent. The very rich have friends and servants, but they are rarely shown assembling the kind of motley crew that, for example, the hero of *Chalte Chalte* (2003) does (comprising the local *paan* vendor, a policeman, a washerman and a neighbour), which his wife's wealthy aunt disdains for class reasons.

---

[7] A *rakhi* is a symbolic thread that a sister ties on a brother's wrist in Hindu families.
[8] A *chawl* is a kind of lower-middle-income neighbourhood typical of Mumbai, characterised by overcrowding. These were houses where factory workers were accommodated in colonial times.

The inextricability of love, friendship and siblinghood emerges most clearly in songs, the primary vehicles of emotion in Bombay cinema. Sibling songs form certain distinctive genres, such as the ubiquitous *rakhi* song (*Chhoti Bahen*; *Anpadh*, 1962; *Anjaana*, 1969; *Be-Imaan*, 1972; *Pyari Behna*, 1985) and the song sung at one another's weddings, which can be either serious ('*Meri pyaari beheniya banegi dulhaniya*' from *Sachaa Jhutha*, 1970; '*Pyaara bhaiya mera*' from *Kya Kehna*, 2000; '*Chhor chali ghar tera*' from *Mere Bhaiya*, 1972) or comic ('*O behna, O behna*' from *Aaj ka Arjun*, 1990; '*Sun, sun, sun didi*' from *Khubsoorat*, 1980). There are also several songs that are simply about sibling love, such as the one from *Majboor* (1974), where the brother declares he cannot see his sister crying, and '*O meri laadli pyaari behna*' from *Aatish* (1979). The words and tropes of sibling songs overlap in significant ways with friendship and romantic love songs. In all three genres, the emphasis is on belonging to one another, lifelong commitment, complementarity and, most significantly, individual love symbolising a larger love.

Take the popular song, '*Behna ne bhai ki kalai se*', from *Resham ki Dori* (1974). The hero, a foreman in a mill, lives with his only sister. He defends the workers' rights and gets into trouble. When his sister is separated from him, the workers' daughters come in a group to tie *rakhi* on him and they sing this song, dancing around him in a circle. In the intervals between the verses, he remembers his sister and imagines her dancing, too. The *rakhi* that links brother and sister thus links men and women in a sibling relationship and also links humans to the cosmos:

Behna ne bhai ki kalai se
Pyaar baandha hai
Pyaar ke do taar se sansaar baandha hai
Resham ki dori se sansaar baandha hai

The sister binds love to the brother's wrist
With two gold threads of love, she binds the world
With a silken thread
She binds the world

These words have mystical resonances. Pearls strung on a thread are an ancient trope for individual selves connected to the larger Self or God; this trope occurs in the *Gita* and is picked up in numerous Bhakti texts, such as the famous devotional song of the fifteenth-century low-caste mystic Raidas: '*Prabhuji, tum moti hum dhaaga, jaise sona charhe suhaaga*'. Raidas here compares the symbiotic relationship of God and his devotees to pearls on a thread and also to the gold adorning a happily-married woman. In the song from *Resham ki Dori*, the sibling relationship stands for the kinship of the world. The *rakhi* thread is also a version of the *puja* thread that binds the world to God.

The song continues with the sister asking the brother to never forget her and to always protect her since he is her whole world. These sentiments are not very different from those of a conventional love song. Likewise, in '*Behna o behna*' (there are several songs beginning this way) from *Shankara* (1991), the brother describes the sister's *bindi* as shining like the sun and her earring as glimmering like the moon, while she says that one who has a brother like she has has all the world's joys. These are conventional romantic sentiments. In perhaps the best-known brother–sister song, '*Phoolon ka taaron ka*' (*Hare Rama Hare Krishna*), the brother declares that his sister is 'one in thousands'. He goes on to say that they will stay together all their lives. Even though, conventionally, the sister must move to another home after marriage, the lifelong emotional entwinement of siblings is suggested in the idea of staying together.

In *Bombai ka Babu*, siblinghood is not biological, but of the larger, adoptive, symbolic kind that is ubiquitous in Bombay cinema. I would not characterise the erotic feelings between the brother and sister as incestuous because the hero is merely pretending to be the heroine's brother, and she returns his feelings only after she discovers the truth about him. The hero's resistance to letting her tie a *rakhi* on him emphasises this.

The motif of siblinghood appears in a predictable fashion at the start of the film, only to take an unexpected turn later. When the protagonist, Babu, emerges from prison, he is welcomed by his friend, Balli, a gangster, who takes him to a gambling den. Soon after hatching plans for a bank robbery, Balli and Babu are seen alone together. Babu enquires about Balli's ring, which Balli tells him is his only memento from childhood when he was separated from his family at the age of five. Immediately thereafter, Babu's childhood friend, Shyam, now a policeman, recounts how, as children, they both picked someone's pocket as a childish prank. Shyam's wealthy father rescued him from the police, but Babu was branded as a thief and grew up to be a gangster. Shyam tries to persuade Babu that there are good people in the world, so he should give up his criminal ways, and Babu finally agrees, with the result that he is suspected of betraying his gang to the police and he ends up killing Balli in self-defence. These initial scenes establish Babu's fraternal relationship with both Balli and Shyam. As Babu is to Shyam, Balli is to Babu—Babu stands between the respectable Shyam and the doomed Balli. Even though eyewitnesses exonerate him from the murder of Balli, Babu is so haunted by guilt that he roams the country in a Cain-like attempt to flee the past. He finally reaches a village in the Himalayas, where a sleazy local character, Lala, enlists him to pose as the long-lost son of the richest landlord in the area. Even though Babu does not realise that it is Balli's family he is entering, the viewer is informed of this. Babu inherits Balli's past and ultimately takes his place, thus fulfilling their sibling-like relationship.

Sister or Beloved?

Babu's relationship with Balli's sister, Maya, is thus set within the larger framework of his brotherly relationship with Balli and the filial relationship he proceeds to develop with Balli and Maya's parents, Shahji and Rukmini; Rukmini's blindness, perhaps, symbolises the blindness of parental love. The dilemma that Babu now faces between a powerful erotic attraction and the equally powerful claims of gratitude and affection is a variation on the great and recurrent conflict in Bombay cinema and in the Indian narrative more generally—between selfish desire on the one hand, and the desire to uphold a supportive affective network on the other. In, perhaps, its most common form, this conflict appears when individuals give up their romantic entanglements for the sake of a deceased sibling.

This type of narrative has been generally viewed as exalting the sacrifice of the individual for the family and, thus, as retrograde. It can indeed function in this way when the film suggests that the protagonist chooses a socially-approved spouse over a socially-disapproved lover only in order to fit in with society's ideal of coupledom (as in *Silsila*, where the turning point for Amit comes in the *gurudwara*[9] where one heterosexual couple after another performs the *aarti*,[10] which he and his lover cannot do). In other films, however (such as *Hum Aapke Hain Koun*, 1994), the protagonist faces a choice, not between a loveless marriage and romantic love, but rather between one love (for the romantic partner) and many loves (family, friends, siblings). While the intensity of sexual desire can make romantic love seem the most important thing in the world temporarily, the network of many loves may ultimately be more valuable and sustaining. Giving it up may be a more painful sacrifice for the individual. The choice of family (in its widest sense) over coupledom may not be self-sacrifice but, on the

---

[9] A *gurudwara* is a Sikh temple.
[10] An *aarti* is a Hindu prayer.

contrary, a choice of that which is more necessary for the individual's emotional well-being. The true lover is one who realises this and, therefore, does not demand that the beloved pay such a high price.

Babu's integration into Balli's family and village signals his psychological and emotional re-integration as an individual. After his release from prison, he tells Shyam: 'You no longer trust me and I no longer trust the world. Maybe there are good people in the world, but I haven't met them'. The song that follows dwells on the hypocrisy of the rich. In the village, Babu meets good people, both rich and poor, and learns to trust them. For his adopted parents, the richest people in the village, love is more important than money, as his mother points out when she refers to money as '*haath ka mael*' (dirt of the hands).The film here plugs into the polarity of unspoilt rusticity versus corrupted urbanity, but this polarity is not absolute because Lala and his goons are also part of the village.

After the family accepts Babu as their long-lost son, Kundan, alternating scenes present the developing conflict between his attraction to Maya and his protective and grateful feelings to the entire family. This is contained within the larger conflict between his selfish desire to flee with whatever money he can grab and his deeper desire for a loving family. Lala and his cronies misinterpret this as Babu being tempted to continue acting as the son of the family in order to grab the entire property. What they do not realise is that along with the property, Babu would also inherit the many responsibilities and obligations of caring for his adopted parents and sister. The conflict between Babu's desire for Maya and his love for her and her parents reflects this larger conflict.

Alternating scenes of Kundan/Babu frolicking with Maya and interacting with her parents depict the two conflicting sets of emotions. Even as the parents demonstrate confidence and affection, terming him *ghar ka chirag* (a traditional reference to an only son), Lala reminds Babu that these are fake (*naqli*) parents and he should not consider them as his real parents. This division between fake or fictive kin on the one hand, and real or biological kin on the other, runs counter to the emotional trajectory of Bombay cinema's construction of kin and is a clear confirmation of Lala's villainy.

Perhaps, the most important overarching and consistent theme of Bombay cinema is the reality of so-called fictive kin. Love, not biology, defines who are kin. This theme structures the narrative arc of film after film and maintains its continuity through the rise and fall of otherwise very different types of male personae (Dev Anand, Rajesh Khanna, Shashi Kapoor, Amitabh Bachchan, Shah Rukh Khan). A character who challenges or trivialises the reality of chosen kin, as Lala does, marks himself as a villain right away.

In lyrical terms, the conflict climaxes in the song, '*Saathi na ko'i manzil*'. Kundan/Babu walks through a field overhung with mist and, at some distance, unbeknown to him, Maya walks a parallel line. The song dwells on Babu's aloneness in the world and, in a larger sense, on the individual's existential isolation in the universe:

>Neither companion nor goal
>Nor any gathering
>Where are you taking me alone, O heart?
>To find an intimate companion
>Is not in my destiny
>The earth is unkind and the heavens far
>These are the alleys of my land
>But they seem strange to me
>Whom can I call mine here?

There are two common ways to partially heal such alienation—one is to follow the trajectory of modernity and find a lover or spouse, and the other, to return to the community. Obtaining both might be ideal, but a protagonist is often forced to choose or at least prioritise one over the other. Bombay cinema, like the Victorian novel, explores the desire to develop a modernity that combines both. Simultaneously, it confronts the anxiety that romantic coupledom may require the sacrifice of other filiative structures.

Sajni: Both Sister and Beloved

Bombai ka Babu presents the dilemma in a stark manner, as the hero cannot have both. Maya as a lover is incompatible with Maya as a sister. And it is as a sister that she carries with her the possibility of community and kinship. Her walking parallel to, yet at a distance from, him neatly symbolises the dilemma. As a romantic partner, she would walk hand in hand with him. As a sister, she must walk at a distance (marry someone else) even while remaining in step with him.

It is, therefore, fitting that the decisive moment arrives in the shape of Maya's wedding. Kundan/Babu is supposed to steal her jewellery; this act would destroy the family's honour and also wreck her marriage. A brother's conventional role, of which the festival of Raksha Bandhan is a symbolic reminder, is to protect his sister in general, but specifically from mistreatment by her husband and in-laws. Thus, in *Anjaana*, the sister's song, '*Hum behnon ke liye mere bhaiya, Aata hai ek din saal mein*', tells her brother to not let her suffer like a nightingale caught in a snare, even as a small boy playfully mimes an overbearing moustachioed husband bullying her. The title song in *Resham ki Dori*, too, alludes to this:

> You are my flower and my sword
> You are the guardian of my honour
> You are my whole world
> Even if fate separates us
> Don't remove me from your heart

Kundan/Babu's dilemma is finally resolved, not by his feelings for Maya, but by his feelings for the lost symbolic brother, Balli, and, through him, for the parents. It is when Kundan/Babu opens the safe to steal the jewellery that he finds the flyer announcing the five-year-old Balli's loss and, after comparing the picture of Balli's ring to the ring that is in his possession, he realises that Balli is the child whose place he has taken. The dilemma is resolved instantaneously and he immediately, without taking any time to think or agonise, puts all the jewellery back in the safe.

Maya, who has discovered that he is not her biological brother, is deeply suspicious of his motives, but is reassured when he proves his genuineness by fighting Lala's goons (being wounded in the process) and brings back all her jewellery, thus enabling her wedding to take place. Kundan/Babu tells Lala that since he killed Balli, this family is now his, the parents are his parents and he is their son.

The film's achievement is in the way it plays new variations on old themes as, for instance, in the wonderfully ironic reversal in the last verse of the haunting '*Chal ri sajni, ab kya soche...*'. Where, earlier, Kundan/Babu was the outsider who felt alone between the earth and the sky, now he displaces not only Balli, but also Maya. The inequity between the brother–brother and sister–brother relationship surfaces as Maya becomes the outsider displaced by the conventions of virilocal marriage. In this same moment, though, she is briefly elevated to the space of the individual alone in the universe; as in the Amir Khusro poem, where the Sufi master is envisioned as a fair beloved ('*Gori sove sej pe*'), and marriage and death are mapped on to one another, pointing towards the soul in search of God; the second line is ungendered and thus hard to translate:

Dulhan ban ke gori khari hai
Ko'i nahin apna kaisi ghari hai
Ko'i yahan ko'i wahan ko'i kahan re

As a bride, the fair one stands
No one of one's own—what a moment this is
One is here, another there, another somewhere else

The refrain of this famous song addresses Maya as *sajni*, which nicely encapsulates the overlap of sister and spouse. *Sajni* derives from the Sanskrit *sa-jan* or *swa-jan*, literally 'one's own', and metaphorically 'dear one'. Either brother or husband could thus legitimately address her as *sajni*.

Maya's name, too, points in two directions—*maya* can signify the delusory glitter and temptation of desirable objects, such as wealth and beauty. However, *maya* is also the divine feminine energy that animates the universe. Likewise, *kundan* means 'pure gold', and also a method of setting precious stones in gold—these literally signify wealth, but metaphorically indicate the value of that which is priceless, as in the song referred to earlier, in which a sister calls her brother her '*anmol ratan*' or priceless precious stone. When Babu is tested and emerges as pure gold, he finally becomes Kundan.

Brotherhood across Borders

If in *Bombai ka Babu* the sibling relationship stands for family and community, in *Naam*, its symbolic meaning expands that community across national borders. The adoption motif here combines with the motif of co-wives, also found in such films as *Main Tulsi Tere Aangan Ki* (1978) and *Sunny* (1984). Ravi and Vicky, raised by their widowed mother, Janaki, find out that Vicky is her biological son and Ravi the son of her husband's mistress, adopted by her when her husband and Ravi's mother died in a car accident. Janaki is, of course, the name of Sita, who raised her sons Lav and Kush in exile; the mistress's name in the film is Radha, who was not Krishna's wife.

Throughout the film, Ravi shoulders the responsibility for supporting both his mother and the ne'er-do-well Vicky. While Vicky feels indebted to Ravi for bailing him out of numerous scrapes and standing between him and their mother's anger, Ravi feels indebted to Vicky because, throughout their childhood, their mother over-compensated for Ravi not being her biological child by favouring him over Vicky. This is a very common narrative pattern in Bombay cinema, but *Naam* extends it in interesting ways.

At the outset, Ravi tells his erstwhile girlfriend, whom he has abandoned without explanation, '*Vicky se mera bhai ke ilaawa ek aur rishta tha—woh tha pyaar ka, mohabbat ka* (I had another relationship with Vicky besides that of brother—that was the relationship of love)'. The two are depicted as deeply co-dependent (I use this term without its pejorative connotations). The film posits intimacy as involving the right to punish—thus, when Ravi's mother slaps him for unwittingly speaking slightingly of his biological grandmother, he kisses her hand, saying that she has now added to their love whatever was missing. Similarly, on more than one occasion, Ravi slaps Vicky repeatedly for his misdemeanours. Vicky endures this unresistingly and the encounters end with repeated embraces.

The film's two most famous songs, although apparently unrelated, are linked through the theme of separation and union. Ravi and Vicky's duet, on the eve of Vicky's departure for the

Persian Gulf, is echoed later, on a more universal scale, by the song about immigrants' ties to their homeland that Vicky and his girlfriend, Rita, hear at a concert along with their friends, a married couple from Pakistan. The half-brothers' relationship thus becomes a microcosm of the macrocosmic relations between South Asians across borders or, perhaps, even of all humanity.

Ravi and Vicky's duet, sung halfway through the film and repeated at the end after Vicky's death, is in the 'I–you' mode of many love songs, especially *ghazal*s, and deploys a number of erotic and romantic tropes. The two get drunk, fall on to each other, embrace, pour wine in each other's mouths and dance together all over Bombay, in many sites where cinematic lovers are generally shown dancing. They look deep into one another's eyes, Ravi touches Vicky's cheek, Vicky puts his head on Ravi's chest, and the camera zooms in, showing them in profile, face to face, as if mirroring one another. The irreplaceability of the brother ('Who else is like you? Who else can I name? When I miss you a lot, what will I do?') morphs into the irreplaceability of homeland and community when Pankaj Udhas sings the song, '*Chitthi aayi hai...*' (A letter has come, After a long time, We homeless ones/Remember the soil of our homeland) to an audience of weeping South Asian immigrants.

In Hong Kong, Vicky and Rita stay in a flat belonging to Aftab Ahmed from Lahore, who tells them that though he left home to earn a livelihood, he has not forgotten his home and so he rents his flat only to Indians and Pakistanis because his aim is not to make money, but to reduce the anguish of having left the homeland (*watan*) by keeping company with people from home. After Udhas' song, Aftab goes onstage and embraces him. Later, when Vicky is arrested on false charges, Aftab pawns his wife's jewellery to bail him out. When Vicky thanks him for helping out a stranger (*ajnabi*), Aftab says: 'You are not a stranger. Those whom one feels happy to be with, those whose joys make one glad and whose sorrows make one sad cannot be strangers. You are my own. You are my brother'. Fraternity between individuals here signifies fraternity between nations of the same stock as well as between Hindus and Muslims.

These two types of brotherhood come together in the last scene, which recalls the last scene of *Anand* (1971). In both scenes, as the protagonist dies, the co-protagonist (Dr. Bannerjee/Babu Moshai and Ravi) is the chief mourner, but their companionship is framed by a loving community. Siblinghood signifies community and derives meaning from it. Thus, Ravi puts his head on Vicky's chest and weeps, while Aftab kisses Vicky on the forehead.

The 'name' of the title acquires increasing significance throughout the film. Vicky's mother gives Ravi, the illegitimate son, his father's name when she adopts him and brings him home. Ravi upholds this name by always coming to Vicky's rescue and by always doing the right thing (standing up to hypocritical and oppressive rich people as well as ruffians). His mother's adoption of him is echoed at the end, when he brings Rita back to India and, after she dies in childbirth, brings her and Vicky's baby home to his mother. Homecoming and naming are thus intertwined, as in the song that says, 'My name is written on the letter [from home]'.

The theme of good siblinghood versus bad siblinghood as symbolic of humankind's fraternal relations is a perennial one, found across the world in many genres (for example, the many feuding brothers in the Old Testament; Cinderella and her sisters in the fairy tale); Bombay cinema's particular take on it is distinctive for its emphasis on adoption. This is in tune with Indian culture's assimilative tendencies. Adoption can be read as a trope for absorbing the outsider. It is also an ancient Indian trope—crucial figures, from Krishna to Sita to Shakuntala, are raised as adopted children.

Despite the many changes in technology and representation as well as in society, the new non resident Indian (NRI) film maintains continuity in this respect, as seen in the hugely successful *Kabhi Khushi Kabhie Gham* (*K3G*) (2001). Here, I agree with those who argue that

Bombay films develop variations on plot and character, but within certain parameters shaped by civilisational imperatives.[11] *K3G* explores the emotional loss entailed in being forced to make the painful choice of spouse over family. As Patrick Hogan points out, conjugality is represented as protective in the way that adoptive parenthood is; the hero, Rahul, intends to obey his father and break off with his girlfriend, but when he finds that her father has died, he fulfils his dharma by refusing to subject her to a double abandonment.[12] Disowned by his father in a fit of anger, Rahul, the adopted son, leaves not just the family, but the country. This devastates his adoptive mother, who loves him more than she does her biological son, and it is the latter who later takes on the task of bringing Rahul back to family and homeland.

As in *Naam*, siblinghood becomes symbolic of kinship between countries. The over-the-top national anthem scene recalls the famous '*Chitthi aayi hai*' song in its evocation of NRI angst as well as in its resolution of this angst, though the kinship this time is not with Pakistan, but with England. Although Rahul sees himself as an outsider, saying that England is now his home and the adopted family was never really his, the anthem works to assure the viewer that the truth is more complex. The modern family, at home in the world, adopts and is adopted both in England and in India. Assimilation works at both the national and the individual level as it is the despised daughter-in-law's highly-Westernised sister who teaches the child and his British schoolmates to sing the Indian anthem. Immediately after they sing it, the brothers are reunited and, in a double whammy for siblinghood, the younger brother finally marries his sister-in-law's sister.

If the word 'romance' indicates an excess of passion, yearning and bliss leading to conflict and drama, and also often pointing to a longing for eternal or mystical union, then it is by no means restricted to sexual love in Bombay cinema. The word imbues many different kinds of emotions and relationships. While heterosexual couplings are the noisiest and most attention-grabbing of these relationships, they are not necessarily always the most important. Indeed, the sound and fury they generate often serve to protect from scrutiny the more cherished relationships that anchor them, much like the foam on the waves masking the still depths beneath. Among these is the subtle thread of chosen kinship as the tie that binds the world.

---

[11] Vinay Lal, 'The Impossibility of the Outsider in Modern Hindi Film', in Ashis Nandy (ed.), *The Secret Politics of Our Desires: Innocence, Culpability and Indian Popular Cinema* (New Delhi: Oxford University Press, 1998), pp.228–59.

[12] Patrick Colm Hogan, *Understanding Indian Movies: Culture, Cognition and Cinematic Imagination* (Austin: University of Texas Press, 2008), pp.191–2.

Aliens, Aliases, Surrogates and Familiars: The Family in Jhumpa Lahiri's Short Stories

DEEPIKA BAHRI

In this essay, I argue that alienation and familiarity serve as mobile matrices for understanding the affectively experienced impact of transnational migration in certain of Jhumpa Lahiri's short stories. While we may think of alienation as a precondition of migrant identity, it is a condition that is familiar to most of us in different contexts. How does alienation, thus plurally conceived, figure in the experience of migrants, producing the relay between heimlich/unheimlich *experiences? Moreover, in the socio-cultural context of globalisation, how does transnational migration challenge conventional notions of family, a word associated with notions of familiarity and filiation that are seemingly antonymous to the idea of alienation? These are the questions I set out to answer, concluding that the 'family' is always a unit composed by its very hauntings, surrogates, and absences.*

Unheimlich is the name for everything that ought to have remained...secret and hidden but has come to light.[1]

The trope of alienation is written into the script of migration, an unwitting irony betrayed in the formulation 'resident alien' in immigration and taxation codes which point to the stranger within. In a further dilation of otherness, 'alien', customarily meaning one who 'belongs to another person or place', is also used in science fiction to mean 'intelligent being from another planet'.[2] In Jhumpa Lahiri's short story 'The Third and Final Continent', the arrival in Boston of the unnamed protagonist on 16 July 1969, the very day of man's landing on the moon, recalls these various connotations of the word alien, effectively conflating journeys of galactic scale, splendid isolation, and Adamic novelty with the migrant's relatively 'ordinary' achievement of surviving in the 'New World'.[3] Although a thorough exploration of the philosophical concept of alienation is beyond the scope of this paper, the understanding of alienation as a state of separation—whether from nature, self, other or the conditions and relations of production—may be sufficient to allow us to recognise that it is a condition at

---

[1] Friedrich Schelling quoted in Sigmund Freud, 'The Uncanny', in *The Standard Edition of the Complete Psychological Works of Sigmund Freud*, Volume XVII (1917–1919) (James Strachey, ed. & trans.) (London: Hogarth, 1923), p.224.
[2] OED Online.
[3] Jhumpa Lahiri, *Interpreter of Maladies* (Boston: Houghton, 1999), p.198. Subsequent references will be cited parenthetically in the text.

once familiar and strange. Additionally, in the Hegelian schematic, alienation, allied with cognitive elevation—the rise above a bounded self—is conceived as a spiritual and philosophical desideratum. The negative dialectic between the alien as at once other and customarily resident and written into the law, is part of the dynamic of the acquisition of identity through processes of negation, with a remaindering of parts of the self that never quite add up to a whole. How does alienation, thus plurally conceived, figure in the experience of migrants, producing the relay between *heimlich/unheimlich* experiences?[4] Moreover, in the socio-cultural context of globalisation, how does transnational migration challenge conventional notions of family, a word associated with notions of familiarity and filiation that are seemingly antonymous to the idea of alienation?

In this essay, I turn to Pulitzer prize winning Indian American author Jhumpa Lahiri's stories about the experiences of post-1965 Indian immigrants to the United States to explore challenges to the limits of the family, expected roles within it, and the ways in which non-family actors infect the traditional family in migration. Many of Lahiri's stories experiment with the boundaries of the family, the threshold of the known and unknown, the familiar and strange. Lahiri's highly regarded debut collection, *Interpreter of Maladies*, performs the legerdemain of seeming at once alien and yet familiar in the larger conspectus of American literature. Despite her primary focus on subcontinental characters and situations, Lahiri has been placed squarely within the tradition of American literature in general, and such masters of the short story as O. Henry in particular. In an attempt to explain why '*Interpreter* [sic] stood out' ('because it didn't try to stand out'), reviewer Matthew Solan writes: 'You can relate to her characters because their plights could easily be your own—a young couple trying to stay together after losing a baby; a housewife yearning to be more independent'. 'Beneath the surface, though', he goes on, 'her fiction takes the pulse of first- and second-generation Indian Americans trying to bridge the gap between the country they call home and the heritage that defines them'.[5] One might argue that the textual effect of an unresolved dialectic between the alien and familiar is produced at least in part by the diegetic narratorial confidence with which the lives of America's supposed others is portrayed, such that the collection seems to do better than merely straddle the India–America divide; it bestrides it like a colossus. Lahiri's narrators command centre stage, speaking of alienation and isolation with a confidence that suggests not only a right to be heard, but a conviction that these seemingly marginal, trivial, and ordinary lives are momentous, and that the endlessly repeated experience of migration and settlement in a new world is in actuality both 'beyond...imagination' *and* part of the fabric of the reader's world.[6]

Although the ability to relate to a broad audience while telling the immigrant's uniquely distinctive story could be ascribed to the writer's unusual narratorial assurance, surface gloss alone cannot account for the impact of the stories. Nor is it sufficient to say that the experiences appeal on the grounds of universality, unless we mean that the sufficiently particularised can sometimes be adduced as the seed from which a sense of the universal may grow. As I argue, 'beneath the surface,' in the innards of many of the stories, the relay between the alien and the familiar functions as a thematic. The making *unheimlich* of the *heimlich*—the coming to light of *heimlich*, homely, family secrets through the 'simple' act of collection and recollection of what has happened in a hitherto unknown life—sets up a relationship between the alien and the familiar that we might liken to the sudden, shocking

---

[4] The meanings of *heimlich* and *unheimlich* are discussed below.
[5] Matthew Solan, 'Catching up with Pulitzer Prize Winner Jhumpa Lahiri', in *Poets and Writers* (Sept./Oct. 2003), p.1.
[6] Lahiri, *Interpreter of Maladies*, p.198.

recognition of something repressed that is nonetheless familiar because it is, after all, recognised. We know, of course, that recollection is not 'simple' any more than it is easy to tell a story well, to relate (in every sense of the word) with success. The lives of others, many of them bona fide 'aliens' at some point in their American sojourn, made familiar to an audience seemingly comprised of those unconflicted about where they belong, sets up a dialectic that warrants examination.

In his essay on the Uncanny, Freud explains the relationship between *heimlich* and *unheimlich* thus:

> The German word *unheimlich* is obviously the opposite of *heimlich* (homely), *heimisch* (native)—the opposite of what is familiar; and we are tempted to conclude that what is 'uncanny' is frightening precisely because it is not known and familiar. Naturally not everything that is new and unfamiliar is frightening, however; the relation is not capable of inversion.[7]

In surveying Sander's *Wörterbuch der Deutschen Sprache*, Freud notes that the first indexed meaning of *heimlich* is what we might expect: 'belonging to the house, not strange, familiar, tame, intimate, friendly'; subsequent meanings offer unsurprising connotations of intimacy, comfort, and in the case of animals, the quality of being tame and companionable. What interests him most, however, is his discovery that 'among its different shades of meaning the word "*heimlich*" exhibits one which is identical with its opposite, "*unheimlich*". What is *heimlich* thus comes to be *unheimlich*'. This secondary meaning is as follows:

> Concealed, kept from sight, so that others do not get to know of or about it, withheld from others. To do something *heimlich*, i.e., behind someone's back; to steal away *heimlich*; *heimlich* meetings and appointments; to look on with *heimlich* pleasure at someone's discomfiture; to sigh or weep *heimlich*; to behave *heimlich*, as though there was something to conceal; *heimlich* love-affair, love, sin; *heimlich* places (which good manners oblige us to conceal).

Freud notes that 'in general we are reminded that the word "*heimlich*" is not unambiguous, but belongs to two sets of ideas, which, without being contradictory, are yet very different: on the one hand it means what is familiar and agreeable, and on the other what is concealed and kept out of sight'. His conclusion is that '*heimlich* is a word the meaning of which develops in the direction of ambivalence, until it finally coincides with its opposite, *unheimlich*. *Unheimlich* is in some way or other a sub-species of *Heimlich*'.[8] The strange, the alien, are not only without, but also within.

The customary sequestration of the immigrant's experience from that of the usually mythical mainstream (not that there is no difference between them, and not to diminish the isolation and trauma of the newly-arrived immigrant in alien territory where s/he longs for signs of the familiar) usually prevents an exploration of the dialectic between *Heimlich* and *Unheimlichkeit* as mutually-relevant states that are only partially resolved in most of our lives. In fact, one might speculate that it is the immigrant's isolation and alienation that provoke deep-seated and secret anxieties that have largely been repressed or domesticated in those more 'settled' in the real, 'true', America. Lahiri says that she has 'often felt' that she is

---

[7] Sigmund Freud, *The Standard Edition of the Complete Psychological Works of Sigmund Freud*, Vol.XVII (1917–1919) (James Strachey ed. & trans.) (London: Hogarth, 1923), p.219.
[8] *Ibid.*, pp.224–6.

'somehow illegitimate in both cultures. A true Indian doesn't accept me as an Indian and a true American doesn't accept me as an American'.[9] Lahiri's self-deprecatory assumption of illegitimacy in both cultures is belied not only by the extraordinary success of her work, but also by her thereby calling into question the salience and value of being 'true' to any one culture, assuming that this were even possible. There are many forms of belonging and unbelonging, and nationally-defined cultural identity can hardly exhaust the various dimensions of our lives. Fears and anxieties that lie deep within us are no less a part of the narrative of displaced, dislocated lives. The immigrant's story is in excess of the fact of migration; for all that it is the experience of migration that is in focus, what lies in the penumbra of this spotlight is hardly less significant. If the 'mainstream' reader encounters the lives of others in these stories, the characters in these stories encounter mainstream American lives with no less a sense of otherness. The mutuality of this transaction demands recognition. In the readings that follow, I want to explore the ways in which the text enjoins us to acknowledge this mutuality in selected stories.

'The Third and Final Continent' is a story told in the first person by an unnamed narrator who sails to England for work and study in 1964, and five years later, arrives in Boston on a fateful day in July 1969, after having 'attend[ed]' his wedding in Calcutta on a week-long break, much as a guest would, for the woman he has married is a stranger to him (p.174). In the weeks before his wife, Mala, arrives to join him, he begins work at his full-time job in the library at MIT (Massachusetts Institute of Technology), and lodges for a few weeks in the home of the 103-year-old Mrs. Croft. At the end of the story, the narrator comments on his journey and the people he has met, and how they have together influenced the life he now looks upon with satisfaction as a family man with a son, a young man who may be the intended recipient of his recollections. 'Mrs. Sen's' tells the story of a young wife of thirty—perhaps something like Mala, at least in that she too comes to the USA after an arranged marriage to a stranger—in what one assumes are the early years of her life on Rhode Island. The third person narrative of the story is focalised in part through the consciousness of an eleven-year-old boy, Eliot, whom Mrs. Sen baby-sits in her fussily-appointed but clean university apartment, since she has not yet learned how to drive. The strangers in each of the two households, Mrs. Croft's and Mrs. Sen's, function for a short while in a surrogate capacity within the makeshift family unit until they part ways, having exposed the secrets of each others' households and lives to the reader, and invited us to speculate on the irresolute line between the alien and familiar.

Although I have described them as makeshift, perhaps it is overreaching to suggest that they are family units in any sense, much less a conventional one. Definitions of the family are hardly stable or uncontroversial, but most of us have a functional sense of what the term implies. Engels' contention that the family develops in conjunction with private property and the need to establish a clear line of inheritance sets up the expectation of a unit with a mother, father, and a child or children.[10] The insertion of the family into the property system, and the association of the monogamous family with property underscore the significance of capital in Engels' formulation. Engels and Marx's joint dismissal of 'the bourgeois claptrap about the family' notwithstanding, the family has been imbued with extraordinary significance in almost every culture, most certainly within the Indian context, and not least when it seems to be in crisis.[11] Anthony Giddens' definition of family as a 'group of people directly linked by kin

---

[9] Barbara Kantrowitz, 'Who Says There's No Second Act?', in *Newsweek*, Vol.142, no.8 (25 Aug. 2003), p.61.
[10] Friedrich Engels, *The Origin of the Family: Private Property and the State* (1884) (London: Penguin, 2010).
[11] Karl Marx and Friedrich Engels, *Manifesto of the Communist Party* (Arthur Baker, trans.) (Chicago: Charles H. Kerr, 1908), p.40.

connection, where the adult members take responsibility for caring for children' eschews precision in favour of the looseness of the idea of 'kin' which might seem vaguely tautological in implying that family is family because it is connected by kinship.[12] Sabatelli and Bartle's definition aims at an identification of interactive features, defining family as 'a complex structure consisting of an interdependent group of individuals who (a) have a shared sense of history, (b) experience some degree of emotional bonding, and (c) devise strategies for meeting the needs of individual family members and the group as a whole'.[13] These definitions of the family together imply expectations of stability, duration, and bonding, although numerous exceptions to these principles would not void a family unit that is recognised by society.

In the liminal space of families transposed internationally, many of the features identified in the definitions above may begin to appear in units much larger than the nuclear family. In the crucible of transnational migration, other filiations may become necessary to compensate for the loss of a larger community in which shared history, food, culture and other quotidian expressions of identity find resonance, support, and confirmation. This is not to say that the idea of family has not been changing in homeland societies in response to historical transformations, especially given the impact of transnational migration on parents and others left behind, but only to demarcate the size of the canvas with which this essay is concerned, and to explore more closely the dynamics within the family in the specific context of migration.

Apart from the aforementioned, other stories in *Interpreter of Maladies* and Lahiri's second collection, *Unaccustomed Earth*, mention chance encounters with fellow subcontinentals who then go on to become part of the family unit for a duration long enough to leave a lasting impression on the narrators ('When Mr. Pirzada Came to Dine' and 'Hell-Heaven', for example). 'Hell-Heaven' opens with a description of the logic that produces a non-familial network of kin figures within the immigrant Bengali socius:

> Pranab Chakraborty wasn't technically my father's younger brother. He was a fellow-Bengali from Calcutta who had washed up on the barren shores of my parents' social life in the early seventies, when they lived in a rented apartment in Central Square and could number their acquaintances on one hand. But I had no real uncles in America, and so I was taught to call him Pranab Kaku. Accordingly, he called my father Shyamal Da, always addressing him in the polite form, and he called my mother Boudi, which is how Bengalis are supposed to address an older brother's wife, instead of using her first name, Aparna.[14]

The diegetic 'I' of 'Hell-Heaven', Usha, remembers that Pranab Kaku showed up for dinner 'almost every night, occupying the fourth chair at our square Formica kitchen table, and becoming a part of our family in practice as well as in name'.[15] The young *émigré* from India is so much a part of the family that the narrator notes: 'Wherever we went, any stranger would have naturally assumed that Pranab Kaku was my father, that my mother was his wife.... In my mind, he was just a family member, a cross between an uncle and a much older

---

[12] Anthony Giddens, *Sociology* (Cambridge: Polity Press, 2nd ed. 1993), p.370.
[13] Ronald M. Sabatelli and Suzanne E. Bartle, 'Survey Approaches to the Assessment of Family Functioning: Conceptual, Operational, and Analytical Issues,' in *Journal of Marriage and the Family*, Vol.57, no.4 (1995), p.1027.
[14] Jhumpa Lahiri, *Unaccustomed Earth* (New Delhi: Random, 2008), p.60.
[15] *Ibid.*, p.62.

brother, for in certain respects my parents sheltered and cared for him in much the same way they cared for me'.[16] Usha notes not only the absence of extended family, and hence the parents' disposition toward experimenting with non-kin in a kinship role, but also the attempt to build into that relationship recognisable elements of traditional family roles and practices. Pranab's cycling through the surrogate roles of husband to Usha's mother, father or older brother to Usha, along with the designated nominally-defined role of uncle, in her eyes or that of others, is an attempt to domesticate and contain irresolute relations within familial norms.

Similarly, although Mr. Pirzada in *Interpreter of Maladies* never serves as 'uncle' to Lilia in the story 'When Mr. Pirzada Came to Dine', the young girl, then ten, recalls that she 'had grown so accustomed to Mr. Pirzada's presence in our living room, that one evening, as I was dropping ice cubes into the water pitcher, I asked my mother to hand me a fourth glass from a cupboard still out of reach'. She notes that he and her parents 'spoke the same language, laughed at the same jokes, looked more or less the same' (p.25). The story might be read as an object lesson in the significance of perspective and scale in the understanding of identity: it is only through a microscopic examination that Mr. Pirzada, who shares so much with Lilia's family (the word 'same' is repeated thrice with almost incantatory insistence), is revealed as distinctive and dissimilar (subcontinental but not Indian, Pakistani but Bengali, Bengali but Muslim, and now soon to be Bangladeshi). We must deduce that Lilia's family is Hindu, since Mr. Pirzada's difference must be explained to the young girl: 'Mr. Pirzada is Bengali, but he is a Muslim', and this is perhaps the reason why he is not 'Uncle' to her as a Bengali but Hindu stranger of a certain age would be. Alternatively, Lilia's family may have grown away from subcontinental practices, including that of naming elders (her mother's hair is 'bobbed to a suitable length for her part-time job as a bank teller' in contrast to many or even most of the Bengali women of that age in several of Lahiri's other stories), but they nonetheless show a great deal of concern for Mr. Pirzada, and he for the young girl who reminds him of his own children, missing in the chaos of East Pakistan's struggle for liberation (pp.26–37). In the worst of the crisis, the family prepares the couch so he can sleep over, and Lilia remembers 'the three of them operating as if they were a single person, sharing a single meal, a single body, a single silence, and a single fear' (p.41). The 'single fear' concerns the fate of Mr. Pirzada's wife and seven girls. One might speculate that Lilia's parents' response to his anxieties is triggered at least in part by a shared knowledge of the importance of children and family, and the incalculable magnitude of their potential loss, fears that are *heimlich* and secret, kept so through repression. The becoming one—the word 'single' is repeated even more insistently here than 'same'—of this family unit and a transient interloper who is never seen again, leaves us with an image of unity, underlining the dissolution of the limit of family and person for a time, precisely when the future of Mr. Pirzada's family is at stake.

Of course it is not only in migration that the boundaries of family are stretched. The subcontinental penchant for extending the bounds of family already exceeds most Western notions of it. The idea of the 'joint family', for instance, cross-hatches the notion of kin family with the dilating modifier 'joint', the extension sometimes stretching quite far by Western standards. Joint families extend not only multigenerationally in a vertical kinship line, but occasionally encompass horizontal and lateral relationships; more typically, however, they do set certain 'limits', commonly characterised by filial and fraternal common purse and property and adoption of women by marriage. The extension of familial relationships beyond even this expansive remit to non-family is something of a subcontinental social tic. Should the identity or relational status of an unfamiliar be in doubt, a filial or fraternal level nominal (Uncle,

---

[16] *Ibid.*, pp.66–7.

Aunty, brother, sister) is most likely to be used by default, especially, though not exclusively, in conventional Bengali interactions.

A collective societal inclination toward establishing familial relationships with non-family members could of course be theorised variously, and need not, in fact should not, be understood either as naïve or unconscious of the limits of family or its functional structure. Indeed, family relationships are named and detailed with extraordinary precision in the Indian social context, establishing the fraternal, maternal, or marital relational co-ordinates of the extended family person in question. Usha, the narrator of 'Hell-Heaven', goes well beyond the generic convention of 'Uncle' in pinpointing the Bengali custom of establishing with exactitude the precise nominal, 'Kaku', that must be given to a young man of Pranab's age and situation. At once precise and hyper-conscious of the relational particulars of all individuals related to the nuclear unit, the custom of extending familial relationships more widely can be read as a tacit recognition of family vs. non-family in the very gesture of extending its bounds or even as an attempt to disarm and contain the threat that the other would pose to the well-being of the family unit by symbolically subsuming him/her within it. In some parts of India, the status of '*rakhi*-brother' can be imposed on a truant young man inclined toward sexual harassment of a young woman, so that the symbolic thread she ties on his wrist (the *rakhi*) binds him to her with the expectation of protection. In the subcontinent the common rejoinder to 'Eve teasing', or sexual harassment of women on the streets, is to demand of the young man or men in question whether they are without shame and have no sister or mother at home: '*Ghar main maa behen nahin hai kya?*' The impulse to recall family relationships in the face of their absence—and that of concern expected in familial relationships—might thus be construed as a recollection of those values and emotional bonds within the family that are calculated to enhance the well-being of its members, although we might cynically concede that neither this ploy nor the family structure can reliably guarantee the desired well-being. Violations of these expectations within the family are coded as 'dysfunctional', with the assumption of functionality as normative, in a mode that might be read as societal judgement and policing in advance of the potential breach of codes naturalised by duration and consensual social contracts which require both expression and repression of our instincts to ensure collective survival.

In other words, a familial nominal comes with the expectation that an individual will behave and function like an uncle, father, son, etc., instead of crossing the line into an inappropriate role. Hence, although a heterosexual relationship is assumed in definitions of family, the father may not sleep with the daughter, the brother with the sister and so on in most societies. Limits apply both beyond and within the family. One might argue that familial names are even *founded* in the idea of transgression, and can be used to forestall it. The hailing of non-family by familial names is similarly designed to interpellate the so-designated individual (the '*rakhi*-brother' for instance) within a socially-defined familial order in which limits must be defined and kept, and inappropriate desires for socially unacceptable relations contained and repressed. In 'Hell-Heaven', when Pranab falls in love with an 'American' woman, Deborah, who begins to use the familial nominals her lover has taught her, Usha's mother Aparna exhibits a jealousy that custom demands should be reserved for her husband. Usha's query, whether she ought to address Pranab's lover as 'Deborah Kakima', elicits a sharp rebuke, with Aparna drawing a line that excludes the American rival for Pranab's affections, but continues to include the latter within the family fold. During their courtship, the couple drive around with Usha in the back seat in 'practice for the future, to try on theidea of a family of their own' while the young girl obligingly participates in the experiment. 'Countless photographs' of Usha and Deborah, with the young child 'sitting on Deborah's lap, holding her hand, kissing her on the cheek', survive as testament to the experiment which includes those aspects of family—emotional bonding, concern and affection—that are its least cynical and most attractive characteristics. Anticipating his parents' opposition to the impending marriage, Pranab asks Usha's parents to advocate his cause. Pranab's parents respond by blaming Usha's mother 'for allowing the affair to develop...as if they were intimate' and asking them to plead with their son. Usha's father refuses the request, insisting to his wife: 'We are not his parents'.[17] Pranab responds by suggesting that their blessings are a sufficient substitute for those of his parents. Although the limits of the family have already been extended and breached, and various simulations attempted, Usha's mother's tragic desire for Pranab, a man who 'wooed her as no other man had, with the innocent affection of a brother-in-law', reminds us that there are limits to the ways in which boundaries can be crossed when she attempts but does not go through with suicide in response to his wedding.[18] The contractual dimensions of co-existence within and beyond the conventionally-conceptualised family require the simulation of a relationship seemingly founded on family-style care and concern, coupled with the taboo against confusing roles within the family.

The heartbreak and tragedy of 'Hell-Heaven' lie in the fact that although Aparna behaves like family with Pranab, she emulates the wrong model in the relationship, that of wife rather than sister-in-law. The latter model permits the possibility of 'innocent affection' and thus flirtation in what might seem an acknowledgment of natural impulses in unrelated young people of the opposite sex placed within close proximity. But it is when secret desires break the surface which was intended to confine them ('in the depths' to use Solan's phrase), that the delicate balance is overturned, turning Heaven-Hell, oppositional but paired in balance, into Hell-Heaven in a tragic overhaul. Aparna's transgression of the expected decorous distance from the man who calls her 'Boudi' is an emotional one. That Pranab, already used to crossing boundaries into a family to which he has not been ritually or biologically bound in a socially-regulated manner, eventually abandons Deborah for a married Bengali woman, suggests that he may have also crossed the line with Aparna, or toyed with its elasticity, his innocent affection not so innocent, or at least not incapable of harm as the word etymologically implies (*in nocere*: incapable of harm).

If we adhere to the etymological connotations of the word transgress ('trans': 'across' + 'gradi': 'to walk, go'), the notion of a spatially-conceived breach applies to the crossing of all boundaries, within the family or beyond it. Indeed, although the visibly-different immigrant's being in a new world points to an original, overwhelming transgression that cannot be erased from the record *vis-à-vis* a sufficiently-homogenous mainstream, s/he is not the only one who crosses over to see what is on the other side. The unnamed narrator of 'The Third and Final Continent' is not the first to transgress, nor will he be the last.

The titular gesture of the last of the nine stories in Lahiri's first collection demands that we learn to shift our scalar expectations and test our collective memory on the subject of historical transgressions. Lahiri's use of an epigraph from Nathaniel Hawthorne's 'The Custom House', exhorting an exploration of 'unaccustomed earth' in the eponymous second collection of short stories, is a similar auctorial bid for an expansion of memory through history. The writer's description of Mrs. Sen's use of a knife with a blade 'that curved like the prow of a viking ship, sailing to battle in distant seas', can be read as a similar narratorial nudge to recall a long history of crossings stretching back to immigrants before the pilgrim fathers, and perhaps even to a time before recorded memory.[19] Beyond the hyphenated Indian-American identities anchored on two major continents, it is Britain—the narrator's second and

---

[17] *Ibid.*, pp.70–2.
[18] *Ibid.*, p.67.
[19] Lahiri, *Interpreter of Maladies*, p.114.

transitional continent in the collection's final story—and the engines of empire that have set in motion both the early pilgrim fathers and the later post-1965 fortune hunters in the direction of the third and final continent. Although the narrator makes no reference to this shared past—for it is his migration and his journey that is in focus and the rest is reserved for another, much earlier migrant's tale—the continental scale suggested in the story's title and the narrator himself gesture at journeys and ventures in which he is not alone in his inter-continental passages, or in his isolation. His first home in north London was occupied, he says, 'by penniless Bengali bachelors like myself, at least a dozen and sometimes more, all struggling to educate and establish ourselves abroad' (p.173). On a different scale, his arrival in Boston on the very day of the moon landing invokes another momentous breach, this time of space, the final frontier. Coincidentally, the first man to walk upon the moon, Neil Armstrong, was also a veteran of the Korean War, in a previous, more terrestrial transgression, which may not have constituted a giant leap but was nonetheless another crossing over onto unaccustomed earth. These historic transgressions rebound on a more domestic scale, infecting private lives, intertwining destinies that geographical distance may otherwise have obliged to remain separate.

All these crossings, some more historic than others, are arguably collectively earth-shattering, and have required a mixing of aliens and familiars, with unexpected discoveries and joinings. Thresholds are crossed despite the threat and danger to self and other, and in the hope of both reward and cost which cannot be calculated in advance. The immigrant who has already transgressed by walking across the boundaries of family, home, culture, and nation knows the price of migration; further crossings into the unknown carry the risk of rejection and tragedy but may also bring the unexpected wages of contact and connection. This joint threat and promise is also offered to the settled, more 'true' American who either crosses a threshold or invites a crossing. The door to the home, bordering inside and outside, is significant for those on either side of it. Mrs. Croft, arguably the deuteragonist of 'The Third and Final Continent', is the elderly woman who hosts the narrator in his first few months in Boston in a home that is formidably and ceremonially barricaded: 'Lock up!' Mrs. Croft commands the narrator as he enters. 'Fasten the chain and firmly press that button on the knob! This is the first thing you shall do when you enter, is that clear?' (p.178). Mrs. Croft, whose name means an enclosed small field, if we were inclined to read more into it to substantiate the theme of enclosure, has been renting rooms to boys from Harvard University and MIT, including at least one other foreigner, a Brazilian, as her daughter Helen mentions. Far from signalling indiscriminate openness, however, this is a compensatory, economically-motivated move for a woman long widowed who raised her family through the dint of her labour (she used to give piano lessons), and who now retains some economic independence by renting a room in a house too large for one, but only to boys she deems acceptable because they have been previously vetted by respectable educational institutions.

In the weeks that follow, the tentative narrator and stentorian Mrs. Croft develop a routine, sharing space, brief, somewhat formulaic conversations, and something like a relationship undergirded by the exchange of rent money but not confined to it. I will not belabour the similarity of some of these features with that of many families—but note rather the narrator's insistence on the *not*-family character of the relationship. The immigrant's mindset is often comparative—the newly-arrived immigrant is constantly comparing the price of things, converting currencies, contrasting behaviours, spaces and people, and looking for the familiar to find comfort in an alien land, even translating alien fears and anxieties into a familiar vernacular. In this vein, Mrs. Croft's wonder at an American landing on the moon, and her insistence that the narrator recognise it by bellowing out 'Splendid!', is baffling and insulting, but immediately compared by the narrator to 'the way I was taught multiplication tables as a child, repeating after the master, sitting cross-legged, without shoes or pencils, on the floor of my one-room Tollygunge school'. He goes on to confide that 'it also reminded me of my wedding, when I repeated endless Sanskrit verses after the priest, verses I barely understood, which joined me to my wife'. Resisting this implicit invitation to join Mrs. Croft—albeit in a context hardly as significant—the narrator says nothing. His obliging murmur of 'Splendid!' the next time she bellows the order satisfies the centenarian, who continues the process by commanding him to 'Go see the room!' (pp.180–1).

Having negotiated the terms of the contract ('No lady visitors' and 'rent...due on Friday mornings on the ledge above the piano keys'), the narrator goes on to the next part of his tale (p.181). What comes next is not what *happens* next, but what has happened recently in his life and which ostensibly offers itself to the narrator for comparison: an account of his arranged marriage, which he has entered into 'with neither objection nor enthusiasm' but rather as a duty (p.181). The segment detailing his first exchange with his new landlady, concluding thus: 'She introduced herself as Mrs. Croft', is followed by the next one, which opens with the disclosure 'My wife's name was Mala' (p.181) in a diegetic move that invites a comparison of the two new entrants into his life. What appears to be a *non sequitur* is offered up not through argumentative logic or through explicit reflection, but through parataxis, such that Mrs. Croft and Mala are narratively juxtaposed. Prior to his departure, 'for five nights...[Mala and the narrator] shared a bed' in his brother's household which would be her home until she left to join the narrator (p.181). 'For the next six weeks', we learn, 'she was to live with my brother and his wife, cooking, cleaning, serving tea and sweets to guests' (p.181). Her six weeks with her new extended family, and *his* six weeks, with a significant portion spent at Mrs. Croft's, his new *un*-family, arrange the two experiences side by side. The narrative interlude dwelling on his five nights with Mala before his departure for Boston concludes with memories of his mother who died six years ago in what appear to be the final stages of dementia.

The similarly elderly (he does not know her age yet) but far more independent, albeit absent-minded and frail Mrs. Croft and the narrator gradually develop a routine which involves his sitting on the bench beside her for some ten minutes every evening upon his return from work. His unfailing courtesy and gentleness appear to be appreciated, for she exclaims, apparently in response to his handing her the rent money earlier that day: 'It was very kind of you' (p.184). A creature of routine and habit, she is visited every Sunday by her daughter, the 68-year-old Helen. Helen's 'short' skirts, worn 'so high above the ankle', and her 'private conversation' with a gentleman (the lodger) to whom she is 'not married', are denounced as 'improper' (p.186). Helen has come with groceries, to wit several cans of soup that she opens and pours into two saucepans for the week to follow. The lodger observes the meagre diet plan with concern, asking: 'Is it enough food for Mrs. Croft?' Mrs. Croft's one-item diet, appropriate to her age according to Helen, but also speaking of a reduced state, reminds the reader (the narrator does not provoke this comparison himself) that in his London home in Finsbury Park he lived 'three or four to a room...and took turns cooking pots of egg curry, which we ate with our hands on a table covered with newspaper' (p.173). One assumes that eggs were chosen by the young bachelors because they were less expensive than meat, and although the final preparation is spicier than Mrs. Croft's canned soups, in both cases the monotonous and diminished diet indicates reduced circumstances, a kind of poverty associated with age and isolation on the one hand and migration and deprivation on the other, a shared secret in two very different lives. In 103 years, in terms of sheer duration, Mrs. Croft, American born and bred, warrants the title 'true American', complete with national pride in America's landing the first man on the moon and its planting of the American flag there, but her life, too, has been one of struggle and want, and is now one of isolation and the comforts of a meagre rent, and brief weekly contact with the only family she has left. In his six weeks in

Boston as he awaits his wife, the narrator also adheres to his strict routine, and lives on a similarly-reduced diet of cornflakes and milk, adding 'bananas for variety, slicing them into the bowl with the edge of…[his] spoon', first in his noisy room at the YMCA, and later at Mrs. Croft's where the kitchen offers no spare utensils for his use (p.176). There is no one to ask of this diet plan or of this routine the question, 'Is it enough?'

We might speculate that the narrator's expression of a sort of family feeling for Mrs. Croft arises from his years looking after his widowed mother, who had 'refused to adjust to life without [her husband]' after his death when the narrator was sixteen (p.187). The narrator has not only shouldered this responsibility while his elder brother has been out earning a living for the household, but he has also stepped in to perform a duty traditionally reserved for the eldest son: the inception of the cremation process which involves touching the flame to the temple of the deceased. Inured to relationships involving responsibility, he tells Helen: 'I am happy to warm Mrs. Croft's soup in the evenings'. Helen declines the offer, explaining that a change in routine is 'the sort of thing that would kill her altogether' (p.188). Having learned from Helen that Mrs. Croft is not in her eighties but a full 103, he begins to worry that he might be accused of negligence if anything should happen to her. Although Helen's nonchalance relieves him of this anxiety to some extent, in the remaining weeks he continues to visit Mrs. Croft every evening, confessing that 'at times I came downstairs before going to sleep, to make sure that she was sitting upright on the bench, or was safe in her bedroom' (p.189). 'There was nothing more I could do for her beyond these simple gestures' he continues, adding: 'I was not her son, and apart from those eight dollars [of rent money], I owed her nothing' (p.189).

The narrator's insistence that 'I was not her son', an obvious fact that should hardly require that it be stated, suggests that he has had to weigh up and then dismiss the relationship that has suggested itself. A dispassionate parting from Mrs. Croft at the conclusion of his tenancy leaves him deflated: 'I did not expect any display of emotion, but I was disappointed all the same' (p.191). Although it is not necessary to exalt his relationship with Mrs. Croft into one of love, the narrator's family feeling seems to arise from the memory of a previously-experienced context that is *familiar*, at least in some ways, but deeply dissimilar in that his mother's response to widowhood was profoundly different from that of his American landlady. In the six or so weeks he has spent with her, the alien and foreign have mingled differently into the familiar. By the end of that time, he is 'used to cornflakes and milk, used to Helen's visits, used to sitting on the bench with Mrs. Croft. The only thing I was not used to was Mala' (p.190). Mala, the woman with whom he has been ceremonially and ritually 'bound together' fails to evoke family feeling, despite her volunteering the troubling information in a poorly-phrased but candid letter: 'Here I am very much lonely' (p.189). The narrator confesses that he 'was not touched by her words' (p.189). This is a repetition of an earlier performance of indifference when she was weeping for her parents on the first few nights they have spent together after their wedding in Calcutta: 'I did nothing to console her' (p.181). He has the model of a mother with which to relate to Mrs. Croft—similar in some ways but not in others, but none to apply to a wife. It is Mala to whom he cannot relate. It is family that is not always familiar; indeed, even the familiar can become alien. As she toys with her excrement in her final days, even his mother crosses the line into unrecognisable territory. In the days that follow his receipt of Mala's letter, a chance sighting of an Indian woman on the street prompts the recognition that '[i]t was my duty to take care of Mala, to welcome her and protect her' (p.190). Irritated by the recollection that 'a five-mile separation from her parents…had caused her to weep', the narrator, himself unconsoled in his early experiences of isolation and alienation that have now been domesticated by familiarity, resents the impending responsibility.

Upon Mala's arrival, he nonetheless offers her what is familiar from his early years away from home: egg curry. They eat with their hands, something he has 'not yet done in America' (p.192), a secret pleasure that would draw unflattering comment beyond the confines of home. A week later, he confides, 'we were still strangers' (p.192). At the end of their first week together, the narrator suggests an outing, regretting the suggestion when Mala prepares for it with ceremonial formality: 'she had put on a clean silk sari and extra bracelets, and coiled her hair with a flattering side part on top of her head' (p.193). Mala observes a formality of dress not customary in American social practice, much like Mrs. Sen does in the eponymously-named short story. On first encountering her, young Eliot observes that Mrs. Sen 'wore a shimmering white sari patterned with orange paisleys, more suitable for an evening affair than for that quiet, faintly drizzling August afternoon. Her lips were coated in a complementary coral gloss, and a bit of color had strayed beyond the borders' (p.112). Mrs. Sen's excessive applications, however, surprisingly elicit in Eliot the recognition that 'it was his mother...in her cuffed, beige shorts and her rope-soled shoes, who looked odd' (p.112). At Mrs. Sen's, '[w]here all things were so carefully covered, her shaved knees and thighs [look] too exposed' (p.113). Similarly, at Mrs. Croft's, a comparable Victorian decorum prevails as the landlady sits next to 'a small round table, its legs fully concealed, much like the woman's by a skirt of lace' (p.179). However, these resonances of 'home' do not suggest themselves to the narrator, either because he has been too long away from it, or because his own childhood home lacked the figure of a householder given his mother's distraction by grief or because of his brother and sister-in-law's straitened circumstances which may have precluded such niceties. It is through a triangulation of Mala, Mrs. Croft and the narrator, then, that recognition unpredictably becomes available.

At their outing, the narrator, 'without thinking', leads Mala down the street where he has lodged briefly with Mrs. Croft, unconsciously seeking a point of familiarity in the city, much as he had sought out Woolworth's, 'a store whose name...[he] recognized from London' (pp.193, 175), a name we might speculate was once alien and then became familiar through repeated exposure. It is on their visit with Mrs. Croft that he experiences his first moment of sympathy for Mala when she is ordered to her feet by the centenarian. He suddenly realises what Mala is experiencing: 'Like me, Mala had travelled far from home, not knowing where she was going, or what she would find, for no reason other than to be my wife. As strange as it seemed, I knew in my heart that one day her death would affect me, and stranger still, that mine would affect her' (p.195). Far from validating his worries about what his former landlady might 'object to', Mrs. Croft recognises in Mala's fussy and scrupulous couture, complete with the end of her sari over her head, something she has failed to find in the daughter she has raised, a quality of modesty that surprises and delights her as she announces: 'She is a perfect lady!' (p.195). Mrs. Croft and Mala, perfect ladies in their native context, connect (to use a modish and often trivialised verb) in what the older woman understands instantly as their joint subscription to values alien to the world beyond her scrupulously locked door. Beyond the particular social markers of the traditional female Bengali alien resident among Americans—the sari, the 'dot painted on her forehead and bracelets stacked on her wrists', or 'the red dye still vivid on her feet'—Mrs. Croft moves up to the cognitive level of an abstract principle to which she herself has adhered for a good portion of her 103 years. If the visibly-different immigrant is someone in the wrong place at the wrong time, unwanted, or even if wanted, dressed and mannered differently, eating alien foods, standing in the thin air of isolation on the barren shores of a life only just beginning in a new world, the long-timer Mrs. Croft is on the point of departure from it, having outlasted her expected expiry date.

It is through Mrs. Croft's eyes that Mala's strangeness is lessened in the light of recognition, recalling us to the connection between the cognate terms, family and relative, and the sympathy-laden analogous active verb, 'to relate to'. Solan's commendation, 'You can relate to her characters because their plights could easily be your own', points to Lahiri's success in awakening this capacity in mainstream readers (clearly, the 'you' excludes a subcontinental audience). In the months to come, it is Mala who consoles the narrator when he comes across Mrs. Croft's obituary. The narrator, so insistent that he 'was not her son', is stricken by the news of this final crossing, and mourns the passing of this all-too-transient presence in his life, much as young Lilia has learned from the absence of Mr. Pirzada at the family table 'what it meant to miss someone who was so many miles and hours away, just as he had missed his wife and daughters for so many months' (p.42). The equation of the loss of non-family with family in both stories begs the question of to what and to whom we can relate, and if there are any real limits to who and what we can recognise as our familiars.

Given the larger question of narratives of immigrant literature, Lahiri's writing, which seems to have succeeded in interpellating more than one sort of reader, prompts the speculation that beyond the threshold, however we might define it, anything can happen, the foreign may be recognised as familiar, the familiar seem alien. Thick descriptions of the lives of others, delivered dispassionately and without reproach or recrimination in a deliberate mode of the factual, recall what may be familiar as an emotion, a feeling, an experience, even as they underscore names and habits and foods and clothes that are alien to a certain 'true', which is to say equally-fictional, America. Encounters with the figure of the immigrant, the resident alien, perhaps 'naturalised' over time, offer encounters with unexpected familiarity, but also with the strangeness and alienation within. In an analogous vein, by virtue of etymology, we might recall that the term 'host' surprisingly connotes its opposite: guest and stranger; and the word familiar, the uncanny connotation of 'a demon supposed to be in association with or under the power of a man'.[20] If the new immigrant's strangeness instigates recognition, included in this response is a recognition of the want, the un-belonging, the dependence reminiscent of states of infancy or as-yet unfulfilled desire, or loss of home and family which the settled 'true' American wants to, but cannot always assume, has been resolved in every context of his or her own life. There is more than one way to be out of place, to be outpaced by developments around us, left behind by a world constantly in motion. There are few who have not suffered some wound of displacement, some encounter with alienation, few who do not struggle for acceptance and a sense of place, few who are understood and heard where they work or live or play. Painful reminders of privation, loss, isolation, repressed desires and behaviours are part of the encounter with stories of the designated alien. It is through *dis*closure, the making known 'of everything that ought to have remained...secret and hidden but has come to light' that the shape and expansive capacity of the limits of our affinities are also revealed to us.[21]

---

[20] OED Online.
[21] Schelling quoted in Freud, 'The Uncanny', p.224.

Contested Representations of Remittances and the Transnational Family

SUPRIYA SINGH and ANUJA CABRAAL

This paper deals with the changing idea of money and the transnational Indian family across generations and life stages. It draws on a qualitative study of 38 first and second generation Indian migrants to Australia. For first generation migrants, sending money home is one of the important ways of expressing belonging and care for the transnational family. Over time, the remittances become contested in terms of their value and their equivalence to physical care, raising questions of belonging. With multiple migrants, the family centres on Australia, which now becomes the source country when children migrate elsewhere. Money and gifts are sent home to Australia or to other countries. The nuclear family is the main reference point for most of our second generation migrants, but there remain some gift exchanges with extended family and charitable donations. These donations reflect a sense of ancestry rather than the locus of family. Hence accounts of sending money to India need to be supplemented by studies of the diffusion of the transnational family across different nodes of the diaspora. The study of remittances has to reflect this diffusion and change in the transnational family if it is to adequately explain how money is the medium of family relationships.

Introduction

Studying migration and the transnational family focuses on some of the most personal and emotional dimensions of globalisation. As Skrbiš says: 'The transnational family is a symptom of our increasingly globalised lives, which take place across borders and boundaries, thereby eroding the possibilities that places of birth, life and dying will coincide'.[1]

The Transnational Family

In this paper, 'transnational family' includes family members who have migrated and those who have been left behind.[2] In a transnational family, people have to negotiate and maintain

---

We gratefully acknowledge the support of the Global Cities Research Institute, RMIT University, for this research. This is a revised version of a paper presented at the Family Ties Workshop, La Trobe University, Bundoora, Australia, on 11 Sept. 2009.

[1] Z. Skrbiš, 'Transnational Families: Theorising Migration, Emotions and Belonging', in *Journal of Intercultural Studies*, Vol.29, no.3 (2008), p.231.

[2] Loretta Baldassar, Cora Vellekoop Baldock and Raelene Wilding, *Families Caring across Borders: Migration, Ageing and Transnational Caregiving* (New York: Palgrave Macmillan, 2007).

family relationships across the boundaries of nation-states. Although these transnational families are separated by distance and national borders, they 'hold together and create something that can be seen as a feeling of collective welfare and unity, namely "familyhood", even across national borders'.[3] The transnational family has much in common with discussions about the continued strength of the joint family in India.[4] Just as most individuals spend some part of their lives in a joint family household, most migrants are members of a transnational family at some point in their history. The issues most often studied for the migrant part of the transnational family—when a nuclear family moves—are those of belonging and caring.[5] Gender has become an increasingly important dimension of migration and the transnational family, particularly in the case of single women migrants.[6]

Studies of the transnational family emphasise the importance of connection and support over distance. As Huang *et al.* note, 'transnationals and their family members often grapple with a sense of liminality—a state of ambiguity, openness and indeterminacy of identity—as they negotiate their transnational life courses'.[7] Other studies point to the tensions that can

---

[3] Deborah F. Bryceson and Ulla Vuorela, 'Transnational Families in the Twenty-First Century', in D. Bryceson and U. Vuorela (eds), *The Transnational Family: New European Frontiers and Global Networks* (New York: Berg, 2002), p.3.

[4] See Veena Das, 'Masks and Faces: An Essay on Punjabi Kinship', in *Contributions to Indian Sociology*, Vol.10, no.1 (1976), pp.1-30; A.M. Shah, 'The Phase of Dispersal in the Indian Family Process', in T. Patel (ed.), *The Family in India: Structure and Practice* (New Delhi: Sage, 2005), pp.214-28; and Patricia Uberoi, 'The Family in India', in V. Das (ed.), *Handbook of Indian Sociology* (New Delhi: Oxford University Press, 2004), pp.275-307.

[5] See Loretta Baldassar, *Visits Home: Migration Experiences between Italy and Australia* (Melbourne: Melbourne University Press, 2001); and Baldassar, Baldock and Wilding, *Families Caring across Borders*.

[6] See Barbara Ehrenreich and Arlie Russell Hochschild, 'Introduction', in B. Ehrenreich and A.R. Hochschild (eds), *Global Woman: Nannies, Maids, and Sex Workers in the New Economy* (New York: Metropolitan Books, 2002), pp.1-13; Ester Gallo, 'Unorthodox Sisters: Gender Relations and Generational Change in Malayali Migrants in Italy', in *Indian Journal of Gender Studies*, Vol.12, nos.2 & 3 (2005), pp.217-51; Michel Gamburd, 'Breadwinner No More', in B. Ehrenreich and A.R. Hochschild (eds), *Global Woman: Nannies, Maids, and Sex Workers in the New Economy* (New York: Metropolitan Books, 2002), pp.190-206; Eugenia Georges, *The Making of a Transnational Community: Migration, Development, and Cultural Change in the Dominican Republic* (New York: Columbia University Press, 1990); Prema A. Kurien, *Kaleidoscopic Ethnicity: International Migration and the Reconstruction of Community Identities in India* (New Delhi: Oxford University Press, 2002); Sarah J. Mahler, 'Transnational Relationships: The Struggle to Communicate across Borders', in *Identities*, Vol.7, no.4 (2001), pp.583-619; Filippo Osella and Caroline Osella, 'Migration, Money and Masculinity in Kerala', in *Journal of the Royal Anthropological Institute*, Vol.6, NS (2000), pp.117-33; Rajni Palriwala, 'Negotiating Patriliny: Intra-Household Consumption and Authority in Northwest India', in R. Palriwala and C. Risseeuw (eds), *Shifting Circles of Support: Contextualising Gender and Kinship in South Asia and Sub-Saharan Africa* (Walnut Creek, CA: AltaMira Press, 1996), pp.190-220; Rajni Palriwala and Patricia Uberoi, 'Exploring the Links: Gender Issues in Marriage and Migration', in R. Palriwala and P. Uberoi (eds), *Marriage and Migration* (New Delhi: Sage Publications, 2008), pp.23-62; Rhacel Salazar Parrenas, 'Caring for the Filipino Family: How Gender Differentiates the Economic Causes of Labour Migration', in A. Agrawal (ed.), *Migrant Women and Work* (New Delhi: Sage Publications, 2006), pp.95-115; Meenakshi Thapan, 'Series Introduction', in N.C. Behera (ed.), *Gender, Conflict and Migration* (New Delhi: Sage Publications, 2006), pp.7-17; and K.C. Zachariah and S. Irudaya Rajan, 'Gender Dimensions of Migration in Kerala: Macro and Micro Evidence', in *Asia-Pacific Population Journal*, Vol.16, no.3 (Sept. 2001), pp.47-70.

[7] Shirlena Huang, Brenda S.A. Yeoh and Theodora Lam, 'Asian Transnational Families in Transition: The Liminality of Simultaneity', in *International Migration*, Vol.46, no.4 (2008), p.7.

arise, particularly due to issues relating to money, reciprocity and gender roles.[8] In countries where patrilocal residence is the norm, the combination of marriage and migration can leave the woman particularly isolated from the support of her natal kin.[9]

Transnational families are studied most often in the context of migration, rather than in the framework of family studies. The transnational family has not been at the centre of family studies because the family has most often been conflated with the household.[10] In Australia the debates range around the increase in de facto, step and blended family households. Census data gives us the number of people with either one or both parents born overseas. However, it is difficult to reach a conclusion about the incidence of the transnational family from such statistics. In India, the relative importance of nuclear and joint family households is still acknowledged. Although patrilocality and family norms influence the migration of married women in India and China, kinship studies have focused on descent, inheritance and prescribed rules of marriage rather than rules of residence and their impact on migration.[11] Studies of family in India do not index migration or transnational families. These topics are left to migration studies, literature and film.

We know that births, weddings, deaths and inheritance are important points in the life-cycle of a family. But the questions seldom asked are: 'how does migration change the idea of family? How do we measure changes in the transnational family in the areas of family practices and belonging to a family? As Levitt *et al.* note:

> religious and family life tend to be more subjective, involving imagination, invention, and emotions that are deeply felt but not overtly expressed. These aspects of transnational lives are more difficult to capture but, nevertheless, critical for the emergence of transnational identities and landscapes.[12]

There has been some discussion as to the appropriate ways of studying the transnational family. As with all families, it is agreed that it is preferable to study a family over time, rather than depend on a snapshot view of it.[13] Although the transnational family includes the migrant and non-migrant members of the family, it is most often studied either in the source or the

---

[8] See Stephanie Riak Akuei, 'Remittances as Unforeseen Burdens: The Livelihoods and Social Obligations of Sudanese Refugees', Global Migration Perspectives No.18 (Geneva: Global Commission on International Migration, 2005); Michele Ruth Gamburd, 'Money that Burns like Oil: A Sri Lankan Cultural Logic of Morality and Agency', in *Ethnology*, Vol.43, no.2 (2004), pp.167–84; Peggy Levitt and Nina Glick Schiller, 'Conceptualizing Simultaneity: A Transnational Social Field Perspective on Society', in *International Migration Review*, Vol.38, no.3 (2004), pp.1002–39; Anna Lindley, 'The Early-Morning Phonecall: Remittances from a Refugee Diaspora Perspective', in *Journal of Ethnic and Migration Studies*, Vol.35, no.8 (2009), pp.1315–34; Sarah J. Mahler, 'Transnational Relationships: The Struggle to Communicate across Borders', in *Identities*, Vol.7, no.4 (2001), pp.583–619; Marcela Ramirez, Zlatko Skrbiš and Michael Emmison, 'Transnational Family Reunions as Lived Experience: Narrating a Salvadoran Autoethnography', in *Identities*, Vol.14, no.4 (2007), pp.411–31.
[9] Palriwala and Uberoi, 'Exploring the Links'.
[10] Bryceson and Vuorela, 'Transnational Families in the Twenty-First Century', pp.3–30.
[11] Palriwala and Uberoi, 'Exploring the Links'.
[12] Peggy Levitt, Josh DeWind and Steven Vertovec, 'International Perspectives on Transnational Migration: An Introduction', in *International Migration Review*, Vol.37, no.3 (2003), p.571.
[13] See *ibid.*, pp.565–75; Vivian Louie, 'Growing up Ethnic in Transnational Worlds: Identities among Second-Generation Chinese and Dominicans', in *Identities: Global Studies in Culture and Power*, Vol.13, no.3 (2006), pp.363–94; and Patricia Pessar and Sarah Mahler, 'Transnational Migration: Bringing Gender In', in *International Migration Review*, Vol.37, no.3 (2003), pp.812–46.

migrant country only. However multi-sited ethnographies are meaningful ways of studying transnational families and kinship networks.[14] As Levitt and Schiller note, connections can be uncovered 'by asking individuals about the transnational aspects of their lives, and those they are connected to, in a single setting'.[15] Levitt *et al.* believe that the 'social field' approach can go beyond national boundaries to analyse the multi-layered connections:

> between migrant and nonmigrant actors—at home and abroad...individuals' transnational experiences must be understood with reference to their families and households; their participation in political, religious and community organizations; and their relation to the national and international policy regimes within which transnational activities take place.[16]

The social field approach needs to be part of life stories. However multiple narratives within the transnational family are more likely to give the necessary depth of perspective and history that can lead us to rethink the idea of family. Though there is a growing body of work on migration and the transnational family in Asia, it is important to note that most of this literature relates to the USA rather than Asia. Hence there is little mention of the long histories of multiple migrations that are found particularly in the life histories of migrants from India. Migration has been part of the Indian landscape and family histories since the nineteenth and early twentieth centuries, with migration taking place to Southeast Asia, Africa, Latin America and the USA. Although the old diaspora has only recently become the subject of literature,[17] these multiple migrations give us a generational perspective, at times going back a century or more. These long family histories reveal changes in the transnational family and its connections with its various home countries.

Family Remittances

In 2011 India received $US64 billion in remittances from abroad, the largest amount received by a developing country. Remittances that go to developing countries through formal money transfer channels are expected to reach $US374 billion in 2012, while total remittances, including those to high-income countries, are expected to reach $US615 billion by 2014.[18] The total value of remittances is even greater because informal remittances are estimated to be at least 50 percent of recorded remittances.[19] In Asia, informal remittances could be anywhere between 15 and 80 percent of the true value of remittances.[20] The International Organization

---

[14] Baldassar, Baldock and Wilding, *Families Caring across Borders*; and Karen Isaksen Leonard, *Locating Home: India's Hyderabadis Abroad* (Stanford, CA: Stanford University Press, 2007).
[15] Levitt and Schiller, 'Conceptualizing Simultaneity', p.1012.
[16] Levitt, DeWind and Vertovec, 'International Perspectives on Transnational Migration', p.567.
[17] See Amitav Ghosh, *Sea of Poppies* (New Delhi: Penguin, 2008); Preeta Samarasan, *Evening is the Whole Day* (New York: Houghton Mifflin Co., 2008); and M.G. Vassanji, *The In-Between World of Vikram Lall* (Edinburgh: Canongate Books, 2005).
[18] Dilip Ratha and Ani Silwal, 'Migration and Development Brief 18: Remittance Flows in 2011—An Update Migration and Development Brief' (23 April 2012) [siteresources.worldbank.org/.../Migrationand DevelopmentBrief18.pdf, accessed 8 May 2012].
[19] Development Prospects Group, 'Migration and Development Brief 2' (2007) [http://web.worldbank.org/ WBSITE/EXTERNAL/NEWS/0,,contentMDK:21124587~pagePK:64257043~piPK:437376~theSitePK:4 607,00.html, accessed 21 Aug. 2007].
[20] Leonides Buencamino and Sergei Gorbunov, 'Informal Money Transfer Systems: Opportunities and Challenges for Development Finance', DESA Discussion Paper No.26 (Nov. 2002) [http://www.un.org/esa/ esa02dp26.pdf, accessed 5 May 2005].

for Migration (IOM) estimates that in 2009, recorded remittances 'were nearly three times the amount of official aid and almost as large as direct foreign investment flows to developing countries'.[21]

Family remittances represent the largest proportion of remittances. Migrants have long sent money home, but the new wave of voluntary migration since the 1960s, particularly to high-income countries, has led to a great increase in the scale of remittances. In India, money is a medium of relationship. Money flows from parents to children and also from children to parents. Money is also a ritual gift to mark life stages such as birth, marriage and death. The giving of money is not just a response to financial need, but an outward expression of filial relationships.[22] In India, sending money home becomes the migrant's overt expression of belonging and caring for the transnational family. As Zelizer says, 'people negotiate coherent connections between intimacy and economic activity'.[23] Among the Indian diaspora, remittances go not only to India, but also from one node of the diaspora to another.

The Qualitative Study

In this research, we focus on eighteen first generation migrants who arrived in Australia between the 1970s and the 1990s, and twenty second generation migrants who were either born in Australia or arrived there before the age of twelve. These 38 persons were part of a larger study of 86 persons from the Indian diaspora in Australia conducted between May 2005 and March 2010. It also included 35 Indian student migrants who came to Australia in 2005 or later and thirteen leaders of the Indian community in Australia.

Our study privileges the perspectives of the migrants in Australia, rather than family members who have remained behind in the home countries or moved to third countries. We are also conscious that this paper focuses on sending money home to India, the traditional direction of remittances from the country of settlement to the country of origin. However with the increase in Indian student migrants and skilled migrants, money is now increasingly remitted from India to Australia as well. We do not know the full extent of these 'boomerang remittances',[24] but Indian families remitted an estimated $A2.1 billion to Australia in 2011 for educational services which generated 21,112 full time equivalent jobs in Australia.[25]

---

[21] William Lacy Swing, *The Director General's Report to the Council* (Geneva: International Organization for Migration, 2010), p.2 [www.iom.int/jahia/webdav/shared/shared/mainsite/about_iom/en/council/99/MICEM-5-2010.pdf, accessed 3 August 2011].

[22] Supriya Singh, *Marriage Money: The Social Shaping of Money in Marriage and Banking* (St Leonards, NSW: Allen and Unwin, 1997).

[23] Viviana A. Zelizer, *The Purchase of Intimacy* (Princeton, NJ: Princeton University Press, 2005), p.2.

[24] Supriya Singh and Anuja Cabraal, '"Boomerang Remittances" and Circular Care among Indian Transnational Families in Australia', in L. Baldassar and L. Merla (eds), *Transnational Families, Migration and Kin-Work: From Care Chains to Care Circulation* (Routledge, forthcoming).

[25] These figures are based on data obtained from Access Economics and Australian Education International. Access Economics estimates that during 2007–08, '[e]ach international student (including their friends and family visitors) contributes an average of $28,921 in value added to the Australian economy and generates 0.29 in full-time equivalent (FTE) workers' (p.i). See Access Economics Pty. Ltd., *The Australian Education Sector and the Economic Contribution of International Students* (Australian Council for Private Education and Training, 2009). According to these calculations, 72,801 Indian students enrolled in December 2011 (down from 120,488 in December 2009); see Australian Education International (AEI), *International Student Data for 2011* [http://www.aei.gov.au/research/International-Student-Data/Pages/InternationalStudentData2011.aspx#2, accessed 30 Jan. 2012]. These students contributed $2.1 billion to the Australian economy and generated 21,112 full time equivalent jobs.

This is a grounded study in that it does not move from hypotheses to verification, but emphasises the fit between data and theory.[26] In our study of the Indian diaspora in Australia, the initial focus was on family remittances in the first generation and issues of identity and belonging in the second. It became increasingly clear that changes in the boundaries of family were important to both sets of research problems as well.

The interview sample was gathered through our personal and professional contacts. We chose to conduct a qualitative study because the issue of family, money and migration was deeply emotional. It was also difficult at times for people to speak frankly about money and family. We sought to discover the questions that were important, particularly to examine the distinctive characteristics of transnational money.

All the members of our sample migrated to Australia in order to further his or her prospects or, in the case of the second generation, their parents had migrated for this reason. Our study is distinctive in that it covers families in which migration was predominantly initiated by the men. All the participants, except one from the first generation, came to Australia with their nuclear families or had their nuclear families join them shortly after in the 1970s, 1980s and 1990s. In some cases, members of their natal families have followed. Therefore, it differs from studies in which women migrated to work in caregiving professions, leaving their children in India to be cared for by their husbands or natal families.[27] Our sample was also not one in which the families were in dire need, as was the case in Akuei's study, which focused on Dinka refugees in the USA.[28]

There was a mix of religions in our first generation sample—six Hindus, seven Sikhs, one Muslim and four Christians. We interviewed nine women and nine men. It was a varied sample in terms of age, too. One interviewee was between 25 and 34, four were between 45 and 54, three were between 55 and 64, eight were more than 65 years old and two did not tell us their age. Thus, fourteen of the eighteen were more than 45 years old. The time since their arrival in Australia was similarly diverse, ranging from eight to 29 years. Annual household incomes varied from under $A25,000 to more than $A100,000: three under $A25,000, five between $A50,000 and $A74,999, five more than $A100,000, and five did not want to say or were not directly asked because it was seen as inappropriate. Our second generation participants were overwhelmingly professional and aged between eighteen and 35. Thirteen of the 38 participants were multiple migrants—families who had migrated multiple times, either within one generation or between generations. In this study, the multiple migrants, or 'twice migrants',[29] had lived in Fiji, Kenya, Malaysia, New Zealand, Singapore, the USA or the UK

---

[26] Anselm Strauss and J. Corbin, *Basics of Qualitative Research: Grounded Theory Procedures and Techniques* (Newbury Park, CA: Sage Publications, 1990).

[27] See Gallo, 'Unorthodox Sisters: Gender Relations and Generational Change in Malayali Migrants in Italy'; Michele Ruth Gamburd, 'Absent Women and Their Extended Families', in C. Risseeuw and K. Ganesh (eds), *Negotiation and Social Space: A Gendered Analysis of Changing Kin and Security Networks in South Asia and Sub-Saharan Africa* (Walnut Creek, CA: AltaMira Press, 1998), pp.276-91; Leela Gulati, *In the Absence of Their Men* (New Delhi: Sage Publications, 1993); Sarah J. Mahler and Patricia R. Pessar, 'Gender Matters: Ethnographers Bring Gender from the Periphery toward the Core of Migration Studies', in *International Migration Review*, Vol.40, no.1 (2006), pp.27-63; Fernando Paragas, 'Migrant Mobiles: Cellular Telephony, Transnational Spaces, and the Filipino Diaspora', in K. Nyiri (ed.), *A Sense of Place: The Global and the Local in Mobile Communication* (Vienna: Passagen Verlag, 2005), pp.241-9; Parrenas, 'Caring for the Filipino Family'; and Cecilia Tacoli, 'International Migration and the Restructuring of Gender Asymmetries: Continuity and Change among Filipino Labor Migrants in Rome', in *International Migration Review*, Vol.33, no.3 (1999), pp.658-82.

[28] Akuei, *Remittances as Unforeseen Burdens*.

[29] Parminder Bhachu, 'Multiple-Migrants and Multiple Diasporas: Cultural Reproduction and Transformations among British Punjabi Women', in C. Petievich (ed.), *The Expanding Landscape: South Asians and the Diaspora* (New Delhi: Manohar, 1999), pp.71-84.

before migrating to Australia. Another two families had children or grandchildren who had moved from Australia to the USA, the UK or Canada.

The open-ended interviews usually took an hour and a half, conducted either at the interviewees' homes or at the office or home of the interviewer. They were conducted in English, or a mix of English, Hindi and Punjabi. The interviews were transcribed and then coded using the qualitative computer program, NVivo8. The data was coded broadly, linked to memos to catch the theoretical and methodological reflections, and then checked for negative cases.

Sending Money Home: A First Generation Phenomenon

Remittances are the currency of care and one of the ways in which migrants maintain their sense of belonging to the transnational family. This sense of belonging has to be visibly displayed in family practices over life stages and generations.[30] The need for display is greater when the family is separated across borders.

In our study, money was routinely sent home via banks, through arrangements with kin in the home country, or taken with migrants when they visited their families. It was predominantly a first generation phenomenon. As all but one of our first generation participants had their nuclear families in Australia, money was sent most often to parents. In two cases, money also went to brothers and sisters, and in one case, to nieces who had been orphaned. The money was primarily sent as a way of caring for the family. In one case, it was specifically for the repayment of debts in Malaysia, and in another three cases, for the purchase of land in India.

Remittances are mediated by the capacity of migrants to send money, the support of their spouses, and the financial needs of the family in the home country. They are also influenced by life stage. The main bulk of remittances stop after the parents die or when they move country to live with their migrant children. Life events such as births and marriages within the family also lead to significant gifts of money.

Our study shows that the centre of the transnational family shifts as it expands across different countries. Thirteen of our first and second generation samples were multiple migrants in that the family had moved from India to other countries before moving to Australia. Another two families saw their children and grandchildren move to the USA, the UK or Canada. So, the different nodes of the transnational family spread across Australia, Singapore, Malaysia, Fiji, the USA, the UK and Canada, bypassing India, although India continued to be seen as the country of origin and at the centre of the migrants' cultural and religious heritage. For three of the six multiple migrants in our first generation sample, money and gifts were received in Australia from Singapore and Canada from children and other kin.[31]

Our study shows that remittances and inheritance remain one of the most male-dominated aspects of transnational money in the first generation. It is men who send money home, continuing the pattern of sons looking after parents in the dominantly patrilineal system of kinship in India. The women send or take gifts and often play a central role in organising gifts for the family. Though women are now entitled to inherit, they often cede their inheritance to their brothers, as they do in India. What is different is that men may also not inherit, which is not uncommon in other migrant groups in Australia.[32]

---

[30] J. Finch, 'Displaying Families', in *Sociology*, Vol.41, no.1 (2007), pp.65–81.
[31] Supriya Singh, Anuja Cabraal and Shanthi Robertson, 'Remittances as a Currency of Care: A Focus on "Twice Migrants" among the Indian Diaspora in Australia', in *Journal of Comparative Family Studies*, Vol. XXXXI, no.2 (2010), pp.245–63.
[32] Baldassar, Baldock and Wilding, *Families Caring across Borders*.

Money is sent home to express caring for the transnational family. This is particularly important in India as money flows in both directions between parents and children, rather than just from parents to children.[33] At the same time, as Levitt and Schiller point out, 'Kin networks maintained between people who send remittances and those who live on them can be fraught with tension'.[34] The conflict revolves around a perceived imbalance of care. Hema (45–54) (the names are pseudonyms), a direct migrant from India, sent three airline tickets to her brothers so that they could attend her son's wedding, but no members of the family came. She says: '[E]very time I need to communicate, I have to go and approach them because I feel the need and they don't really feel it...'. This perceived imbalance in communication was heightened when it came to the valuation of money sent for 'caring for' the family and the physical hands-on care that kin in the source country were able to provide.

The Dollar Sent is Not the Dollar Received[35]

The first instance where remittances can contribute to conflict is where the dollar sent is not the dollar received. Ishaan (25–34), who migrated to Australia from Kenya with his parents when he was six months old, relates how his father sent money home regularly to support his parents and help educate his siblings and help them set up a business. Ishaan's father saw himself as having financial opportunities that the rest of his family did not have, but sometimes he had to go into debt to honour these obligations. Finances were so tight that everyone in the family could not visit India at the same time. At times, his father would try to keep secret how much money he sent home but his mother would find out because it was taken out of her housekeeping budget. Ishaan thinks his mother found it especially frustrating because she felt their contribution was not 'widely recognised or appreciated'.

This difference between the value of the money sent, the sacrifice it represents for the senders and the value of the money received, is often at the centre of tension for familial migrants. This sense of not being valued is heightened if there is uneven reciprocity in terms of communication and gift relationships, which signal a lack of 'caring about' the migrant offshoot of the transnational family. It is part of the 'money tree' syndrome, where people in the home country think that money is earned easily in a foreign country.[36]

Silences around Inheritance

Baldassar *et al.* point out that in some cases, tensions over care and money flow into issues of inheritance, one of the most significant expressions of belonging in the family.[37] Money sent home is pitted against the day-to-day physical 'caregiving' provided by other family members,

---

[33] Supriya Singh and Mala Bhandari, 'Money Management and Control in the Indian Joint Family across Generations', in *The Sociological Review*, Vol.60, no.1 (2012), pp.46–67.
[34] Levitt and Schiller, 'Conceptualizing Simultaneity'.
[35] The following two sections draw partially on Singh, Cabraal and Robertson, 'Remittances as a Currency of Care: A Focus on "Twice Migrants" among the Indian Diaspora in Australia', pp.245-63.
[36] Personal communication from Dulari, a migrant from Trinidad to the USA (New York, 22 July 2008). A comparative study of migrants and refugees in Australia also found that Afghani refugees were inundated with requests, sometimes for luxuries that they themselves could not afford. See Baldassar, Baldock and Wilding, *Families Caring across Borders*. Akuei, writing about Dinka migrants to the USA, details the stress caused by demands from the extended family at home, the moral imperative to help and the financial needs of settlement. See Akuei, *Remittances as Unforeseen Burdens*. The experiences of Somali migrants in London are equally stressful. See Lindley, 'The Early-Morning Phonecall'.
[37] Baldassar, Baldock and Wilding, *Families Caring across Borders*.

usually siblings in the home country. This conflict is often at the centre of the division of property when the parents die,[38] and can spill into the legal arena.[39] The conflict is not only 'over who gets what but also over structure and meaning'.[40] The conflict goes to the heart of inclusion in the transnational family and its consequent rights and responsibilities.

This conflict is avoided if there is nothing to inherit. Murali (45-54), who migrated from Malaysia to Singapore to Australia, inherited only debts. Niranjan's family home has already been given to his eldest son because Niranjan and his wife invited him to come and look after them when they were still in India. In one case, a migrant and his siblings agreed that the family home would go to the unmarried sister who had looked after the parents. She, in turn, has willed it to them and their children.

Even when women have ceded their claims in favour of their brothers, it is important to them that they be mentioned in the inheritance. Where this is not clear, there are silences around inheritance. In our first generation sample, Hema laughed off the issue of inheritance, saying: 'I am not even in the picture'. Her son, Hemat, said: 'It definitely is a touchy issue', and it has led to a family rift. Daya, who migrated from India with her husband in the early 1980s, was silent when asked about her husband's inheritance, although she spoke openly of her decision to renounce her claim in favour of her brother. It was often difficult for a person to talk about inheritance when the issue was still raw.

Ishaan's father also did not inherit anything. It is not clear whether a share was offered or whether he himself renounced all claims because he was financially better off than his siblings. Ishaan says: 'I think my Dad was largely ambivalent to an inheritance'. One reason was that his father was not able to attend the funeral of his father in time, but Ishaan also thinks 'that he always felt, from a financial point of view, that he was not really expecting anything because he was the strongest at the time'.

Even when men have inherited agricultural land in India, there are difficulties in holding on to the land.[41] Bhagwan, who is in his seventies now and was a multiple migrant from India to Singapore and then to Australia, inherited land from his father. The trouble started after his father's brother died and Bhagwan had to depend on his paternal cousins to look after the land. On one of his routine visits back to India, he moved the management of the land to his sister's son. His own sons and his surviving brother are not interested in the land, and Bhagwan and his wife will not be retiring to India as they had hoped. Bhagwan realises he has to sell the land, but he feels that it is like selling his family history. He says: 'On the deeds, there is my great grandfather's name, my grandfather's name, my father's name'. There is also increased pressure from relatives in India for him to sell the land to them at a preferential price.

Ambika, also a multiple migrant from India, Malaysia and Singapore, knows how difficult it was for her husband to sell his family land. Communication had already deteriorated between him and his paternal uncle and cousins, despite her husband continuing to send money for Deepavali and weddings. In the end, he agreed to sell the land to his cousins at half the market price, but insisted that the transaction be completed in Singapore where his younger brother lived. Even in Singapore, his brother would only sign the deeds in a hotel, fearing poisoning by pesticide or murder.

---

[38] Karen Fog Olwig, 'A Wedding in the Family: Home Making in a Global Kin Network', in *Global Networks*, Vol.2, no.3 (2002), pp.205-18.
[39] Zelizer, *The Purchase of Intimacy*, p.225.
[40] *Ibid.*, p.225.
[41] Supriya Singh, 'Sending Money Home—Maintaining Family and Community', in *International Journal of Asia Pacific Studies (IJAPS)*, Vol.3, no.2 (2007), pp.93-109.

Changes in Gifts and Remittances over Life Stages and Generations

The direction of remittances and gifts shifts over life stages and generations as members of the transnational family die or move to another country. The relationship between source and destination countries becomes complex due to multiple migrations. The transnational family also becomes diffused across different nodes of the diaspora as children migrate to other countries. The source country may remain the reference point for communication, family practices and issues of identity, but Australia becomes part of the idea of home. Sending money home then no longer necessarily means sending money to family in India. These complexities of the transnational family are not captured in the remittance figures, which concentrate only on money sent to India.

A Changing Centre with Multiple Migrations

When children migrate to other nodes of the diaspora, Australia becomes the centre of the transnational family. This is true of our six first generation multiple migrants. The direction of gifts and remittances changes as one or two of the 'home countries' disappear from active family networks, perhaps because there are no effective kin left in the birth country, although land or a home in the birth country slows this pulling-away process.

Ambika moved from India to Malaysia as a young child, from Malaysia to Singapore when she got married, then with her husband and child to Australia. Her brothers were already in Australia. Soon her father joined her. As a result, she seldom visits Singapore, while Malaysia is no longer part of her family sphere. Before the death of her husband, her visits to India used to involve suitcases filled with gifts for the family and occasional remittances to his siblings for festivals. Now she visits India only for pilgrimages although while in India, she might look up some natal family that remains there. For twice migrants like Ambika, as family ties lessen over the generations India becomes a place of childhood memories and the 'cultural heart' of her sense of religion rather than 'home'.[42] Weddings are now held in Australia, drawing in kin from Canada as well as a few from India. At the last family wedding, Ambika's maternal kin came from India, the UK and Canada. Her first cousin—her father's younger brother's son—and his family stayed with them on this occasion. They brought gifts when they came. When they were leaving, Ambika's cousin gave Ambika and her daughter $US100 each. Ambika says: 'I said "No, no, I am the older". But they said: "Brothers give to their sisters". My daughter also said: "No, no, I am working". But they gave. The love was there. The connection was there'.

For other twice migrants such as Banta, however, the birth country might drop out, but the interim countries of destination remain important because of nuclear family and property there. Banta was born in Malaysia, married in Singapore and then moved to Australia. Malaysia is no longer a part of her transnational family network as her kin have moved to Singapore. Yet, connections with India and Singapore remain through the presence of kin and ownership of land and property. Her network has also expanded to Canada because her son has migrated there. So, Banta and her husband, Bhagwan, receive money and gifts in Australia from her sons in Australia, Singapore and Canada. They accept only gifts, not money, from their daughter, keeping to the traditional patterns of remittances.

The exception to these accounts is that of Murali, who migrated from Malaysia to Singapore to Australia. Malaysia remains important because his brothers and their families

---

[42] M-A. Falzon, 'Bombay, Our Cultural Heart: Rethinking the Relation between Homeland and Diaspora', in *Ethnic and Racial Studies,* Vol.26, no.4 (2003), pp.662–83.

live there, but for him the emotional core of home lies in India, the country of his parents' birth. This is reflected in his strong emotional experiences when he visited first his father's village and then his mother's village when she died in India. He talks of taking his children there as a sort of pilgrimage.

Diffusion with Continued Migration

Over time, transnational family ties become more diffuse as children migrate to other countries. Anita migrated from India to Australia. When her mother died she brought her father to live with her in Australia. When Anita connects with family, she no longer travels to India, but to the USA, where her eldest daughter lives with her husband and children. So, Australia is now at the centre of the transnational family for Anita and her children. Her husband's father still lives in India, so her husband goes to India for a week or two every year. But his longer visits are to the USA to help their daughter with childcare. In Anita's case, there are no remittances coming from the USA to Australia. She recoils even at the question. They have sufficient income themselves and the idea of receiving money from a daughter remains unacceptable.

Niranjan, 91, is a direct migrant from India. He came with his wife to join his son's family in Melbourne. More than twenty years later, two of his four sons have families in Melbourne, and Niranjan has a number of grandchildren there, too. His family is diffused across India, Australia, Europe and the USA, although there is some movement to Australia as the centre. But there is no dilution, for he remains a revered elder and the anchor of the transnational family. He lives in Australia mainly with his son and family, though his grandson and family keep asserting their right and desire to have him live with them. Niranjan is the person who ensures that communication among his far-flung family remains continuous and frequent and he is still the person whose advice is sought for weddings in the family.

Transnational Family, Gifts and Donations for the Second Generation

The literature on second generation migrants shows that transnational family ties weaken in most cases. Keeping to distinctive cultural patterns may add more to their identity in the migrant country, rather than make for transnationalism.[43] The exceptions are migrants who have spent long stretches of time with their families in the home country. Rumbaut observed in a decade-long longitudinal study of 1.5 (those who arrived in the US when they were 17 years or younger) and second generation young adults (those born in the US to two foreign-born parents) from Mexico, the Philippines, Vietnam, China and a host of other Latin American and Asian countries, that transnational attachments are 'always under 10 percent'.[44]

---

[43] Pawan Dhingra, 'Committed to Ethnicity, Committed to America: How Second-Generation Indian Americans' Ethnic Boundaries Further their Americanisation', in *Journal of Intercultural Studies*, Vol.29, no.1 (2008), pp.41–63; Louie, 'Growing Up Ethnic in Transnational Worlds'; Martin O'Flaherty, Zlatko Skrbiš and Bruce Tranter, 'Home Visits: Transnationalism among Australian Migrants', in *Ethnic and Racial Studies*, Vol.30, no.5 (2007), pp.817–44; Ramirez, Skrbiš and Emmison, 'Transnational Family Reunions as Lived Experience'; Shalini Shankar, *Desi Land* (Durham and London: Duke University Press, 2008); Edna A. Viruell-Fuentes, '"My Heart is Always There": The Transnational Practices of First-Generation Mexican Immigrant and Second-Generation Mexican American Women', in *Identities: Global Studies in Culture and Power*, Vol.13, no.3 (2006), pp.335–62.

[44] Rubén G. Rumbaut, 'Severed or Sustained Attachments? Language, Identity, and Imagined Communities in the Post-Immigrant Generation', in P. Levitt and M.C. Waters (eds), *The Changing Face of Home: The Transnational Lives of the Second Generation* (New York: Russell Sage Foundation, 2002), p.89.

He notes that 'unlike their parents...there appears to be no "tingling" sensation, no phantom pain, over a homeland that was never lost to them in the first place'.[45]

The nuclear family is at the centre of the idea of family for the second generation in our sample, although visits to family in India were part of the experience of most of the second generation whose parents were born in India. In our study, four of our twenty second generation participants speak of the loss of the extended family, and five said they would go on their own to visit family in India. These five had come to Australia when they were eight to twelve years old and had memories of spending time with their cousins and having a close relationship with them. They have valued memories of connection revolving around aunts and/or grandparents who were important to them in their early years in India. Once these family members die, the ties loosen. For the second generation there is none of the first generation's dwelling over imbalance of care, for there are no unfulfilled expectations. This change in the relationship with the transnational family is reflected in the move from remittances to gifts.

India is no longer the locus of family for the second generation migrants in our sample. Like the multiple migrants, they often see India as a reference point for ancestry rather than home. They see themselves as both Australian and Indian.

Gifts for the Transnational Family

It is gifts, rather than remittances, that express connections with the transnational family for the second generation. Individual gifting comes into the picture when second generation migrants begin working and travel independently of their family to India. But most often, it is the parents who are the givers of gifts to the transnational family, rather than the second generation. When Hemat (in his late twenties or early thirties) went to India, he took presents from his parents. And he felt that even the gifts he bought for the family after he arrived were 'like following instructions to make sure we're doing it on their behalf; it's more like—it's really them; we're just physical couriers of it'.

Mahesh's story, too, reflects how second generation giving—even when done in an individual capacity—is usually done on advice from parents. Mahesh is a doctor in his early thirties and recently married. He and his family migrated from India when he was eight years old. He has remained connected to his extended family through visits to India with his parents, and his wedding was celebrated in Delhi. When he and his wife went to Nepal recently, they also went to India, particularly to meet up with his paternal grandfather, who could not attend the wedding because of a broken hip. Mahesh says it was important for his wife to meet his grandfather. He also feels close to his mother's sisters, especially as they have visited the family in Melbourne. But as he is older than most of his cousins, he did not know how to handle the gift giving. He says: 'We asked Mum and Dad, "What should we do? Should we give things to people, or what?"' They had taken gifts when they used to visit, but everything was now available in India. He says:

> we decided we'd give a certain amount of money to all of our cousins. Now, there are too many cousins to give things to, so Malini and I made envelopes for all of the cousins.... Most of my aunties and uncles didn't want it at all, so they actually took the envelopes away from the cousins and gave them back to us. If not straight away at that time, but in another way, by giving us cash in return.... So, in a way, they didn't want to take it from us because they still regard us as the kids.

---

[45] *Ibid.*, p.91.

Brindha's story is one of personal gift-giving on her own behalf, reflecting a strong emotional connection with her family in India. She was the only one who lent $A2,000 to an uncle for his son's study in Australia. Brindha is in her late twenties and works in information technology. She continues to have a close relationship with her maternal aunt in India, with whom she stayed as a child. She told us: 'If I go to India, the only place I really want to eat at is my auntie's house'. 'I honestly love going to India and love buying them presents, and taking them out for dinner'. She says:

> ...we go sari shopping and I buy them a sari.... And they get more out of that than anything else. They go, "That's too expensive", and I'll go, "Don't worry, aunty, this one's for my promotion that happened last year, and this one's for something else, don't worry about it".

Brindha does not think she will go back once her aunts and uncles have died: 'I wouldn't necessarily go back to see my cousins'. When she goes to India for her cousins' weddings, she says, 'I don't really go to my cousins' weddings because of my cousins. I actually go for my aunt and uncle. They invite me, so I go for them'.

Donations for Indian Causes

Donations for Indian causes are connected with a sense of being Indian, although it is most often a comfortable hybrid identity in that they feel Indian and Australian. So, the donations are also for Australian and for more global causes. The four second generation participants who spoke of diaspora philanthropy say they most often gave through Australian charitable organisations which have a focus on India. One gave through a community organisation of which she and her parents were members. Another gave through her religious organisation. Only one sent money directly to India. This contrasted with their parents, who usually gave directly when they visited India or through their religious organisations in India and Australia. The connection between a sense of Indian ancestry and identity and community donations came through most clearly in the two cases where India does not consciously figure in the giving. Harsh (24), a professional, has difficulties with her parents, who expect her to do everything the Indian way in Australia. She does not have many Indian friends and sees herself as Australian, particularly when dealing with her parents. She says she assesses the need when she donates:

> I wouldn't think so much about whether this is an Indian cause or an Australian cause. If it was a religious cause, maybe I would question it and think, why are we discriminating based on religion? I'm not comfortable with that...I think I'd be more likely to consider what cause the money is going to, rather than what culture it is going to support.

Dahlia (29) says she gives to Muslim countries that are most troubled at the moment. Growing up as an Indian from Kenya, her sense of self shifted to identifying herself as a Muslim when she first moved to Melbourne. She says:

> I'll tick those boxes...usually Palestine and Indonesia...and Sri Lanka. Again, these aren't countries which are devoutly Muslim or necessarily Indian. But I think

the...deciding factor was how dire the need was and, you know, if there were a lot of people suffering. That would be my issue.

Chitra, who is in her late twenties and a multiple migrant from Malaysia, sends money to India for community work through a religious organisation in Australia and also through Oxfam. Although she visited India once with her family, her connection to India comes from her membership of an Indian religious organisation in Australia, and she has gone back to India several times because of it. She thinks it 'stems from the fact that you want to know your origins.... That's where your family or your lineage comes from'.

Together with the Rajasthani community in Australia, Jaya, in her early twenties and still a student, helped raise $A10,000 for India after the 2004 tsunami. She says there is always something special about being from India. But when Melbourne was ravaged by bushfires in 2010, she gave for that, too. Lena, a married professional without close connections with her transnational family, sponsors a child from India and another from elsewhere. She has visited India on her own once for volunteer work and said India was part of her background.

Etash, in his late twenties, contributed directly to an organisation in India when the tsunami struck India. He says: 'I guess it was more a national contribution because the one state that was affected was the state I was from. So, I wanted to get something there'. Etash migrated with his parents from India to the USA, then back to India, and then to Australia when he was eleven years old. Except for his first few years in Australia, he has had continuous involvement in India through his extended family and his interest in music and dance. In Melbourne, he has been involved in community service in a Hindu temple. When he was at a university in Melbourne he led an Indian club which sponsored a child in India. Etash was struck by the difference in community giving between the second generation in India and the USA when he went to study in the latter as part of his graduate programme. In the USA, Indian organisations were involved in serious fund-raising for social causes. He said:

> I saw a lot of organisations that were giving back to the community in India. A friend of mine used to run a marathon...as part of an organisation which sets up schools in India.... I went to a concert where they got a band from India to come and play and again the proceeds...were going to some organisation which was giving money back to India.

Conclusion: Money and Family across Borders

In this paper, we have focused on the meaning of money and the transnational family for direct and multiple Indian migrants in Australia. In the first generation of migrants, money can change from being an expression of belonging and caring for the transnational family to an issue overwhelmed by emotion and conflict. This conflict calls into question the nature of family and belonging when families cross borders. As transnational family relationships become more diffuse, remittances and gifts, too, change direction. Money is no longer sent home to India, but travels along different nodes of the diaspora.

When a couple with or without children migrate, at first the cross-border connections between families are intense. These connections are diluted most often at the death of parents in the home country and/or the migration of siblings, accompanied by the cessation of remittances being sent to the source country. As the second generation of migrants grows up in the host country, our study supports other research which suggests that there is a lessening in the intensity of transnational family relationships. Hence, remittances are rare among the second generation in our sample. Occasional gifts remain important as long as strong relationships with aunts or grandparents remain, most often going back to the early years of the second generation migrant. The second generation donates for Indian causes, often in an indirect way, through Australian community organisations. This diaspora philanthropy reflects a sense of common ancestry, rather than closeness with family.

This study has shown the different ways in which money is the medium of family relationships. The relationship becomes complex and changes when the nature and composition of the transnational family changes over generations and life stages. Money and gifts continue to be sent home, but the location and sense of home changes in the transnational family. Figures for remittances that only take into account money sent from a destination country to a source country do not include the money and care that travel along different nodes of the diaspora; they depend on the intensity of relationship, the composition and locations of the transnational family and a sense of identity and heritage. Just as migration patterns have become more complex, rather than linear, money relationships through remittances and gifts travel in myriad ways across the diaspora.

In/dependence, Intergenerational Uncertainty, and the Ambivalent State: Perceptions of Old Age Security in India

SARAH LAMB

This essay examines competing perspectives on old age security within contemporary Indian families and society. Ideas and policies concerning old age security are intricately connected to broader cultural meanings and values—surrounding personhood, the life course, family moral systems, and perceptions of the very nature and identity of a wider society and nation. The family in India has long been viewed as the central site of ageing and elder care, yet there is a widespread perception that family-centred elder care is on the decline. Market-based options such as for-pay old age homes are on the rise among the solvent urban middle classes, along with discourses emphasising the need for older individuals to rely on themselves. At the same time, recent parental care legislation and limited state-funded social security programs emphasise that family care is best. Confronting such developments, this essay explores competing Indian perspectives on: where is the best site of elder care: the family, the market, the state, or the individual? The aim is not only to illuminate important values, practices and policies being contested and fashioned in India today, but also to subject ostensibly a-cultural international models of old age security to cross-cultural scrutiny.

Kalyani-di[1] and Uma-di sat with me one evening on the front verandah of their modest old age home on the outskirts of Kolkata, West Bengal, India, reflecting on what they saw as the 'huge transformations, enormous transformations' (*pracur paribartan, sangatik paribartan*) taking place in their society, changes that had led them to life in an old age home, an institution they had never even dreamed of when young. 'Now everyone wants to live alone', Kalyani-di mused. 'All the new flats being built are just for two people, two people—and soon they'll be for just one person!' She and Uma-di both laughed. 'Even husbands and wives will live separately!' Uma-di added: 'So much change has happened—we are startled seeing it all' (*amra dekhe abak hoe jacchi eto paribartan hoe gelo*). Kalyani-di went on: 'Some people say these changes are good because there used to be a lot of arguing in large joint families; but— don't people need others to live?'

Narayan Sarkar, a retired engineer who at age seventy resides independently with just his wife in a spacious middle-class south Kolkata home, their two children both settled abroad in the USA, reflected: 'In our families, we raised our children—why? Our idea, our dream was that when we grew old, our sons and daughters-in-law would serve us (*seva karbe*). And it is

---

[1] The suffix '*di*' is short for *didi*, 'older sister' in Bengali, the primary language spoken in the Indian state of West Bengal (of which Kolkata is the capital) and neighbouring Bangladesh. Along with *da* for *dada* (older brother), *di* is used commonly as a sign of respect, and warmth, when addressing a senior person. Like other South Asians, Bengalis generally find it disrespectful to address a senior person by the first name only, so epithets such as 'older sister', 'older brother', 'uncle' and 'grandmother' are regularly used. Kalyani, Uma and the other names used in this essay are pseudonyms.

our dream, and a natural thing, to hope for this, to want this. We did this for our parents, and they for theirs.... In my day, parents *had* to depend on their children. There was no other option and we imagined it no other way'.

An editorial by Bollywood superstar Aamir Khan published in the *Hindustan Times* on 16 July 2012 picks up this now widespread theme of remarkable changes underway in India which impact upon forms of ageing and elder care:

> I think India must be one of the few countries/societies where culturally, and traditionally, there is so much respect for elders. It is probably the only country where we touch the feet of our elders as a mark of respect. Yet on a practical level and in our infrastructure we are far behind many other countries and societies in looking after our elderly. With Indian society changing and with the gradual shift from [the] joint family system to the nuclear family system, our relationship with the elders in our own family is also changing. Today a person working and living in a large city has many demands on him. He or she has very little time for himself and his own immediate nuclear family (children and spouse). In this changing scenario what happens to our elderly?[2]

The Bengali-language daily paper *Anandabajar Patrika* proclaims disparagingly: 'The majority of people in old age in the country today are helpless'.[3] *The Times of India* calls the Indira Gandhi National Old Age Pension Scheme a 'cruel joke', offering just a meagre 6.66 Indian rupees per day only to recipients living below the poverty level who are able to prove they qualify.[4] A headline in *The Times of India* on 1 May 2012 pronounces straightforwardly: 'Can't depend on kids in sunset years', and moves on to offer advice on how to invest and save, and how to make independent living a feasible and successful option for old age.[5]

These discourses display the intensity and variety of perspectives on old age security within contemporary India. 'Security' when referring to old age is most commonly taken to refer—internationally and to some extent within India—to 'social security', a phrase that has come to signify government forms of financial support for persons with inadequate or no income, including (often paradigmatically) older and retired persons. Security in old age can more broadly refer to the expectation that one will receive the kinds of material, social and/or emotional support one envisions one will need in later life. Akiko Hashimoto, in 'Cultural Meanings of "Security" in Aging Policies', articulates a dimension of security relevant especially to the experiences of many elders in contexts of dramatic social change: 'the feeling of being part of a social world that revolves around a familiar order with some predictability'.[6]

This essay examines competing perspectives on old age security within contemporary Indian families and society. It explores how ideas and policies concerning old age security are intricately wrapped up with broader cultural meanings and values—surrounding personhood, the life course, family moral systems, and perceptions of the very nature and identity of a wider society and nation. The family in India has long been viewed as the central site of ageing and elder care; and the majority of Indian elders today, as in the past, does continue to

---

[2] Aamir Khan, 'Rewire, Don't Retire', *Hindustan Times* (Kolkata) (16 July 2012), Nation section, p.10.
[3] *Anandabajar Patrika* (31 May 2012), p.4.
[4] Rukmini Shrinivasan, 'This Pension is a Cruel Joke', *The Times of India* (Kolkata) (8 June 2012), p.10.
[5] Vishal Dhawan, 'Can't Depend on Kids in Sunset Years', *The Times of India* (Kolkata) (1 May 2012), p.11.
[6] Akiko Hashimoto, 'Cultural Meanings of "Security" in Aging Policies', in Susan Orpett Long (ed.), *Caring for the Elderly in Japan and the U.S.: Practices and Policies* (New York: Routledge, 2000), p.20.

live in a multigenerational family setting. Yet there is a widespread perception that family-centred elder care is on the decline. Such perceptions have spurred recent legislation and judges' opinions proclaiming that children are not only morally but also legally obligated to support their parents. Such parental care legislation comes in the context of highly-limited state-funded social security for the elderly. Market-based options such as for-pay old age homes are also on the rise among the solvent urban middle classes, but with accompanying intense debates about their appropriateness in the Indian context.

Confronting such developments, this essay explores competing Indian perspectives on: where *is* the best site of elder care: the family, the market, the state or the individual? And what kinds of social, cultural, moral and economic principles, and models of personhood and the life course, are entailed by the rival answers to this enduring question? I draw on case studies and insights I have gleaned from over twenty years of anthropological fieldwork conducted with older Indians and their children in both rural and urban areas of West Bengal, as well as an analysis of recent legislation and court cases pertaining to parental care in India. Many in India view debates regarding the proper site and nature of elder care as speaking profoundly not only to ageing *per se* but also to the very nature of Indian morality, society, modernity and nationhood.

My aims in this essay are not only to illuminate important values, practices and policies being contested and fashioned in India today, but also to subject supposedly a-cultural international models of old age security to cross-cultural scrutiny. Although international development discourses frequently depict the availability of state and market-based programs for old age security as 'progress'—the sign of a 'developed' rather than 'developing' nation (as developing nations rely inordinately on the family)—Indian perspectives are more complex and critical. Exploring such perspectives can help make interventions into presumed universal frameworks, unsettling the certainties of Eurocentric models surrounding matters such as elder care policy, old age security, and progress.

Is Old Age Security in the Family?

If the family looks after them they are quite comfortable, otherwise the life becomes a curse for the aged people.[7]

In a world where the joint family is breaking down, and children are unable to take care of their parents, millions of elderly face destitution.[8]

The family has long been the central site of ageing and mode of old age security in India. Although multigenerational families were of course never ubiquitously present or perfectly harmonious, prevalent perceptions across India are that the family has for generations and generations been the most normal, natural, familiar and traditional site of ageing and elder care for Indians. A family in which elders live with their sons, daughters-in-law and grandchildren is often referred to as a 'joint family', an institution commonly represented in India as quintessentially Indian. Despite contemporary social changes, and widespread public discourse that the joint family is fast breaking down, co-residence across generations is still by

---

[7] Women's Studies Centre, Punjabi University Patiala: 'Women and Aging: Problems and Prospects' report (2012) [http://www.wscpedia.org/index.php?option=com_content&view=article&id=789%3Acomminity-care&catid=17%3Acompleted-projects&Itemid=29, accessed 24 July 2012].

[8] 'OASIS (Old Age Social and Income Security): A Report' (1 Feb. 1999) [http://www.seniorindian.com/oasis__.htm, accessed 24 July 2012].

far the most common living arrangement for elders in India; according to recent surveys, about eighty percent of India's population aged sixty or older lives with adult children.[9]

Those of both older and younger generations relate that in a joint family system, adult children, in particular sons and daughters-in-law, provide care for their ageing parents—out of love (*bhalobasa*), a deep respect for elders (*sraddha*), and a profound sense of moral, economic and even spiritual duty to attempt to repay the inerasable debts (*rn*) they owe their parents for all the effort, expense and affection the parents expended to produce and raise them. Conventionally, this offering of parental care (or *seva*, service) would take place in the elder parent(s)' home, as a son would bring his wife into the family home upon marriage rather than departing to set up a new residence. As it has become increasingly common for adult children to travel to different cities or abroad for work, some elder parents are alternatively moving to their sons' homes after retirement or when they need care. Depending on the circumstances, daughters (especially if unmarried), grandchildren, nephews and nieces may also offer elder care or *seva*. Elders and their juniors often state that it is precisely what parents once gave to their young children—including co-residence, food, material support, love, time together, assistance with daily routines, and toileting—that adult children will later reciprocate to their parents when the parents become old.

From such a perspective, not only children but also elders can be very appropriately dependent on kin for material, emotional and bodily support, and in fact Bengalis often explicitly compare the acts of caring for both elders and children. One afternoon I spoke with a group of older ladies living in the village of Mangaldihi where I had done research for many years, telling them about my new project on the rise of old age homes in and around the city of Kolkata. They exclaimed: 'We would *never* throw our parents in an old age home! That's only a matter of cities'. They went on effusively: 'When we grow old, we live right with our sons and daughters-in-law! We receive care from them, love from them. If we are sick or weak, they tend to us, just like we tended to them'.

Although it is highly usual for middle-aged and older adults especially to describe such a mutually interdependent intergenerational relationship as natural, sustaining and obligatory, such elder care can certainly be experienced as difficult, particularly by daughters-in-law. Pratima, a professional Kolkata woman in her middle adult years, remarked: '*I* could be a case study for you. I live alone with just my mother-in-law (*sasuri*) and husband. My husband is the only brother, and our children are abroad'. One son is studying neuroscience in a PhD program at Cornell University, and the other son is at Massachusetts Institute of Technology. Pratima went on to describe her care practices:

> Every day after work I go to sit with my *sasuri* for at least one hour. This is my commitment. I hear about the details of her day—it is so boring that I almost fall asleep. I insist that my husband visit with her at least once per day, but he doesn't spend much time with her. My *sasuri* will say, 'I can't live without seeing my son's face' (*cheler mukh na dekhe bacte pari na*). I tell her that I haven't seen *my* sons for months.... She is with maids all day, but she doesn't find fulfillment and companionship from them.

---

[9] See S. Irudaya Rajan and S. Kumar, 'Living Arrangements among Indian Elderly: New Evidence from National Family Health Survey', in *Economic and Political Weekly*, Vol.38 (2003), pp.75–80; D. Jamuna, 'Issues of Elder Care and Elder Abuse in the Indian Context', in Phoebe S. Liebig and S. Irudaya Rajan (eds), *An Aging India: Perspectives, Prospects and Policies* (New York: Haworth Press, 2003), pp.127–8, and Saumitra Basu, 'Some Social, Economic and Behavioural Problems of the Aged Inhabiting Calcutta City: An Anthropological Approach', unpublished PhD dissertation, University of Calcutta, 2006.

Pratima detailed how they employ three maids to care for the older woman, one to cook, and the other two to provide two shifts of companionship during the day while Pratima and her husband are out working. 'This is expensive and a hassle. Maybe an old age home would be a good solution, but the social stigma! What would people say? I could never do it'.

Yet the widespread perception across India is that joint families are fast breaking down.[10] On the one hand, many perceive profoundly that the family is best: not only for elders, but also as a means to uphold core *Indian* forms of morality, identity and sociality. On the other hand, there is a pervasive sense that due to the (good and bad) changes of modernity and globalisation, family care for elders is no longer fully expected or feasible. The growth of nuclear-family lifestyles and flats,[11] the preponderance of children moving abroad, the fostering among both generations of generational and gendered equality, rising incomes (allowing the financing of separate residences), the ageing of the population (more elders with fewer juniors to provide care), and other factors cluster together to create a milieu in which so much uncertainty and ambivalence surrounds the intergenerational family that (the narratives go) those of the junior generation are no longer able or willing to provide care, and those of the senior generation are no longer preferring or expecting such care. These changes in practice and sentiment are especially prevalent among India's urban middle and upper-middle classes.

One spring evening in 2006, I gave a lecture comparing Indian and US ways of ageing to a gathering of members of the Dignity Foundation in Kolkata. This foundation aims 'to create an enlightened society in which the 50+ feel secure, confident and valued, and can live with Dignity',[12] and comprises largely well-educated, middle-class members from a variety of Indian regions who speak mostly English in their gatherings. After my talk, an elegant middle-aged woman with long grey hair tied up in a loose attractive knot, dressed in a becoming ash-green *salwar* pant suit, came to sit next to me as the program was winding down. She said that she had enjoyed the talk (though I had gone a little too fast), and then offered her perspectives: 'You see, we looked after our parents, *but*, I don't expect my children to look after us. If I did, I would be disappointed. You see, the modern educated people are realising this in the cities. I don't want to be a burden on my children—it would not be fair. I *do* look after my own parents and my husband's parents, but I don't expect my children to look after me'. I asked: 'How do you think you came to have this perspective?—such a significant change in expectations in your one lifetime?' Her soft reply, after thinking for a moment: 'You see, we *educated* them (our children) to move out. In fact, we *financed* them to move out also. We raised them in such a way, educated them, and then sent them out to find good jobs and live on their own'. She paused again, contemplating, then offered in a somewhat emotional tone: 'It's just that as parents, we *hope* that they will feel for us'.

The family is wonderful, natural, intimate, Indian. Yet at the same time, the family is disintegrating, uncertain and, perhaps, even backward.

---

[10] Lawrence Cohen and Sarah Lamb explore such perceptions in further detail in their respective works, *No Aging in India: Alzheimer's, Bad Families and Other Modern Things* (Berkeley: University of California Press, 1998) and *Aging and the Indian Diaspora: Cosmopolitan Families in India and Abroad* (Bloomington: Indiana University Press, 2009).

[11] See Raka Ray and Seemin Qayum, *Cultures of Servitude: Modernity, Domesticity, and Class in India* (Palo Alto, CA: Stanford University Press, 2009) for a compelling portrait of some of the many transformations entailed by the rise of nuclear-family lifestyles and flats in contemporary Kolkata.

[12] The Dignity Foundation vision statement can be found at http://www.dignityfoundation.com/about-us/mission-statement.html, accessed 24 July 2012.

Is Old Age Security in the Market?

If the family cannot unquestioningly be counted on to provide old age security, can private institutions in the market do so? In fact, in India the past several decades have witnessed the emergence of old age homes and other private elder-care institutions, offering social, emotional and practical support for urban middle-class elders living apart from junior kin. The most dramatic occurrence is the near flood of elder residences that has risen in India's major urban centres. Until the 1990s and early 2000s, 'old age homes' as they are commonly referred to in English, scarcely existed in India, save for a handful established by Christian missionaries largely catering to the Anglo-Indian community and the very poor.[13] Now, old age homes number nearly one thousand or more across India's urban centres, catering primarily to the Hindu middle and upper-middle classes.[14] Run by non-profit organisations as well as private entrepreneurs, the rates range from about Rs1,000 to Rs5,000 per month (a little over $US20–$US100), and often require a sizable joining fee or security deposit of anywhere from about Rs5,000 to Rs300,000 (about $US100 to $US6,000). The monthly fees of a modestly-priced old age home are similar to that of the salary of a full-time domestic servant in the region, and are affordable by those with pensions, substantial savings, or salaried children wishing to pay the bills.

Non-profit non-government organisations (NGOs), as well as private businesses, are also emerging to help support elders living independently, offering services such as around-the-clock telephone help lines, escorts to late-night wedding receptions and doctor appointments, visits to chat over tea, meal delivery, help completing tax forms, and the promise of a presence at the time of death. It is often NRI or 'non-resident Indian' children who fund the services for their parents in India, able to supply money but not time or proximity. The director of one such NGO, Agewell Foundation, compared their hired elder-care counsellors to 'surrogate sons', commenting: 'A sad situation indeed when children cannot gift their parents time. But this is a contemporary reality that has to be faced'.

In my home nation of the USA, such forms of private market-based elder care have been widely available since the early twentieth century and form an important dimension of American old age security. Private elder-care services work to help American elders maintain their keenly-valued sense of independence. Although the commonly-accepted ideal is to be able to care independently for oneself throughout adulthood and old age, if elders do come to require co-residence or intimate bodily care (such as help with dressing, toileting or bathing), American elders will tend to prefer to pay for such care rather than to depend on an adult child. If care is paid for on the market, the elder is not demeaningly dependent on the caregiver, but rather engaging in a reciprocal market transaction. In India, market-based elder care is regarded with a good deal more ambivalence—as a novel, even peculiar, in some ways damaging, development—at the same time as some find it a practical and welcome old age

---

[13] See Lamb, *Aging and the Indian Diaspora*, pp.55–8; and Phoebe S. Liebig, 'Old Age Homes and Services: Old and New Approaches to Aged Care', in Phoebe S. Liebig and S. Irudaya Rajan (eds) *An Aging India: Perspectives, Prospects and Policies* (New York: Haworth Press, 2003), pp.159–78.

[14] HelpAge India's 2002 guide to old age homes lists 800 across India [http://www.helpageindia.org, accessed 16 Aug. 2012]. See also Maneeta Sawhney, 'The Role of Nongovernmental Organizations for the Welfare of the Elderly: The Case of HelpAge India', in Phoebe S. Liebig and S. Irudaya Rajan (eds), *An Aging India: Perspectives, Prospects and Policies* (New York: Haworth, 2003), pp.179–91; since its publication new elder residences have been springing up at a fast pace. From 2004–06, I was able to locate 71 old age homes in Kolkata and its suburbs (Lamb, *Aging and the Indian Diaspora*). I and others' research has as yet uncovered no homes for the aged in India dedicated to Muslims (Lamb, *Aging and the Indian Diaspora*, p.59, and Liebig, 'Old Age Homes', p.166).

security option for those able to pay and unwilling or unable (for varying reasons) to depend on family.

Two middle-aged women friends from Kolkata's high society social circles spoke of their motivation to found a serene, up-scale elder residence on the outskirts of Kolkata adjoining a guava orchard on old family land: 'We are trying to begin to wipe out the stigma of living in an old age home', Sanjita explained. '"Come *happily* stay with us", is our motto. It's not that the children are throwing away their parents—it's not *always* that.... These are just the circumstances of modern society.... Children are eager to pay, *more* than eager to pay, for their parents' happiness, and parents are also able to pay. We arrange for mental peace as well as physical peace'.

Over 2004–06 I spent much time in several of Kolkata's old age homes. One of my friends and research subjects, Purnima Bhattacharya, a retired professor in her late sixties who had never married and lived entirely alone, was becoming worried about her future as an old woman. Purnima asked me to take her to see several old age homes that I might recommend, to help ease her mind about the future. 'Sarat Chandra Niketan' was one place I thought she might like, a place not so terribly far from her home in the Dhakuria neighbourhood of Kolkata, and a bit less intimidatingly posh than 'Retreat', the first elder home I had taken Purnima-di to see; this new home was more affordable and more traditionally Bengali as well. I picked up Purnima-di at 10 a.m. She was ready and waiting, dressed in a fine hand-embroidered raw silk sari, and with a garland in hand; she asked if we could stop by a *sraddha* funeral service on the way—it would only take 15 minutes. It was the *sraddha* for one of her brother's dear friends who had died just now, although her own brother had died 21 years before, at such a young age. After the *sraddha*, we made our way through the crowded streets to 'Sarat Chandra Niketan', and stopped in to see one of my acquaintances, Gauri Chattopadhyay, who resided in the elder residence in a double room with her ailing husband.

Purnima asked Gauri-di to please tell her frankly all about the good and the bad of the home. After all, Gauri-di had lived there for six years, since the very beginning; she must know all about it. Gauri-di started with the good: for instance, that it is perfectly safe:

> You can stay here without worry at all, if you are concerned about security, or being on your own. The *ayah*s (nursemaids, assistants, nannies) will look after you. All your meals will be delivered and they will be fine and safe and healthy. There are security guards at all times. If you fall, someone will know it. In those regards, you can live here completely without worry.

Gauri-di went on to discuss some things she did not like about living in the home—she had not found a close rapport with many of the other residents, for instance; the staff did not seem to have a sense of who Gauri-di and her husband are and were as persons—her husband, who was now quite bedridden and unable to communicate well, had been such a highly-regarded doctor and community leader—no one had a sense of that now; the food, though perfectly adequate, was not like home cooking. However, from the perspective of security, the home offered all she wanted. Their only son had died as a young man so they did not have the option of living in a family home. She was relieved to have found the institution of an old age home to meet her basic needs during this phase of her and her husband's life.

Many elder-abode residents do speak very appreciatively of the security and amenities provided by old age home living, including the regular delivery of meals and tea, the presence of security guards, rooms cleaned and clothes washed—all this without having to worry about hiring and managing household servants on one's own, a task which can be tedious, expensive and, some believe, risky: news stories and public discourse these days are full of stories of domestic servants taking advantage of the elderly. Elder residences can provide valued social and emotional security as well. For instance, *seva*—or respectful care for and service to elders—is widely regarded by proprietors, staff and residents as one of the most central and valued features of elder home living. Indeed, many of the elder homes I visited were set up expressly to offer *seva*, and several were succinctly named 'Seva'. The manager of 'Gurujan Kunja' (Garden Abode for Respected Elders) explained his home's name: 'It indicates the home's purpose; to serve and honour the old people living here. You see, they are all revered people living here'. Residents speak appreciatively of how much *seva* they receive from the hands of the staff and proprietors, especially in smaller homes set up similarly to ordinary family households: bed tea each morning; breakfast; a full Bengali noon meal; tiffin or snack in the early evening; supper; delivery of warm bath water; combing of hair; massaging of tired feet; hanging of mosquito nets; washing of clothes; the offering of comfort and even love. Other elders observe positively that old age home living offers a familiar joint-family-like feel and sociality, reminding residents of childhood days in crowded, overflowing households, where (in both settings) all eat food cooked from the same hearth, people sleep in groups of two to six to a room, and one almost never has to be alone. Some develop very intimate, supportive relationships over the years, especially with co-residents, describing each other as 'like sisters'. And many say that living in an old age home is less culturally alien and bizarre than what for some would have been the alternative option of living alone, offering reflections such as 'human beings have never lived alone' and 'it is not natural for human beings to live alone'.

But for very many in India, old age home living is profoundly associated with stigma, shock, and—especially for those with sons—an acute sense of having been thrown away or abandoned by families. *Phele daoya* is the term most commonly used in Bengali public discourse to refer to the act by which a family, son, or son and daughter-in-law place an elder in an old age home. Meaning literally to 'throw out', 'throw away', or 'abandon', it is the same verb used to refer to the 'throwing away' of garbage. Kalyani Chatterjee had been placed or thrown away into an old age home, against her will, by her only son about four years before I first met her in 2006. Widowed at a young age, Kalyani-di had been employed throughout her adult years, raised three children, arranged and paid for the marriages of her daughters, and brought a daughter-in-law into their modest family home. For sixteen years, both her daughter-in-law and Kalyani-di had worked to earn money while sharing the household duties. Shortly after the older woman's retirement as a Rotary Club secretary, and after her son had unexpectedly lost his own job, the son suddenly told his mother that he did not feel comfortable having her reside with them, living off his wife's money. He gave his mother just one day's notice and asked her to be prepared to go to a home for the aged. Kalyani-di had never before even heard of such an institution. Whenever Kalyani-di's son makes a rare visit to the home, Kalyani-di begs him to get her 'released'. She reflects: 'If we had grown up with the idea that we might live separately from our children, then it might not be so hard to get used to now. But with our own eyes we had never seen or known anything like this. We never could have even *dreamed* that an abode for elders existed, that we would be here, in a place like this!' What most profoundly thwarts the sense of security for many old age home residents is just this kind of acute feeling of not 'being part of a social world that revolves around a familiar order with some predictability'.[15]

Many of those in the Indian public who have not yet had any close interaction with elder-care institutions similarly have trouble getting their arms around the idea that old age home

---

[15] Hashimoto, 'Cultural Meanings of "Security" in Aging Policies', p.20.

living could be a normal, viable and morally-acceptable option for Indian individuals and families. Pratima reported to me the provocative discussion of the notion of old age homes that had recently transpired at a meeting of her ladies' group, which Pratima described as 'ordinary middle-class women' from her neighbourhood. After an opening conversation in which the group had been vociferously criticising the rise of old age homes in their country, one member aged about thirty, who had a child of five, began to argue in favour of the idea, comparing old age homes to crèches and boarding schools for children:

> When I was young, my parents both worked. There was no shortage of money, and I went to a very good crèche and then to a very good hostel [at a boarding school]. I was perfectly well (*bhaloi chilam*), and no one said anything critical. My parents would come to get me for vacations. They would visit me, and I would visit them. They loved me, and I loved them. So what's the problem with old people going to old age homes?

Everyone was silent, Pratima reported. 'Really, she spoke very well, compellingly', Pratima confided. Then someone broke the silence: 'This isn't a simple math problem with a certain answer, like two plus two equals four'. 'Really', Pratima said to me, 'this is such a big concern (*boro baepar*) for our society now'.

Another factor to consider is that to date the majority of India's old age homes are not for the truly physically and socially helpless; they are closer to American 'assisted living' institutions than to 'nursing homes' that provide daily medical care and a good deal of assistance with the activities of daily living. In many cases, India's elder home residents must be sent 'home' or away if they do end up requiring such extensive care. After visiting with my acquaintance and resident Gauri Chattopadhyay at 'Sarat Chandra Niketan', Purnima went to speak to Mr. Das, the manager of the home we were considering for her own future needs. The first time we had ventured to an elder residence together, Purnima had seemed not to be able to admit to the manager (and/or to herself? to me?) that she was considering the institution for herself. But this time she was more direct and asked lots of questions, with a degree of anxiety, about the rates, foods, rooms, services and conditions of admission. When Mr. Das mentioned that to move in, one needs to list two 'guarantors'—guardian-types who can be called upon if one becomes unable to make decisions for oneself, who could make medical decisions and manage finances, and take the ill person away if necessary—Purnima became quite distressed. She phrased her comments in terms of 'we'—presumably, 'we' old people who have no one, the types who may wish to come to an old age home:

> Purnima: So, let me understand, you are saying that those who come here must have two guardians who must take care of them if the need arises.
>
> Mr. Das: Yes.
>
> Purnima: But don't you understand? We who have no one, we who if we had someone to look after us, then we wouldn't even be coming to an old age home, then you are saying that you will only take us when we are in good health, when we can make decisions for ourselves, when we are in the condition that we in fact could take care of ourselves on our own. And then only when we get to the condition that we really *need* an old age home and someone to take care of us, *that's* when we have to find someone else to depend on?
>
> Mr. Das: I understand.

Purnima: But if we had someone to depend on as a guarantor, we wouldn't need to be coming to the old age home. Why would someone agree to take on that burden? We thought we were going to an old age home so we could free others of that burden.

So, market-based elder care, on the rise in India, is welcomed by some as a modern, convenient and practical way to acquire old age security, through purchase. Yet, are such institutions ethical, *Indian*, certain enough to provide answers for those questioning their future needs, and familiar enough to be bearable?

Is Old Age Security in the State?

If family and market are both uncertain, does or should old age security lie with the state? Social security programs for the aged are often taken to be one sign internationally of a modern nation, and the United Nations Universal Declaration of Human Rights recognises the right to social security, in old age and other parallel circumstances, as a basic human right, the responsibility of both national governments and international co-operation.[16] Does India concur? A report from the India-based Project OASIS seems to support such an ideology, proclaiming: 'India has been among the *enlightened nations* which recognised the need for social security during old age quite early'.[17] Yet much ambivalence surrounds the project of state-backed old age security in India, both morally and economically, and recent Indian state interventions into old age care have aimed much more at ensuring family care than at replacing it.[18]

In India, there are three main avenues through which the government has become involved in the matter of old age security: first, it has instituted modest old age pension schemes for the poor. Beginning in the 1950s, India's states initiated old age pension programs for destitute older persons, and in 1999 the federal government instituted the National Old Age Pension Scheme (NOAPS) now offering Rs200 per month to persons aged over 65 who are considered destitute in the sense of having 'no regular means of subsistence from his/her own source of income or through financial support from family members or other sources'.[19] Second, in December 2007 the Indian parliament, seeking to enforce family care of the elderly as a legal obligation, passed a bill titled the Maintenance and Welfare of Parents and Senior Citizens Bill, 2007. Under this law, implemented in October 2009, children may be fined Rs5,000 and jailed for up to three months if found guilty of neglecting their parents. Relatives other than children are also obligated to support childless senior citizens (any citizen of India aged sixty or older), if they stand to inherit property from their aged kin. The bill in addition gives

---

[16] The principle of social security as a human right is articulated in Articles 22 and 25 of the Universal Declaration of Human Rights. Article 22 reads: 'Everyone, as a member of society, has the right to social security and is entitled to realization, through national effort and international co-operation and in accordance with the organization and resources of each State, of the economic, social and cultural rights indispensable for his dignity and the free development of his personality'. Article 25 reads: 'Everyone has the right to a standard of living adequate for the health and well-being of himself and of his family, including food, clothing, housing and medical care and necessary social services, and the right to security in the event of unemployment, sickness, disability, widowhood, old age or other lack of livelihood in circumstances beyond his control' [http://www.un.org/en/documents/udhr/, accessed 27 July 2012].

[17] 'OASIS (Old Age Social and Income Security): A Report', italics added.

[18] See also Bianca Brijnath, 'Why Does Institutionalised Care Not Appeal to Indian Families? Legislative and Social Answers from Urban India', in *Ageing and Society*, Vol.32, no.4 (2012), pp.697–717.

[19] Old Age Solutions: Portal on Technology Solution for Elderly, an Initiative of Ministry of Science and Technology, Government of India: National Old Age Pension Scheme (NOAPS) [http://www.oldagesolutions.org/facilities/Noaps.aspx, accessed 27 July 2012].

parents powers to disinherit errant children and other kin. Third, intergenerational family disputes can be brought to local courts, which tend to side strongly with elderly parents, stipulating that children have both a legal and moral obligation to provide care and respect for their parents. In each of these cases, one can find the Indian government interventions to be much more about enforcing family care than substituting it.

One example of this claim can be found in the opening remarks prefacing the senior citizens and maintenance bill. Under 'Need for the Legislation', it declared straightforwardly: 'It is an established fact that family is the most desired environment for senior citizens/parents to lead a life of security, care and dignity', and 'Unfortunately, the time has come when the moral obligation of children to look after their parents in their old age has to be backed by a legal obligation'.[20] What 'used to' happen 'naturally'—intimate support within the haven of the sustaining Indian joint family—may need now to be mandated by the state although not discarded.

An analysis I conducted of several years of newspaper coverage of intergenerational family disputes brought to the courts[21] indicated the strong sense of appropriate family values among the judges who again and again stipulated that junior children must support their elders. In one case, a widowed mother, son and daughter-in-law were called to court after the mother complained that her son and daughter-in-law did not take care of her or provide her with food, but yet were renting out her portion of the family home, while keeping the proceeds. The *Anandabajar Patrika* staff correspondent reported:

> Today, right at the beginning of the case, the judge asked [the son], 'What is this? You don't take care of your mother, give her food? This old woman had to come to the court—aren't you ashamed?' With folded hands, [the son] replied, 'Sir, I have committed a wrong, my Lord. I apologise. From now onwards, I shall take care of my mother'.

The judge decreed that the mother must be paid each month the full proceeds from the rental, speaking with an emotion-filled voice as he proclaimed: 'A mother cannot be compared with anyone. You wait and see, your mother will save from that amount and give to you at your hour of emergency'. The judge then asked the aged woman whether Rs4,000 a month would suffice for her maintenance. The woman replied meekly: 'I have small expenses. Whatever I save I will give to him. I am advancing toward death'. In closing, 'the Judge spoke to [the son] affectionately: "Take care of your mother. You see, you will be happy"'.[22] Another judge ordered a son and daughter-in-law to grasp their parents' feet and beg for forgiveness, and then come back to report to the court after the quarrels had been settled, warning: 'Remember, your own children will be grown one day. I hope you will have no regrets'.[23]

It is also striking that the National Old Age Pension Scheme limits its support to elders who can document that they have no support from family members. Consider, in contrast, the

---

[20] The text of the 2007 bill is available at http://www.prsindia.org/uploads/media/1182337322/scr1193026940_Senior_Citizen.pdf (accessed 27 July 2012). See also MWPSC.pdf [http://www.tiss.edu/tiss-attachements/downloads/maintenance-and-welfare-of-parents-and-senior-citizens-act-mwpsc/view, accessed 25 Oct. 2012].
[21] Lamb, *Aging and the Indian Diaspora*, pp.242–9.
[22] '*Make dekhen na, lajja kare na! Mucaleka nila court*' ('You Don't Take Care of Your Mother—Don't You Feel Ashamed?! Court Requires Son to Post Bond'), *Anandabajar Patrika* (19 March 2008), p.1.
[23] '*Atyacar karay bhartsana, ma-babar pa dhare kshama caite nirdes korter*' (Court Reprimands Son and Daughter-in-Law for Torture and Orders Them to Embrace Parents' Feet and Ask for Forgiveness), *Anandabajar Patrika* (27 June 2003), p.1.

US Supplemental Security Income (SSI) program for the indigent aged; an elderly recipient could have children making millions and still qualify, as the assets of one's children are not taken into account when calculating eligibility for this aged welfare program.[24] So it is plain that although the government is increasingly involved in matters of old age care in India, a central premise underlying its involvement is that care of the aged by the family is best, most normal, most appropriate—culturally, morally and economically.

Yet such a premise does not go entirely unchallenged, as some assert that it is time for India to de-emphasise the role of the family, and others argue that if a family does not out of its own volition wish to care for its elderly, will the existence of laws accomplish the task? One newspaper editorial, 'Present Tense, Future Imperfect', asks of the new parental maintenance bill: 'But will this Bill be able to better the lives of the elderly? If the intent is missing, will any law, rule, regulation bring any change in the way children mistreat their elderly parents?'[25] A *Telegraph* editorial, spurred by a report of a middle-class elderly woman abandoned on the streets by her sons, criticises the absence of a viable welfare system in India, which creates 'inordinate dependence on the family.... To blame [the current situation of the elderly] on the demise of the joint family is to misrepresent the complex, systemic and political nature of the problem—an evasive moralism behind which governments often hide'.[26]

So, it is with complex ambivalence that members of the Indian public approach recent developments regarding state involvement in elder care in India.

Is Old Age Security in the Individual Self?

If the family, market and state are all uncertain sites of old age security, what about the self-reliant individual self? The 1999 OASIS (Old Age Social and Income Security) Report declares that, as family and government support are both inadequate in India, the nation must work to develop modes of individual self-reliance:

> The problem [of old age security] will have to be addressed through thrift and self-help, where people prepare for old age by savings accumulating through their decades in the labour force.... We must educate people that old age is inescapable and that saving for old age could be a painless process if started early in life.... The government should encourage fully funded old age income security systems that emphasise the values of thrift and self-help.[27]

Some Indian gerontologists likewise advocate the development of self-sufficiency among the aged in India today. S. Irudaya Rajan, U.S. Mishra and P. Sankara Sarma recommend, for instance, that ageing individuals should cultivate a dependence on the self—through savings, exercise and an open-mindedness about living in old age homes—as one can no longer count on, and *should* no longer count on, if one is modern and educated, depending on children in

---

[24] See Lamb, *Aging and the Indian Diaspora*, pp.256–67.
[25] Sarah Salvadore and Roshni Mukherjee, 'Present Tense, Future Imperfect', *Times of India* (28 Feb. 2007), Calcutta Times Leisure section, p.1.
[26] 'Unaccommodated', *Telegraph* (11 Mar. 2006), p.18.
[27] 'OASIS (Old Age Social and Income Security): A Report'.

old age.[28] Peer-oriented senior citizens' clubs are on the rise in India's urban middle-class milieu, promoting self-developing activities and hobbies, and notions of 'successful ageing' as an individual project.

However, such a project of crafting an independent way of life in old age is not one that most Indians I know find unambiguously easy or natural, practised as part of their familiar, unremarked culture. Rather, it is a project that they engage in with critical reflection, self-consciousness, effort and, generally, some ambivalence. At the same Dignity Foundation gathering I introduced above, where I had been invited to give a talk comparing US and Indian ways of ageing, a lively discussion ensued debating the merits and demerits, the possibility and impossibility, of living independently and apart from one's children in late life. One gentleman commented favourably:

> With the passage of time, we have witnessed so much change, and so parents have become cleverer now. For example, they are now not *so* generous to their children. Modern parents will give some things to their children, but will also keep property in their own name. Because they know that they cannot count on their children to provide for them. So, you see, I am more or less self-sufficient. At the same time, I love my children, and they love me. I pay visits to my children, and they pay visits to me. But, I do not expect them to support me.

Another man described how he tells his daughters not to do too much for him, otherwise he will become completely dependent. His tone and words evoked a sense of how seductive and enjoyable it is to be waited on, visited, tended to and loved, so much so that one must aspire very purposefully if one wishes to maintain strength and independence in the face of that allure. 'That was a very sweet relationship', another member added, referring to the mutual interdependence of the joint family system, 'but it is dying now'. Another commented: 'But we can't get rid of that expectation level. The problem is that we have grown up *expecting* our children to care for us'.

In 2003, an older Bengali gentleman wrote to a Kolkata newspaper commenting disparagingly on the trend of generations living separately, reacting to a judge's decision that if a daughter-in-law wants to live separately from her in-laws, she should be allowed to: 'The human society is being transformed into an animal society (*pasusamaj*). Like animals and birds, in the present society, the role of parents will be simply to educate the son effortlessly until he can be on his own'.[29] According to this man's vision, in a society where children grow up to live separately from their parents, people become like animals—among whom neither generation, following a short-lived period of dependent infancy, depends on or maintains intimate ties with the other.

Concluding Notes

Models of old age security are embedded in profound cultural and moral visions of the human project and the best ways to live. These visions pertain not only to old age *per se*, but also to

---

[28] S. Irudaya Rajan, U.S. Mishra and P. Sankara Sarma, *India's Elderly: Burden or Challenge?* (New Delhi: Sage, 1999).

[29] From a collection of letters to the editor assembled under the title 'Let Aged Father and Mother Go to Hell' (*buro bap-ma culoe jak*), published in *Anandabajar Patrika* (16 Oct. 2003). *Culoe jak* literally means 'go to the funeral pyre' or to the 'oven' (*culo*), and carries a meaning similar to the English idioms 'go to hell', 'go to the dogs', or 'go to ruin'.

the very nature and identity of a society and nation. Examining the diverse and complex ways older middle-class Indians and their communities are critically reflecting upon the problem of old age security illuminates competing understandings of personhood, family and the social-moral order: where *is* the best site of ageing and elder care: the family, the market, the state and/or the individual? We see that there are no simple answers to this compelling question.

In country after country around the world, not only in India, there has been a dramatic transformation in the key sites of ageing and elder care—from the multigenerational family to the market, state and individual. This transformation is often understood as 'progress'. International bodies such as the World Bank and the United Nations, for instance, have taken the existence of elder care institutions beyond the family as one of the signs of a 'developed' nation. In this vein, economist Robert Palacios of the World Bank remarks: 'In the past fifty years, policymakers in India have made precious little progress towards providing a viable alternative to the family as the main source of income security for the elderly'.[30] We see here a clear developmental teleology: as a nation progresses from being poor to rich, developing to developed, its elders will progress from relying on the family to reliance on the state, market and individual self.

Yet, a key point I wish to make is that such transitions and policies are not simply 'natural' or 'right' or constitutive of 'progress', but carry profoundly different meanings across cultural, political-economic and historical contexts. Barbara Ehrenreich and Arlie Hochschild, in their introduction to *Global Woman*, reflect: 'The Western culture of individualism, which finds extreme expression in the United States, militates against acknowledging help or human interdependency of nearly any kind'.[31] Such a cultural model has influenced international ageing policies, I believe, though often with insufficient critical scrutiny. For India, and likely elsewhere, it is not so obvious that to turn away from the family and to shun human interdependence is best—not in a simple, straightforward way, at least. For India, what will likely work most successfully for old age security over coming years is the forging of a creative combination of family and extra-family policies and practices, as elders, their communities and policymakers find new ways and rationales to negotiate remarkable societal transformations, striving to craft meaningful lives and forms of ageing in the present.

---

[30] Robert Palacios, 'The Challenge for India: Do New Initiatives Go Far Enough?', Global Action on Aging, New York (2002) [http://www.globalaging.org/pension/world/india.htm, accessed 27 July 2012].

[31] Barbara Ehrenreich and Arlie Russell Hochschild, 'Introduction', in Barbara Ehrenreich and Arlie Russell Hochschild (eds), *Global Woman: Nannies, Maids, and Sex Workers in the New Economy* (New York: Henry Holt, 2002), p.4.

Contractarianism and the Ethic of Care in Indian Fiction

IRA RAJA

Through close readings of recent fiction from English, Hindi and Kannada sources, this paper analyses the feminist ethic of care with reference to adult daughters caring for their critically-ill or dying mothers. The discussion focuses on problems associated with the care ethic and examines some of its assumptions, particularly its inability to account for the emotional complexity of adult caregiving relationships, which can make the invocation of relationality difficult; its focus on responsiveness to needs, such as those of helpless infants, which prevents adequate engagement with ideas of reciprocity; and, finally, its extraction of the caregiving relationship from the network of social and familial relationships in which it is embedded. Alongside my critique of the ethic of care, I will also examine the extent to which mainstream moral concepts, such as rights and contracts, may continue to be relevant to the dynamics of intergenerational relations in old age.

The Intergenerational Contract

The right of parents who have no means of supporting themselves to be cared for by their children is widely accepted in Indian culture, where children are socialised from an early age to understand their role and commitment to the idea of interdependency and support across generations.[1] Gerontological literature in India generally refers to this informal filial understanding as an 'intergenerational contract'. Given the paucity of alternative old age guarantees and services to complement or substitute for family support (for example, state welfare), the elderly are almost completely reliant on this contract.[2]

Traditionally, the responsibility for honouring this contract lies with the son. It is sons, rather than daughters, who are said to continue the bloodline, provide old age support and perform ceremonies when parents die, so guaranteeing them salvation.[3] By convention, a

---

[1] Rajib Lochan Dhar, 'Caregiving for Elderly Parents: A Study from the Indian Perspective', in *Home Health Care Management and Practice*, Vol.XX, no.X (October 2012), p.1. Also see Leena Mary Emmatty, Ranabir S. Bhatti and Mathew T. Mukalel, 'The Experience of Burden in India: A Study of Dementia Caregivers', in *Dementia*, Vol.5, no.2 (2006), pp.223–32.

[2] E.J. Croll, 'The Intergenerational Contract in the Changing Asian Family', in *Oxford Development Studies*, Vol.34, no.4 (2006), p.478. Although perceptions are changing, it is generally true that even when such services exist, children who allow parents to avail themselves of them are viewed critically. See also M. Larsen, N. Hatti and P. Gooch, 'Intergenerational Interests, Uncertainty and Discrimination: Conceptualizing the Process of Declining Child Sex Ratios in India', in *Lund Papers in Economic History* (Lund, Sweden: Media-Tryck, 2006), p.6.

[3] *Ibid.*, p.23; and A. Collins and P. Desai, 'Selfhood in the Indian Context: A Psychoanalytic Perspective', in T.G. Vaidyanathan and J.J. Kripal (eds), *Vishnu on Freud's Desk: A Reader in Psychoanalysis and Hinduism* (Delhi: Oxford University Press, 1999), p.382.

married daughter has no reciprocal obligations to her own parents: in fact, reliance upon a married daughter may even be considered 'shameful and demeaning'.[4] Particularly in the patrilineal North, the quasi-religious belief that a daughter is '*paraya dhan*' (literally, wealth that belongs to someone else and must, therefore, be returned via marriage) entails parents' non-reliance on daughters for support in old age.[5] These attitudes have been shifting in recent years and, although the preference for and privileging of sons remain high across South Asia and discrimination against girls is often extreme, daughters are slowly beginning to be seen as a potential source of support in old age.[6] This paper will examine some of the issues that make it difficult for daughters to assume such roles *vis-à-vis* their parents. In particular, it will analyse four recent short stories from India, which focus on adult daughters caring for their critically-ill or dying mothers, from the perspective of the feminist ethic of care.

The View from Literature

In his critique of the patriarchal bias in anthropological research, Sudhir Kakar observes that it is difficult to assess how daughters fare in 'mother India'. Anthropological studies largely focus on the development of boys, but overlook the subject of female childhood. Myths, too, tend to neglect daughters for 'in a patriarchal culture myths are inevitably man-made and man-oriented'. Since myths address the unconscious wishes and fears of men, Kakar argues 'it is the parent–son rather than the parent–daughter relationship which becomes charged with symbolic significance'.[7] The mother–daughter relationship appears to have suffered particularly from this bias. As Radhika Mohanram notes, scholarly research in India has failed to demonstrate formal and sustained interest in this relationship.[8] Mohanram attributes this silence to the relative absence of the mother–daughter relationship as a distinct category in the Indian family.[9] Holding imaginative literature up to scrutiny, she claims that 'not even a skeletal blueprint exists for the narrative of mother–daughter relationships within the master-discourse of Indian fiction'.[10]

More recently, mainstream Indian literature has begun to place the mother–daughter relationship at the centre of its concerns. Conditions in the late twentieth and early twenty-first centuries—such as opportunities for education, travel and new forms of interpersonal relationships—have worked to provide a narrative impulse for reframing and re-examining the mother–daughter relationship as a significant issue for women's writing from India, forcing us now to revisit Mohanram's contention that 'the most significant difficulty is not interpretation

---

[4] Sylvia Vatuk, '"To Be a Burden on Others": Dependency Anxiety among the Elderly in India', in O.M. Lynch (ed.), *Divine Passions: The Social Construction of Emotion in India* (Berkeley, CA: University of California Press, 1990), p.77.

[5] See Dhar, 'Caregiving for Elderly Parents', p.6. This prohibition is less applicable to the matrilineal traditions of the South and the Northeast. Also, in the North, the prohibition on a married daughter supporting parents is not uniform everywhere. It is much stronger in Haryana, for instance, than it is in Maharashtra. Also, when a married daughter is an only child, there is a tradition of *ghar jamai* even in the North: since the daughter stands to inherit everything, she is expected to support her parents and her husband is expected to join her in her parents' house.

[6] Croll, 'The Intergenerational Contract in the Changing Asian Family', pp.480–1.

[7] Sudhir Kakar, *The Inner World: A Psycho-Analytic Study of Childhood and Society in India* (Delhi: Oxford University Press, 1978), p.57.

[8] Radhika Mohanram, 'The Problems of Reading: Mother–Daughter Relationships and Indian Postcoloniality', in Elizabeth Brown-Guillory (ed.), *Women of Color: Mother–Daughter Relationships in 20th-Century Literature* (Austin, TX: University of Texas Press, 1996), pp.21–2.

[9] *Ibid.*, pp.20–1.

[10] *Ibid.*

of texts but location of materials'.[11] A quick overview of recent writing makes it clear that stories addressing the theme do exist and in increasing numbers, and that it is scholarly writing that has failed to keep pace.[12]

This article will analyse stories by four prominent women writers in English, Hindi and Kannada. Githa Hariharan's 'The Art of Dying', Shashi Deshpande's 'Lucid Moments', Vaidehi's 'The Confession' and Krishna Sobti's 'Listen, Girl' are all stories about adult daughters caring for their terminally-ill and ageing mothers. Drawn from a small selection of texts focused mainly on the urban middle classes, the daughter in these and other such stories is an enabling presence who attempts to retrieve the sense of her mother's marginal life as she herself approaches her mother's perspective, registering emotions that range from love and longing to anger and resentment, but rarely rejection. Not quite the perfect subject of a bourgeois patriarchal family, the daughter in this fiction is mostly depicted as unmarried, divorced or childless—social positions that endow her with the means and the 'freedom' to care for her mother. Conversely, in stories where the daughter is well-adjusted as a wife and mother, her caregiving relationship with her own mother is depicted as ending in grief.

My discussion of this fiction will undertake a critical engagement with the ethic of care—a theoretical approach first formulated in the course of Anglo-American feminist debates over ethics in the 1980s. It sought to rescue the supposed feminine inclination towards relationality from the realm of the natural and accord it the status of a legitimate ethical position from which to critique mainstream moral concepts such as rights and contracts. Central to the ethic of care are the concepts of relationality and interdependence. As Selma Sevenhuijsen elaborates, '[P]eople need each other in order to lead a good life and…they can only exist as individuals through and via caring relationships with others'.[13] Since the mother–child relationship is seen to be characterised by nurturing and dependence, rather than competition and autonomy, it is singled out by feminist ethicists as an ideal illustration of the care ethic.[14]

The maternal paradigm is especially relevant to the four stories discussed in this paper, where adult daughters caring for dying mothers consciously invokes mothers caring for young children. My discussion, however, will focus on problems associated with the care ethic and examine some of its assumptions, particularly its inability to account for the emotional complexity of adult caregiving relationships, which can make the invocation of relationality difficult; its focus on responsiveness to needs, such as those of helpless infants, which prevents adequate engagement with ideas of reciprocity; and, finally, its extraction of the caregiving relationship from the network of social and familial relationships in which it is embedded, instead of an attempt to understand it from within those contexts. Alongside my critique of the ethic of care, I will also examine the extent to which mainstream moral concepts, such as rights and contracts, may continue to be relevant to the dynamics of intergenerational relations in old age.

The Ethic of Care

The maternal approach to ethics, or what Sara Ruddick calls maternal practice,[15] was first theorised by feminist ethicists in the 1980s as a challenge to the social contract theory of

---

[11] *Ibid.*, p.20.
[12] See Ira Raja and Kay Souter (eds), *An Endless Winter's Night: Mother–Daughter Stories from India* (New Delhi: Women Unlimited, 2010).
[13] Selma Sevenhuijsen, 'The Place of Care: The Relevance of the Feminist Ethic of Care for Social Policy', in *Feminist Theory*, Vol.4, no.2 (2003), p.183.
[14] Tom Cockburn, 'Children and the Feminist Ethic of Care' in *Childhood*, Vol.12, no.1 (2005), p.77.
[15] Sara Ruddick, *Towards a Politics of Peace* (New York: Ballantine Books, 1990).

Hobbes, Locke, Rousseau and Rawls, which had shaped the understanding of human relationships in the West at least since the eighteenth century.[16] A contractarian approach employs the metaphor of contract to characterise broad political, social and moral relationships between people. The ideal subject of this approach is understood to be an autonomous individual who is focused on maximising his self-interest. Assumed to be part of an association of equals, all of whom can function independently, this individual is fortified with rights and reason and is actually or potentially in competition or conflict with others who are equally situated with respect to power.[17] But as the mother in Krishna Sobti's 'Listen, Girl', a text I discuss below, points out: '[I]n a family, the game is never amongst equals'.[18] More formally, the contractual approach was first challenged in 1982 by Carol Gilligan who examined the language of care associated with women to argue that it constituted a legitimate moral voice. Life, as Virginia Held put it, was not just about maximising self-interest, it was also, as mothers knew, about caring for others,[19] not least those who are left out of the domain of rights because they cannot function independently, such as infants and the elderly.[20] Real care, according to feminist ethics, grows not from good intentions, but actual relationships between embodied persons, the 'one-caring' and the 'cared-for'.[21]

One relationship seen to be particularly conducive to the fostering of a relational self, which is defined as being endowed with mutually compatible needs for both recognition of self and understanding the other, is between mothers and daughters. Scholars and clinicians, especially those affiliated with the Stone Center for Developmental Services and Studies at Wellesley College in the 1980s, argued that the traditional gender system led men to seek autonomy and power over others, preventing adult male–female relationships from achieving the goal of mutuality. The mother–daughter relationship, on the other hand, with its reciprocity contributing not only to the satisfaction of individual needs, but also the affirmation of the 'larger relational unit', offered a better model for the growth of the healthy, interdependent self.[22]

While the projection of ideal adult mutuality onto the mother–daughter relationship subsequently came in for much criticism,[23] mothering itself has continued to provide the basis for ethical theory, even if it is now rarely associated with the literal experience of giving birth and much more with the 'mothering role' that can theoretically be assumed in equal measure by both men and women. As feminist philosopher Sara Ruddick argues, caring for children, because they are dependent and fragile, encourages a certain type of thinking, feeling and

---

[16] 'Feminist Ethics', Part 3, *Stanford Encyclopedia of Philosophy* (1996) [http://plato.stanford.edu/entries/feminism-ethics/, accessed 18 Mar. 2007]; and L. Huey-li, 'Environmental Education: Rethinking Intergenerational Relationship', in *Philosophy of Education* (1994) [http://www.ed.uiuc.edu/eps/PES-Yearbook/94_docs/LI.HTM, accessed 8 April 2007].

[17] Eva Feder Kittay, 'A Feminist Public Ethic of Care Meets the New Communitarian Family Policy', in *Ethics*, Vol.111, no.3 (2001), p.528; Samantha Brennan, 'Recent Work in Feminist Ethics', in *Ethics*, Vol.109, no.7 (1999), p.866; Huey-li, 'Environmental Education'; and C. Whitbeck, 'A Different Reality: Feminist Ontology', in Carol Gould (ed.), *Beyond Domination* (Totowa, NJ: Rowman & Allanheld, 1983), p.79.

[18] Krishna Sobti, 'Ai Ladki' ('Listen, Girl'), trans. from Hindi by Shivanath, in *The Little Magazine* (May 2000), p.76.

[19] See 'Feminist Ethics', *Stanford Encyclopedia of Philosophy*.

[20] Brennan, 'Recent Work in Feminist Ethics', p.866.

[21] J. Wall, T. Needham, D.S. Browning and S. James, 'The Ethics of Relationality: The Moral Views of Therapists Engaged in Marital and Family Therapy', in *Family Relations*, Vol.48, no.2 (1999), p.139.

[22] Virginia Held, 'Feminist Transformations of Moral Theory', in *Philosophy and Phenomenological Research*, Vol.L, Suppl. (1990), p.342.

[23] See Marcia Westkott, 'Female Relationality and the Idealized Self', in *The American Journal of Psychoanalysis*, Vol.49, no.3 (1989), pp.239–50.

reflecting that may be labelled 'maternal thinking'. Attentive love, which refers to the mother's intellectual capacity to know and care about a child, is extended beyond maternal practice in the work of Katherine Allen and Alexis Walker to include other forms of caring labour such as adult caregiving, teaching and nursing.[24] In particular, Allen and Walker explore the similarities between caring for frail elderly mothers and the work that mothers do in meeting the demands of their dependent children. The focus of moral obligation in such relationships, it is argued, is not the rights of the dependent person, but the relationship that exists between the one in need and the one who is best placed to meet that need.[25]

Most recent developments in feminist ethics have renounced the scepticism about the capacity of mainstream moral concepts, such as rights and contracts, to generate a serious critique of women's oppression. Increasingly, the tendency is to revise moral concepts, rather than to reject them outright.[26] My paper continues this line of thought to argue that neither the social contract theory with its basis in the notion of a self-interested individual, nor the ethic of care with its emphasis on an 'other-focused relationality', provides an adequate model for capturing the intricate relationship between ageing mothers and adult daughters. Instead of seeing contractarianism and relationality in terms of an overriding opposition, this article points to the need for thinking about them in relation to each other.

Resisting Relationality

Githa Hariharan's 'The Art of Dying' is a grim story about a middle-aged woman who has temporarily left her husband, adult children and a job to come and tend to her mother, who is dying of causes related to her deep mourning for her dead son.[27] Like a good mother, the daughter preserves her mother's life through her caregiving: '[My mother] lets herself be cleaned, bathed, and dressed. She lies there, neither resisting nor actively cooperative, while I sponge her, pat her dry, and turn her over' (p.190). There is an apparent calmness to their routine: 'My mother shuts her eyes as I massage her scalp lightly with a thick, green oil. We are a quiet family. Doctor, nurse, mother: creatures of habit, dedicated to the housekeeping of the body' (p.192). But all is not well. The daughter harbours a great deal of hostility towards the mother.

Two years after the death of her doctor brother, with whom she had competed for the mother's love, the daughter trains to be a counsellor. She wants her mother 'to see that I too am a healer of sorts' (p.195). Her subsequent self-confessed flirtation with death, which is enacted in the course of her professional counselling of 'suicidal cases', is at once an expression of a desire to follow in her dead brother's footsteps and a dramatisation of her guilt at having harboured an inchoate desire to displace him in her mother's affections in the first place. The daughter thus speaks from a deeply contradictory position: the unwitting bearer of her mother's grief for having outlived her brother, she is at the same time her self-appointed carer.

While the ethic of care exhorts us to look at the relationship between caregiver and care receiver in terms that are individualised rather than impersonal, the mother–daughter

---

[24] K.R. Allen and A.J. Walker, 'Attentive Love: A Feminist Perspective on the Caregiving of Adult Daughters', in *Family Relations*, Vol.41, no.3 (1992), p.284.
[25] 'Feminist Ethics', *Stanford Encyclopedia of Philosophy*.
[26] Brennan, 'Recent Work in Feminist Ethics', pp.861, 865. Also see Cockburn, 'Children and the Feminist Ethic of Care', pp.84–5.
[27] Githa Hariharan, 'The Art of Dying', in Ira Raja and Kay Souter (eds), *An Endless Winter's Night: An Anthology of Mother–Daughter Stories* (New Delhi: Women Unlimited, 2010), pp.186–202.

relationship in this story is so intensely mediated by the missing son that the personal approach cannot offer the daughter any straightforward way of proceeding with the mother. It is so deeply mired in emotional confusion that the only way in which the daughter can seem to go on caring for her mother is by denying the personal—a project in which her training as counsellor comes in especially handy: 'I say nothing. I deftly slip on a mask of listening, all smooth, unknotted, withholding judgement' (p.194). The daughter's desire to find ways of approaching the mother that are not completely grounded in their past history is also evident in a series of other roles she chooses for herself: a mere listening post, a surgeon, a good Samaritan, a doctor, a healer—all detached modes that draw more on the logic of contractarianism than the ethic of relationality. Unfortunately, by her own admission, she is not always successful in her efforts: 'But I cannot summon up, at least not yet, my disinterested counsellor's voice in this well-dusted room crowded with familiar ghosts' (p.192).

To the extent that her desire to get away from her mother is rooted in their difficult and shared past, the daughter is caught in a situation from which she can never escape. At the same time, the only way in which she can get her mother to acknowledge her is by stepping into her brother's shoes, by mimicking not just his life and career as a professional caregiver, but even his death. The point of this especially bleak story, of course, is precisely that this daughter will never be able to step into her brother's shoes as her mother's 'real' or paradigmatic child.

The story takes an even more disturbing turn towards the end, when the daughter obliquely entertains the idea of ending her mother's life, which she then attributes to the mother herself: 'It would take only a minute or two to give her [the mother] what her heart yearns for' (p.202). According to Martha Minow, the main challenge of the relational approach is the sustained commitment to mutual interaction between individuals. But as 'The Art of Dying' shows, this interaction may not be possible where relationality between individuals is articulated only through great effort. In the absence of such interaction, Minow warns, 'acts of care may unwittingly express the self-interests or biases of the actor who claims to know what is good for the recipient'.[28] While the story ends on an inconclusive note, where the reader is not quite sure if the daughter went any further with her idea, it nonetheless manages to drive home the point about the potential abuse of the relationality approach.

Limits of Maternalism

Shashi Deshpande's 'Lucid Moments' is the story of a childless woman who has temporarily left her job and husband to tend to her dying mother.[29] In a self-conscious invocation of the maternal paradigm, the daughter sponges her bedridden mother's face, neck and arms, completing the routine by applying a decorative *bindi* to her forehead. '"There", she says, "you are all ready now"', her words and gestures unconsciously recalling those of her sister, Shilpa, just after she has finished giving her little daughter a bath. 'And like Tiny after her bath, my mother sleeps' (p.177). The parallel is developed right through the story: 'I am now as finely tuned to her suffering as a mother to her child's' (p.183). The mother's suffering in death is likewise viewed as a rite of passage comparable to birth: 'I feel I am sharing it with her, the pain of dying, as we had once, perhaps, suffered together the pangs of my birth'. And again: 'Tears collect in pools in the two wells of her eyes, brim over and run swiftly into her

---

[28] Quoted in Brennan, 'Recent Work in Feminist Ethics', p.871.
[29] Shashi Deshpande, 'Lucid Moments', in Ira Raja and Kay Souter (eds), *An Endless Winter's Night: An Anthology of Mother–Daughter Stories* (New Delhi: Women Unlimited, 2010), pp.175–85.

hair. We don't wipe them; we have as little right to blot them as we have to stifle the cry of the newborn' (p.183).

Their deathbed intimacy notwithstanding, the daughter's relationship with her mother has been a difficult one. Women's mothering, for her, is an activity structured by patriarchal social relations, connecting the figure of the mother with continued subservience to men and patriarchy. This connection is captured in a childhood memory of her mother wiping her feet endlessly on a rag kept at the threshold, while her grandmother raged at her mother. As a young girl at the time, the daughter had asked her mother why she was being reprimanded and the mother had replied: 'What's the use?', becoming in the eyes of her little daughter a woman who was resigned to her powerlessness in the face of existing social hierarchies of age and gender within the family. To the daughter, her mother had seemed to fit perfectly the role of a suffering woman who, like young children, was unable to speak for herself.

As the story progresses though, the sickbed becomes a site for the daughter to gain a new perspective on her mother, revealing her subjectivity to be less unified than the daughter had first assumed. The first big challenge to the daughter's reading of her mother comes while she is watching her mother's struggle to remember the name of her own mother—a reference to the pre-wedding rite, in which priests call out the names of a couple's male ancestors—which underscores the mother's desire to know, as against the patriarchal injunction to erase, a woman's maternal legacy. As the older woman labours unsuccessfully to recall her mother's name, she wants to ensure this legacy of loss is not repeated for the following generation:

'You know my name?' she asks [her daughter] with an odd anxiety.
'Oh yes.'
There seems to be enough breath in her wasted body for a small sigh. Is it a sigh of relief? (p.176).

The story ends with the narrator introducing her little niece to her deceased mother's photograph on the wall: '"She is your grandmother", I tell her. "Her name was Sumati"' (p.185).

In asking her daughter whether she knew her name, the dying mother had called for the recognition of a self that lay outside the family plot. In finally pronouncing the mother's name in the presence of her young niece, the narrator delivers on that expectation, re-imagining new relationships among women which alter the mother–daughter plot as she has known it for most of her life.[30]

The sombre mood of the above scene starts to shift as it unfolds. Thus the young girl responds to the pronouncement of her grandmother's name by uttering her own:

'And I', Tiny points a little finger towards herself, 'I am Karuna'.
'And I', I imitate Tiny's gesture, 'am Sujata'.
'And I', Shilpa joins in the game, 'am Shilpa'.
We laugh in unison, Tiny's delighted chuckles going on longer than ours. The darkness and despair lift. I can imagine my mother's pleasure in our laughter (p.185).

Drawing on Kathleen Woodward's work, we may view this picture of familial intimacy as an implicit critique of the two generational triangle of desire propagated by Freud, in which power was firmly vested in the parents. The introduction of the little girl in the midst of a

---

[30] Ruth E. Ray, 'The Uninvited Guest: Mother–Daughter Conflict in Feminist Gerontology', in *Journal of Ageing Studies*, Vol.17, no.1 (2004), p.126.

complex adult mother and daughter dynamic in the above scene links the three generations in a way that is suggestive of a straight line more than a triangle, pointing towards 'a heritage based not on struggle for domination but on pleasurable interaction (play) and care'.[31]

The deathbed exchange with the mother then gives the narrator a new perspective on the older woman. She now draws strength from her mother's new spirit, seeing her for the first time as a woman who has an identity outside her role as mother. However unlike her younger sister, Shilpa, who loves her mother dearly, but who sees her (merely) as a sick person whose needs must be met for her own good (i.e. she treats her mother as one of her children and, therefore, does not think that the questions her mother raised on her deathbed need to be answered after she is gone), the narrator incorporates her mother's struggle into her own search for identity: 'Can I prove to my mother—my mother? no, myself—that even if they never chant a litany of their names in a wedding, these women are real?' (p.185).

Towards the end of the story, the narrator, who, as a young girl, had rejected her mother for her father—that wisest and most dignified of men, to be admitted to whose companionship had been the greatest honour (p.178)—returns to her mother, to discover that she can after all invest the mother with part of her own identity. Her desire for freedom, agency, the spirit of questioning and contact with the outside world, for which the daughter had sought the companionship of the father, are now revealed as a part of the mother's identity.[32] In its non-material conceptualisation of reciprocity, the story allows us to perceive even the dependent mother as an active intergenerational partner in relation to her caregiving daughter, rather than simply a recipient of care or a mere footnote to the daughter's process of individuation.[33] The story thus explores the limitations of the care ethic, with its focus on one party meeting the needs of the other, which hinders an understanding of the dynamic nature of the intergenerational exchanges being explored in this story.[34]

The Burden of Care

In both the stories discussed above, the caregiving daughter expresses, if only obliquely and in passing, a wish to end the mother's fragile hold on life. In the following passage from 'The Art of Dying', the daughter surmises that since it is only the memories of her dead son that keep the mother alive, the daughter has a case for hastening her end:

> She is, whatever the doctor says, a terminal patient. Her fragile body is chained to the life-support machine of her memory.... To come back, nurse her again, relieve her burden, feel the same remorse: who says she should be kept breathing at any cost?
> It would be simpler to help her forward. It would take only a minute or two to give her what her heart yearns for.
> ...
> He awaits her, his chest as broad, his face as unlined as in his framed photograph, the eternal lover (p.202).

---

[31] Kathleen Woodward, 'Inventing Generational Models: Psychoanalysis, Feminism, Literature', in Kathleen Woodward (ed.) *Figuring Age: Women, Bodies, Generations* (Bloomington, IN: Indiana University Press, 1999), p.151.

[32] See Suzanne Juhasz, 'Towards Recognition: Writing and the Daughter–Mother Relationship', in *American Imago*, Vol.57, no.2 (2000), p.168.

[33] See A.J. Walker, C. Pratt and N.C. Oppy, 'Perceived Reciprocity in Family Caregiving', in *Family Relations*, Vol.41, no.1 (1992), p.82.

[34] Cockburn, 'Children and the Feminist Ethic of Care', p.73.

The daughter in 'Lucid Moments' likewise expresses a wish to kill the mother, if only to put her out of pain:

> In the afternoon it begins again. I hear the moans before the nurse does.... My body goes cold, my insides begin twisting into coils. I can't go through it again, I won't, I'll kill her myself... (p.183).

These fleeting references to the possibility of matricide receive much fuller treatment in the third story I discuss in this paper. Vaidehi's 'The Confession' is an account of two women's chance encounter in a train compartment.[35] We first meet Narmada while she is on her way to see her young children, whom she has sent to live with her own mother in a distant town where they have access to a better school. Narmada is just settling in for the long journey when she notices the presence of another woman in her compartment. The stranger is returning from a three monthly visit to her bedridden mother in the village, where she had arranged for a hired nurse to take care of the older woman. The story ends with the stranger's shocking admission to Narmada that she has killed her mother. For three years, she claims, she has struggled to bear the strain of travelling back and forth between her own family home and the village where the old woman lived on a piece of land that belonged to her son-in-law, who reportedly could not stand her (p.253). 'Caught between two worlds and unable to sever her links from one or the other', she has finally killed her mother:

> This time when I went to the village, I finished off my mother...killed her...are you listening...I murdered her myself. When she was asleep, I smothered her...I consigned her to the fire...all that's finished now...I don't ever have to go back to that place. There's no one there... (p.255).

The daughter's choices in this story are presented with brutal clarity: 'Tell me.... Whom should I have killed if not her? Myself? Or my husband...or whom?' (p.255). Even as Narmada is absorbing the full horror of the confession, the stranger lurches out of the compartment to get off the train at a station long before the one she had said she was going to. Moments later, Narmada hears a sound outside her compartment and wonders if the woman has returned, only to be met with the sight of a young couple, proudly cradling an infant. Narmada lets out a small shriek as she holds on to the bars of the window to steady herself.

While the first two stories discussed above focused on mother and daughter to the exclusion of other characters, spectres of brothers, sons, fathers and grandfathers were, in fact, never far away. What the third story shows is how fathers, husbands and sons do not just hover on the margins of the mother–daughter plot; they can actively change its course. The stranger's experience of being her mother's carer in 'The Confession' is thus characterised by an inability to go on caring for her in the face of difficulties brought about by her conflicting responsibilities towards her own family. While research shows that even in mainstream Western cultures, daughters have difficulty taking care of their mother's relational and instrumental needs because of socio-cultural norms that privilege husbands and children,[36] the daughters' experience of the contested nature of care in India is often peculiar to its cultural

---

[35] Vaidehi, 'The Confession', trans. from Kannada by Vanamala Vishwanatha, in Ira Raja and Kay Souter (eds), *An Endless Winter's Night: An Anthology of Mother–Daughter Stories* (New Delhi: Women Unlimited, 2010), pp.250–5.
[36] Lori A. McGraw and Alexis J. Walker, 'Negotiating Care: Ties between Aging Mothers and Their Caregiving Daughters', in *The Journals of Gerontology*, Vol.59B, no.6 (2004), p.S325.

context on at least two counts. Firstly, the overriding opposition between a woman's role as wife and her role as sister/daughter (i.e. a patrilineal kinswoman)[37] adds to the daughter's problems of balancing the conflicting demands made on her time and resources. Secondly, this balancing act has to be performed on a day-to-day basis because caregiving in India is still 'entirely family based', rather than provided in an institutional setting.[38] Together, these two conditions have the potential for making the daughter's task of caregiving in Indian families a great deal more onerous compared to developed Western countries, where the prevalence of institutional care tends to be much greater and where caregiving daughters, while still wrestling with the intense demands of their roles, can nonetheless put some level of physical distance between the needs of their mothers on the one hand and their husband and children on the other.

But the stories discussed in this paper do more than simply assert that even when a daughter wants to care for her parent, in many parts of the patrilineal North the odds are stacked against her. What really amplifies the contested nature of care in these stories is how they oppose the woman's role as wife, not to her role as a patrilineal kinswoman, but to her role as her *mother's daughter*—the one dyadic relationship that finds no mention anywhere among the issues that have dominated cross-cultural research, especially on changes in family in India.[39]

'The Confession' also raises important questions about the ethic of care. If the care ethic expressed through a maternal paradigm prevents a conceptualisation of autonomy and reciprocity, it also, at the same time, assumes that the 'larger relational unit' constituted by mother and daughter is an autonomous unit that can be abstracted from its wider cultural context.[40] As Marcia Westkott notes, scholars at the Stone Center did describe a cultural context, but they limited discussion of its consequences to adult male–female relationships, wherein the goal of mutuality was understood to be rarely achieved, and identified the interaction that occurs in mother–daughter relationships as the best source of insight into the promotion of the healthy, relational self.[41] What these stories foreground are the ways in which the traditional gender system also mediates relationships between women.

And there is a further challenge, delineated most vividly in 'The Confession': the relational turn in ethics grew out of a reaction against rights-based morality on the argument that the people most in need of morality's protection are often left out of the domain of rights because they are in no position to claim them.[42] While it appears that the mother in Vaidehi's story is not in a position to claim her rights, it is not clear that the relationality approach has come to her rescue either. The matricidal daughter's enormous love for her mother, expressed primarily through the enormity of her guilt at having ended her life, urges her in a direction that is more self-serving than anything else. It is far from clear that her last attempt to meet her mother's needs in fact corresponded to the needs of the mother. By all accounts, the daughter's narrative appears to follow a process of selection that is organised as a function of her own needs and abilities, more than her mother's.[43] As Veronique Munoz-Darde notes:

---

[37] See Lynn Bennett, *Dangerous Wives and Sacred Sisters: Social and Symbolic Roles of High-Caste Women in Nepal* (New York: Columbia University Press, 1983); and Irawati Karve, *Kinship Organization in India* (Poona: Deccan College Monograph Series, 1953).
[38] Emmatty et al., 'The Experience of Burden in India', p.224.
[39] Patricia Uberoi, 'The Family in India: Beyond the Nuclear versus Joint Debate', in Veena Das (ed.) *The Oxford India Companion to Sociology and Social Anthropology* (Delhi: Oxford University Press, 2003), p.1088.
[40] Westkott, 'Female Relationality and the Idealized Self', pp.239–50.
[41] Held, 'Feminist Transformations', pp.341–2.
[42] Brennan, 'Recent Work in Feminist Ethics', p.866.
[43] Bernadette Bawin-Legros and Jean François Stassen, 'Intergenerational Solidarity: Between the Family and the State', in *Current Sociology*, Vol.50, no.2 (2002), pp.251–2.

'[J]ustifying moral action through special ties may be plausible in easy cases, but that relatedness provides little guidance in difficult moral dilemmas'.[44]

Reciprocity in a Lifelong Calculus

While the above three stories are told from the viewpoint of mothering daughters, the fourth speaks from the place of the mother who is being mothered. Krishna Sobti's 'Listen, Girl' is structured as a dialogue between an old woman immobilised by a fracture and her unmarried, successful artist daughter with whom she lives.[45] The story is set in an urban, liberal and upper-class Punjabi family, where the mother takes pride in not discriminating between her children on grounds of gender.

Accordingly, she seems happy to be looked after by her daughter, invoking the notion of a generational role reversal between mother and daughter (now that she is old), taken as a matter of parental right: 'Listen, Girl! In the beginning parents hold their children's hands and teach them how to walk. But, when parents grow old, they become the children of their children' (p.66). And yet, while the mother seems willing to submit herself to a position of considerable dependency, she makes it quite clear that she does not want the daughter to forget that it is her mother she is mothering, not an infant. If the maternal paradigm structures mother–child relationships in terms that read like an interaction between equals, this story underscores the difference between the needs of an ageing adult and the needs of an infant or a child, and shows how these cannot be conflated without distorting the care needs of both.[46] A child, for instance, may reasonably be expected to draw attention to discomfort in a way the mother in the story finds a violation of her dignity and self-respect:

'Ammu, you should have told us that you were in pain'.
'Don't be silly. Let the patient retain at least some self-respect. Did you expect me to groan to let you know?' (p.70).

Like the first three stories discussed in this paper, this story too invokes the ethic of care. However, unlike the previous stories, which focus on the limitations of the care ethic, 'Listen, Girl' gestures towards a new model for understanding intergenerational dynamics, a model that seems to combine features *both* of intimate relationality and 'contract'. Generational inversion (where an adult child takes on the role of 'mothering' the ageing parent), in Sobti's story, is only partially understood in terms of the model of relationality. The ageing mother and her adult daughter here share a complex relationship that draws upon, in addition to intimate relationality, a long-term familial and relational history expressing reciprocity.

The terms in which the intergenerational contract, with which I began this paper, is articulated in 'Listen, Girl' also addresses feminist criticism of the contractarian approach within the mainstream Western moral tradition. Feminist ethicists charge that since the contractarian approach assumes maximising self-interest is the primary human motivation, it fails to account for the moral dimension of personal relationships, which are characterised by

---

[44] Veronique Munoz-Darde, 'Rawls, Justice in the Family and Justice of the Family', in *The Philosophical Quarterly*, Vol.48, no.192 (1998), p.344.
[45] Sobti, 'Ai Ladki', pp.65–85.
[46] Westkott, 'Female Relationality and the Idealized Self', p.244.

a direct concern for others.[47] But as Samantha Brennan notes, this criticism fails to engage with the logic of contractarian evaluation. When the mother in 'Listen, Girl' says to the daughter 'I am glad you have looked after me in my last days. As your mother, I had to suckle you and as my daughter you had to drink my milk' (p.65), her point is not that the reason why parents look after children is so that the children look after them when the parents are old. The mother here is not *explaining her motives* for having suckled her daughter so much as *justifying* the reversal of roles in later life.[48]

Affection and reciprocity, which sustain caregiving in the context of this family, are clearly rooted in past relationships.[49] As with the contractarian framework, this model concedes the right of older parents to receive care from their adult children, but this is now understood not in terms of unilateral individualism so much as the sacrifices that parents make in raising their children. In an anthropological study of dependency anxiety in a North Indian community, Sylvia Vatuk notes that parent–child reciprocity is perceived in terms of a life-span calculus. Typically, Indian elders take great pride in having children who can and do support them in comfort.[50] The mother in 'Listen, Girl', a story set very much within the North Indian milieu, takes filial obligation on the part of her daughter so much for granted that at one point in the narrative, when she is feeling particularly satisfied with how well she is being looked after by her daughter, she suddenly turns on her with suspicion: 'I hope you are not trying to pay off all your debts in this life itself so that the cycle of giving and taking comes to an end' (p.68). The mother here is alluding to the idea that long-term bonds of reciprocal indebtedness extend throughout life and even after death. A similar belief is found in Sarah Lamb's study of Bengali family relations, where children are required to 'provide care for their elderly parents, reconstruct relations with parents as ancestors after death, and ritually nourish these ancestors as a means of repaying the tremendous debts owed for producing and caring for them'.[51] Intergenerational reciprocity in this conception continues even when an aged person can no longer make material returns to other family members for their support and care.[52]

Parents and children, in such accounts, are seen to participate equally in the practice of giving or receiving at different points of the life-cycle and the generational history. As both generations contribute to the establishment of harmonious relations between them, both also earn the right to expect support from each other in their time of need, a support that may be deferred, but not denied.[53] The fulfilling of obligations towards their parents on the part of adult children is one such example of deferred support, which is seen to mitigate their sense of

---

[47] See Virginia Held, 'Non-Contractual Society', in *Canadian Journal of Philosophy*, Vol.13, Suppl. (1987), pp.111–38; and Virginia Held, *Feminist Morality: Transforming Culture, Society, and Politics* (Chicago, IL: University of Chicago Press, 1993).
[48] Brennan, 'Recent Work in Feminist Ethics', p.875.
[49] Catherine Ward-Griffin, Abram Oudshoorn, Kristie Clark and Nancy Bol, 'Mother–Adult Daughter Relationships within Dementia Care: A Critical Analysis', in *Journal of Family Nursing*, Vol.13, no.1 (2007), pp.13–4.
[50] Vatuk, 'To Be a Burden on Others', p.68.
[51] Sarah Lamb, *White Saris and Sweet Mangoes: Aging, Gender and Body in North India* (Berkeley, CA: University of California Press, 2000), p.46.
[52] Vatuk, 'To Be a Burden on Others', pp.65–6.
[53] Bawin-Legros and Stassen, 'Intergenerational Solidarity', pp.257–8.

personal indebtedness,[54] thus allowing for the re-establishment of egalitarian sharing of intergenerational contributions to happen naturally and gradually over time.[55]

But relations within the family are not based on the repayment of debt alone. And to view intra-familial reciprocity as only based on the dynamics of exchanges, i.e. to consider the help that children give to their parents as a 'fair return of things' towards those who supported them in the past, prevents one from seeing that 'reciprocity also exists upstream, as a foundation of the norms'.[56] Indeed, parental duties cannot be defined in isolation from children's duties. That said, though, in practice the two groups of obligations function independently of one another.[57] The mother who looks after her young children thus does not have any guarantee that she will be looked after by them in her old age. It is the *'potential reversibility'* of the dependency situation between the generations which gives meaning to the ideas of equivalence.[58] Reciprocity, that is to say, is inscribed more in the norms than in the acts. As all of the four stories discussed above show, reciprocity only finds expression in social behaviour according to individual needs, resources or differing capacity to accept the norms. And yet, as Bawin-Legros and Stassen suggest, without the norm of reciprocity, it would not be possible to conceptualise any acts of intergenerational support.[59]

For social contract theorists, self-interest could be considered the key motivation for a rational individual to surrender to the rules of the social contract. But the familial contract of intergenerational reciprocity, as demonstrated in 'Listen, Girl', clearly does not work along those lines. Although, as Vatuk observes, the concept of long-term intergenerational obligation is communicated to children at an early age, in a very direct and explicit manner,[60] the intergenerational contract in this story is viewed in terms of a history of past relationships, where the focus is not on maximising self-interest, but on relations of reciprocity, thus situating contractarian logic within a long-term relational perspective.

The terms in which the intergenerational contract is articulated more generally in these stories, and the fissures or limitations in the ethical models examined in my discussion of them, may be seen to point towards an irreducible cultural specificity of the stories themselves. This, however, is not to imply that the lessons one is able to draw from these stories are exclusive to Indian culture as revealed here; mutated forms of the intergenerational contract, wherein the relationship between the generations is characterised as much in terms of the logic of contractarianism as of intimate relationality, may be found in many other cultures, even the 'mainstream' Western one.[61]

---

[54] C.H. Stein, V.A. Wemmerus, M. Ward, M.E. Gaines, A.L. Freeberd and T.C. Jewell, 'Because They're My Parents: An Intergenerational Study of Felt Obligation and Parental Caregiving', in *Journal of Marriage and the Family*, Vol.60, no.3 (1998), p.613.

[55] Bawin-Legros and Stassen, 'Intergenerational Solidarity', pp.257–8.

[56] *Ibid.*, p.258.

[57] *Ibid.*

[58] *Ibid.*, p.257.

[59] *Ibid.*

[60] Vatuk, 'To Be a Burden on Others', p.66.

[61] See L.J. Beckman, 'Effects of Social Interaction and Children's Relative Inputs on Older Women's Psychological Well-Being', in *Journal of Personality and Social Psychology*, Vol.41, no.6 (1981), pp.1075–86; Joanne M. Pohl, Carol Boyd and B.A. Given, 'Mother–Daughter Relationships during the First Year of Caregiving: A Qualitative Study', in *Journal of Women and Aging*, Vol.9, nos.1–2 (1997), pp.133–49; Stein *et al.*, 'Because They're My Parents'; McGraw and Walker, 'Negotiating Care', pp.S324–32; and Laura K.M. Donorfio and Kathy Kellett, 'Filial Responsibility and Transitions Involved: A Qualitative Exploration of Caregiving Daughters and Frail Mothers', in *Journal of Adult Development*, Vol.13, nos.3–4 (2006), pp.158–67.

Feminist Mothering? Some Reflections on Sexuality and Risk from Urban India

SHILPA PHADKE

Post-globalisation India has seen the rise of several moral panics around questions of sexuality and safety. In this paper, I ask how women who see themselves as feminist mothers in urban India reflect on a variety of concerns, including clothing, fashion, consumption, sexualisation, sexuality education and sexual choices. I reflect on the complex ways in which young women are exercising choices around sexuality and how feminist mothers reflect on these choices in relation to questions around risk and morality. This paper represents the beginning of an inquiry into the question: what does it mean to be a feminist mother raising daughters in twenty-first-century urban India?

My daughter and I were visiting a four-year-old girl and her mother. The little girl was slouching on the sofa, one leg dangling over the armrest, when the mother told her daughter to sit properly as that was no way for girls to sit. I found it very hard to hold my tongue and not suggest that it might not be a good idea to inculcate ideas of shame and modesty in a four-year-old. On another day in a busy park with a friend and her eight-year-old, who was playing on the jungle gym, I found myself itching to tell the little girl that, maybe, we should come back another time when she was wearing slacks or jeans, for there were many men, possible predators to my mind, hanging around the park.

I open with these personal anecdotes because they frame in one sense the complexity, indeed the impossibility, of the terrain of contradiction and dilemma I traverse in this essay. The last two decades have seen questions of morality assume centre stage, especially in relation to young women: their clothing, food and drink habits, transportation, romantic partners and sex lives have been the locus of celebration, anxiety, censure and even violent attack. If it is not easy to be a young woman in *these times*, it is equally difficult to be a mother navigating the maze of choices open to and constraints imposed upon them. In this essay, I reflect on how feminist mothers negotiate questions of sexuality and risk in raising their daughters.

Here, I am pointing to the particular kinds of sexual risks that confront us, rather than suggesting that the 'sexual risk' of our times is a cause for panic or that sexual risk itself is unique to the early twenty-first century. Along with moral panics, there is also a very real sense that we live in times that are full of risk for young girls and women—health risks that

---

I would like to thank Ira Raja whose suggestion that I think about families led me to conceive this ongoing project. I would also like to thank Abhay Sardesai, Amit S. Rai and the anonymous reviewers of my paper for their critical insight and intellectual generosity. Special thanks to the feminist mothers who shared their experiences and dilemmas, some of whom also commented on the essay.

come from anxieties about body shape or unsafe sex, risks of assault and risks of making choices that undermine self-esteem. When I refer to risk here, I refer to particular kinds of sexualised environments that make children or adolescents vulnerable to attack—contexts in which information is seen as dangerous, thus denying adolescents access to knowledge (for instance, education about sexuality), and contexts in which giving consent may be seen as immoral.[1]

I focus on mothering daughters, but this does not mean that feminist mothering is not valuable for sons, nor do I assume that mothering sons does not involve complex and nuanced negotiations around issues of sexuality and risk, requiring a similar analysis. This choice is partly logistical in order to keep the focus manageable and partly personal—as the feminist mother of a daughter, I am implicated in the concerns of this paper.

I intentionally use the term mothering in preference to the more neutral term, parenting. The term, feminist mothering, suggests the necessity of joint parenting and the involvement of men,[2] various ways of child rearing that are gender neutral, and the effort to bring up both boys and girls as human beings without socialising them into rigid gender roles. It might also indicate women claiming for themselves a life and identity outside of motherhood and domesticity.[3] I use the term mothering because I am interested in how feminist *women* locate the intersection of their gender politics with their ideas and everyday practices around parenting. When I say feminist mothering, I refer to a commitment to an egalitarian gender politics in raising a child as well as the effort to create an environment where a child is able to make choices and exercise agency, given various contexts.

Reading around the theme, I found little scholarly engagement with either feminist mothering or raising daughters in India. The conversations that do exist are in the form of blogs and newspaper articles. Therefore, I used a mix of methodology, auto-ethnography and in-depth interviews.[4] I have also included, where relevant, comments that were part of conversations with friends, colleagues or acquaintances, which often resulted from my talking about my research.[5]

I interviewed eleven women currently living in Mumbai, New Delhi and Hyderabad, though one of my interviewees had brought up her daughter in a smaller city. Four of these women are academics, three are journalists, two are activists, one is a writer of fiction for children and one is a facilitator of workshops for children.[6] All my respondents have at least one daughter (four of them have two each), ranging in age from two to twenty-four. All the women interviewed belong to the middle class and possess the cultural capital of being professionals and educated and identify themselves as feminists. This is not a representative sample of mothers or even of feminist mothers, but my concern in this paper is not so much

---

[1] Since the feminist mothers I interviewed all belong to the middle class, this dictates that the kinds of risks explored are most relevant to middle-class young women. I am aware that lower-class young women are subject to both similar as well as different kinds of sexual risks not addressed here.

[2] Nancy Chodorow, *The Reproduction of Mothering: Psychoanalysis and the Sociology of Gender* (Berkeley, CA: University of California Press, 1978).

[3] Adrienne Rich, *Of Woman Born: Motherhood as Experience and Institution* (New York: W.W. Norton, 1976).

[4] One of the reasons I chose to engage with online blogs is a 2001 essay by Amy Koerber, who researched an online community of feminist mothers and argued that this space facilitated a conversation not easily addressed in the offline world (p.230). See Amy Koerber, 'Postmodernism, Resistance, and Cyberspace: Making Rhetorical Spaces for Feminist Mothers on the Web', in *Women's Studies in Communication*, Vol.24, no.2 (2001), pp.218–40.

[5] This group of women belongs to a similar class and educational cohort as my interviewees.

[6] All names have been changed to ensure the anonymity of my interviewees. I am myself one of the persons cited as interviewed. For the purposes of this study, the women interviewed are called (in alphabetical order) Isha, Kamila, Kyla, Maya, Meera, Nina, Priya, Ramya, Rose, Sapna, and Vani.

with a representative sample as with engaging with some of the contradictions that feminist mothers confront over questions of sexuality and to draw on these to ask the question: what does it mean to be a feminist mother raising daughters in twenty-first-century urban India?

How do feminist mothers think through various dilemmas and competing desirable goals such as freedom and safety? Some of these dilemmas include the idea that the sexualisation of girls and adolescents objectifies them and puts them at greater risk of abuse, and the simultaneous hope that they will be able to exercise agency in sexual expression and exploration. Another dilemma occurs in addressing consumer culture—Barbie dolls, clothing, wandering around malls—all of which are fraught with complex sub-texts from a feminist perspective, but, at the same time, are activities daughters may 'choose' to do.

I focus on the contradictions that emerge from these dilemmas: feminist mothers wary of the dangers of 'malling', for instance, are labelled 'conservative' for restricting their daughters' access to malls, as are mothers who refuse to sexualise their little girls. Awareness of risks and dangers and the commitment to an egalitarian gender politics sometimes oddly places feminist mothers in the position of appearing illiberal.

Attempting to engage with the dilemmas and contradictions outlined above, I examine first the sexualisation of young children, particularly through clothing. In the second section, I reflect on the pressures to consume and be seen in the new spaces of consumption and the kinds of negotiations these may entail for mothers. In the next section, I ask how feminist mothers discuss sex with their daughters. The last section looks at the complex ways in which young women exercise choices around sexuality and how feminist mothers reflect on these choices in relation to questions of risk and morality. This paper does not have definitive answers; in fact, it raises more questions than it answers.

Two Little Triangles: Sexualised Clothing and Little Girls

In the swimming pool, I watch my two-year-old daughter and another slightly older child in 'conversation'. As the older child steps out of the pool, I notice immediately the two little triangles across her (approximately) four-year-old chest. The bikini top simulates the future presence of breasts and thus suggests the need to 'clothe' this site already imagined as sexual and, therefore, shameful.

I mention this to a woman I sometimes meet in the playground, adding that if the child were to simply wear the bikini bottom, it would be fine because a '*chaddi*' on a child is simply a *chaddi*.[7] She looks at me strangely: 'What's wrong with a bikini? You shouldn't be so conservative'. I find the framing of conservatism in this context interesting. The new regime of the public sexual persona now suggests that anything sexual, particularly in relation to clothing, is 'progressive' and by this definition any attempt to problematise this new regime of sexualised clothing for little girls is then viewed as conservative.[8]

Priya tells me that she is deeply uncomfortable with some of the clothing sold for little girls that appears to sexualise them either implicitly or explicitly. She expresses outrage that there are T-shirts for girls as young as eight and ten that bear the message 'Eye-Candy'. She contends: 'It's not like I'm a prude, but these are simply not suitable. I cannot imagine that mothers buy these for their children'.

A blog written by someone who calls herself Utbtkids echoes this view: 'Why does a seven-year-old child want to wear thong underwear with words "cute" or "eye-candy" printed

---

[7] *Chaddi* is a colloquial term in Hindi and Marathi for underwear, devoid of any sexual overtones.

[8] This framing of conservative versus progressive and the contestations around it is a recurrent theme to which I will return.

across it? Why does a nine-year-old need a push-up bra? What exactly is she trying to push up?'[9]

Ramya says: 'Pink is a pleasant colour. I understand if a mother wants to overdo pink. I may not do the same, but I understand. But the obnoxious wording on clothes, I just can't digest! Probably they fancy these wordings for themselves. And for an eight-year-old, they think it is cute or funny. I don't think they interpret the sexual innuendo behind these wordings'. She adds: 'Yesterday, I was asking other mothers in the playground why do children need this artificially created "pre-teen" segment? It is not like age-sensitive, context-sensitive clothes or products are being provided to them. It is just becoming a market to be exploited. I understand a babies section—they need different clothes for crawling. But why pre-teen? It is not like an "eight-year-old *pre-teen*" has drastically different needs compared to a "seven-year-old girl"'.

In her racily titled *Cinderella Ate My Daughter*, Peggy Orenstein suggests that Americans live in a prematurely-sexualised culture in which young girls are invited to dress largely in pink and identify with narrowly-defined images of princesses.[10] The debate on the sexualisation of children, particularly girls, is one that has been raging recently in the UK as well. In 2011, the UK government released a report on the commercialisation and sexualisation of childhood by Reg Bailey entitled 'Letting Children be Children', which suggested introducing new regulations, including covering up sexualised images on the covers of magazines and requiring retailers to offer age appropriate clothing for children.[11] Meg Barker and Robbie Duschinsky critique the Bailey report, arguing that it conflates the issue of sexism and a concern with teenage sexuality and 'deviant' sexuality, which subverts any feminist agenda.[12] They argue that such a perception problematises the sexuality of young people, especially young women, without necessarily expressing similar anxiety about gender stereotyping. This argument is echoed by a blogger who calls herself 'Ragged Robin' and engages some British websites: 'We are told that young girls shouldn't face these pressures at such a young age, yet the presenters offer no alternative. We are told that young girls are growing up too quickly, that they will *have* to worry about heels and make-up when they are older but this isn't challenged. They don't explore the assumption that all women will groom themselves, with make-up, fake tan, heels and hair extensions. It is simply taken for granted that this is what *all* women do and the problem is what we can do to stop it from taking over the lives of girls age six'.[13] Maddy Coy and Maria Garner articulate a need for an 'explicit gendering of the debate about sexualisation' and a questioning of approaches that focus on prematurity, and to make explicit the overlaps and differences between sexism, sexual harassment and sexualisation.[14] As Mary Jane Kehily points out, the question of premature

---

[9] Utbtkids.com, 'Sexualization of Young Children' (17 Nov. 2007) [http://utbtkids.com/2007/11/17/sexualization-of-young-children/, accessed 15 May 2012].

[10] Peggy Orenstein, *Cinderella Ate My Daughter* (New York: Harper, 2011).

[11] Reg Bailey, 'Letting Children be Children: Report of an Independent Review of the Commercialisation and Sexualisation of Childhood' (2011) [https://www.education.gov.uk/publications/eOrderingDownload/Bailey%20Review.pdf, accessed 8 Aug. 2012].

[12] Meg Barker and Robbie Duschinsky, 'Sexualisation's Four Faces: Sexualisation and Gender Stereotyping in the Bailey Review', in *Gender and Education*, Vol.24, no.3 (2012), pp.303–10.

[13] Ragged Robin, 'The Sexualisation of Children Debate' (1 June 2011) [http://theraggedrobin.wordpress.com/2011/06/01/the-sexualisation-of-children-debate/, accessed 15 May 2012].

[14] Maddy Coy and Maria Garner, 'Definitions, Discourses and Dilemmas: Policy and Academic Engagement with the Sexualisation of Popular Culture', in *Gender and Education*, Vol.24, no.3 (2012), p.259.

sexualisation must be framed within questions of the context of time, place and the lived experiences of girls.[15] Rosalind Gill reminds us that 'sexualisation does not operate outside processes of gendering, racialisation, and classing, and works within a visual economy that remains profoundly ageist, (dis)ablist and heteronormative'.[16]

Another recurrent theme in my interviews is the sheer desire on the part of girls to be someone else, to masquerade, or to simply fit in. How does one address this without casting this desire as illegitimate, but also without allowing it take over the entire conversation on how young girls grow? Meera articulates this when she says: 'As a child of about eleven–twelve, my daughter would drive me crazy in clothes shops—she would keep on trying all kinds of stuff—she just wanted to see herself in them'.

Vani talks about how her four-year-old daughter threw a tantrum in a FabIndia store, saying she didn't want 'any more of these clothes'. Vani adds: 'For parties, I used to dress my daughter in clothes I thought were appropriate, but she would often be the only girl there who was not in sequins and shiny clothes. She rarely said anything, but I could see as she grew older, she was aware of the difference. Sequins have become important to just simply fitting in'. She says: 'When one sees the mothers, one sometimes knows where it's coming from. There are mothers who are in full make-up and tight fitting clothes in the afternoon just to pick up their kids from school. I know some of these are stay-at-home mothers and I don't grudge them the right to dress up, but when they dress their children the same way, I feel really uncomfortable'. Vani shows me her daughter's wardrobe—the clothes she would like her to wear and I recognise in them my own taste for my daughter, a demonstration of Indian feminists' penchant for handlooms, cottons and block prints.[17] There are also clothes sent by Vani's cousin, who lives in the West—dark shiny dresses that she says her daughter loves. And then the ones her daughter has chosen herself, full of sequins. There is one that she bought for her daughter that Vani says finally earned *her taste* some approval—a synthetic blouse full of multi-coloured embroidery and sequins. Vani says she has evolved a lot as a parent and now feels that it is important for her child to be happy even if it is at the cost of hurting her own aesthetics.

What Vani is articulating here is something much more layered than simple aesthetics—she is suggesting that she is allowing her daughter to *choose* something that she herself experiences as being against her politics. Vani is making a complex decision of feminist mothering to prioritise her daughter's agency over her own understanding of what might be appropriate clothing for a child.

Sapna says: 'Of course, I do want to protect them and shield them from a world that looks at the body and appearance above all else. But we try to voice our fears and discuss them as frankly as possible. About over-sexualisation, the anxiety exists where my daughter is concerned, partly because her own body has developed very quickly and she loves dressing up to show off her body. If I suggest she change into something less revealing, she is capable of turning around to tell me I'm being a fraud feminist, so I do need to explain firmly that she needs to be more aware of what she wears for cycling or dance class! We

---

[15] Mary Jane Kehily, 'Contextualising the Sexualisation of Girls Debate: Innocence, Experience and Young Female Sexuality', in *Gender and Education*, Vol.24, no.3 (2012), p.257. Much of this scholarship is from the UK, but it resonates with some of what my interviews reveal—that the field is deeply complex.

[16] Rosalind Gill, 'Sexism Reloaded, or, It's Time to Get Angry Again!', in *Feminist Media Studies*, Vol.11, no.1 (2011), p.65.

[17] The preference for cottons and handlooms reflects a particular economic as well as cultural and political class since these products are far from inexpensive.

just try to get the kids to wear clothes that are appropriate to the occasion and the environment they will be in. So the mini-skirts and spaghetti straps are okay for a party, but not for a walk with the dog'.

Meera says: 'In regard to wearing shorts, I have two kinds of reservations—one is about how safe spaces are for these kinds of expressions of individuality. The other is a concern with social sensitivity. What happens when upper-middle-class girls start wearing *what they like* in contexts where others are made uncomfortable or as a demonstration of class privilege? When I objected, my daughter would say that this is an inversion of my feminist principles that women should be able to wear what they want. Also, it's more difficult for women to be taken seriously and clothing might add to this. Though, of course, women should be taken seriously no matter what we wear'.

Kyla argues: 'It's not really about what age it's okay for girls to wear some kind of sexualised clothing. For me, it's about understanding the politics of it—the politics of halter necks, for instance—if she understands how women are looked at in a particular way—as sluttish, for example—sees the gender politics and still chooses to do it, as her choice, then it's okay. I don't want her to fall into the trap of trying to become what society thinks she should wear. And in the same vein, I would be also upset if she decided to cover herself up completely in a burkha or something'.

Sapna's, Meera's and Kyla's comments point to yet another contradiction. On the one hand, feminism supports precisely women's right to wear what they want, but, on the other hand, as mothers, women are motivated by the need to keep their daughters safe from the pressures of over-sexualisation. But their very protectiveness may be experienced by their daughters as exactly the kind of restrictions against which they, as feminists, have been arguing. And often, as the articulate young women they have been raised to be, daughters are perfectly capable of turning around as Sapna's daughter did and accusing their mothers of being 'fraud feminists'. Here, Kyla makes the point that *choosing* to be sexualised is alright if one does it within an understanding of gender politics—it must then include not just agency, but also 'knowledge'.[18]

Returning to the suggestion made by Coy and Garner, Kehily, and Gill, that we need to be careful of the ways in which we use the term 'sexualisation' in feminist discourse, I see a range of different voices in the concerns voiced with regard to 'sexualisation', from those concerned about the dangers to those articulating a greater ambivalence in relation to it.

Meera's comment brings into sharp relief the notion that we must reflect on the class contexts within which our daughters 'choose' to wear various kinds of clothes. Similarly, it is also important for us to confront the very privileged contexts within which our own aesthetic sensibilities have been shaped. These often demonstrate our cultural capital, which is reflected

---

[18] Angela McRobbie suggests that young women are located as individual agents and as subjects of consumption. She argues that a certain level of sexual freedom, which is allowed in the discourse of new femininities, must be read as 'new technologies of the self' rather than celebratory expressions of female subjectivity. Responding to both MacRobbie as well as the ongoing debates that draw on the work on Michel Foucault on the creation of disciplined bodies and the idea of power as constitutive, one needs to consider how and where this particular kind of sexualisation fits into the larger picture of globalised consumer citizenship in Indian cities, where, increasingly, wearing particular kinds of clothing has come to represent a politics of modernity and belonging in a context where those who cannot buy (the have-nots) are being not just marginalised, but also vilified and seen as responsible for their poverty because they are unable to be part of the new economies of desire. There are several other concerns that came up in my interviews which I do not have the space to explore here—concerns about weight issues and skin colour are only two of them. See Angela McRobbie, *The Aftermath of Feminism: Gender, Culture and Social Change* (London: Sage, 2009).

in our responses of both discomfort and disdain (to sequins, for instance), based on our assumption of our own superior understanding.

What anxieties are we articulating when we are uncomfortable with children who look 'prematurely' sexual? How do we articulate the nuances between sexualisation and gender stereotyping? How do we understand a feminist position on clothing? What are the class affiliations implicit in our discussion of appropriate clothing? Finally, as feminist mothers, what is our responsibility in terms of contributing to this debate in the spirit of dialogue, rather than being alarmed and pessimistic?

Negotiating Spaces: The Question (Often) of Consumption

My daughters kept pointing out to me that their friends went to the mall on their own all the time. One of the pastimes of these trips was to enter expensive boutiques and try on clothes that they had no intention of buying. While this is not a problem in itself, when the girls doing it are as young as thirteen, I think of all the possible things that could go wrong (Kamila).

Here, I want to return to an argument begun in the previous section—on how ideas of 'conservative' and 'progressive' mothering are increasingly perceived in a mainstream upper-middle-class discourse. Kamila points out that the way girls dress at malls makes her particularly uncomfortable—the kind of clothing and also the assumption by other mothers that this is a safe space. She feels her concerns about such spaces, and her articulation of them, have made her appear a more conservative mother. She says: 'Other parents/mothers who are more permissive might come across as more liberal because they let their daughter loaf in the malls, but because one is more aware of the dangers, one comes across as strict and monitoring'. She adds: 'On the other hand, these parents are in complete denial about their daughter's sexuality and won't even allow their daughters to talk about boyfriends, whereas in our home, they are welcome'. Priya contends that 'because we are somehow more clued in and aware of the dangers, we come across as "paranoid", "over-protective" and maybe "inadequately modern", for modern then is being *laissez faire*, isn't it?'

Kamila and Priya are indicating a vision of consumer-led progressiveness and modernity. Both women seem to suggest that 'other mothers', who presumably are not feminist, are inadequately aware of the risks of permitting their daughters to hang out in malls, for instance. Further, Kamila suggests another notion of what constitutes progressiveness, in this case an acceptance of one's daughters as sexual beings. This 'other modernity' then is viewed as being skin deep. Both Kamila and Priya implicitly reject the vision of themselves as 'conservative', though Priya's comment appears to acknowledge that there is a huge chasm between the more mainstream notions of mothering and those of feminist mothers. Is the curtailment of our daughters' choices, even in their best interests, or at least what we perceive to be their best interests, an anti-feminist act? The language of 'best interests' is often used by those whose politics we may consider regressive. Can we divide restrictions into 'progressive' and 'regressive'? Do our feminist politics make our boundaries more acceptable than those of people who are not feminist?

As feminists, many of the mothers have an ambivalent relationship with the joys of consumption itself. On the one hand, some (though not all) could see the often textured pleasures it offered, but, at the same time, they felt acutely that consumption, especially as displayed in malls, might alter the ways in which their daughters engaged with the world with problematic consequences. Kyla puts it thus: 'I see malls in relation to the idea that you can buy anything...without understanding the value that goes into it. The mall gives you a warm fuzzy feeling of being anything, buying anything and imagining that branded things have a value'.

Vani recounts how she would allow her daughter to play with a Barbie doll in a shop, but not buy her one until, one day, her daughter threw another huge tantrum in a shop. She then asked one of her friends to buy a Barbie doll for her daughter as she did not want to be seen endorsing the Barbie phenomenon. Meera frames the concerns broadly, pointing out: 'It's not just about feminist mothering, but also about how the whole notion of childhood is undergoing a change—the idea of children as consumers and the complexity of talking about an autonomous agential childhood'. The conversation on consumption and agency is also clearly an expression of class experience, which mediates the conditions for mothering.

Meera put her finger squarely on the dilemma posed by consumption and new consumer spaces such as malls: the idea of childhood agency is being increasingly invested in the power to consume, much like the kind of citizen-consumer agency being offered to middle-class women. Consumption then suggests the free individual agent (making and expressing oneself through buying and displaying) and, certainly, for many women, the act of buying has come to represent a form of agency. For feminist mothers, the dilemma lies in their own discomfort both with this limited and limiting notion of agency as well as with the ways in which it sexualises and objectifies their daughters, making them more vulnerable to a variety of risks.

How do feminist mothers engage with the dubious pleasures of Barbie dolls without dismissing them, but without also imagining that they mean nothing, even as we know that children use the dolls in a variety of often creative and unorthodox ways? How does one think of the space of the mall itself in cities where young women in particular have little opportunity to hang out in public spaces and malls offer a privatised space to stroll? At the same time, how does one reflect on the fact that the mall is a private space, not a public space, and comes with its own complex ideologies? How do feminist mothers respond to their daughters' desires in ways that point out their limitations without suggesting that they are illegitimate or even frivolous? Also, how do we think through the post-globalisation notion of what is 'progressive', which, within consumer capitalism, has increasingly come to stand in for 'modernity'? Are our feminist ideas 'modern', or at least 'progressive', simply because they are feminist? How has feminism engaged with the idea of consumption and what do these reflections offer us as feminist mothers? As one works through the complex layers of pleasure, risk, ideologies, choices and ideas about agency reflected through the prism of feminist mothering, the questions only multiply.

'There's Something You Should Know': Talking about Sex

I was in the ninth standard when my mother tried to have the sex education conversation with me, and I was...like...eeugh, please don't...I already know all this and I don't want to discuss it with you.... And even if I don't know it, I can't ask you.... (Conversation with a twenty-year-old).

The sex education conversation is often fraught with tension, as mothers are awkward and daughters are not necessarily keen. The dissemination of information about sex and sexuality is a contentious one. The Indian Ministry of Human Resource Development collaborated with the National AIDS Control Organization (NACO) to develop the Adolescence Education Programme (AEP) focusing on life skills education, including comprehensive sexuality education (CSE). The AEP began in 2005, but was suspended in several states in 2007 because objections were raised by teachers, parents and policy-makers, especially with regard to the need for CSE in India.[19]

All of the women I speak to say they have made or plan to make efforts with sex education.[20] Sapna says they do not 'do' sex education in a formal way, but always try to answer questions: 'From a fairly early age...there was always an atmosphere where they could ask questions and would get answers as close to the truth as their young minds could understand—we always tried to make explanations simple and if we felt they were not at the right age to understand some part of it, we would tell them. Of course, if kids feel we are not telling them everything, they can be very persistent. So we have had situations when the kids would say, "Okay, we know about the egg and the sperm, but how do they meet?" So then we'd say: "It is an act of love. So when mama and papa make love..." and they'd go: "Eeugh...like when you kiss?" Basically, we'd get to this point and the conversation would end. Once they grew up after about ten–twelve years, then, we could talk about the actual act of sex'.

Maya says: 'I think that at home, we had a natural kind of environment where we could talk openly. Also, as parents, we're easy about our own relationship, our bodies and could discuss issues of love, sex and attraction in front of the children, and with them. More specifically, we saw films together, asked them to read articles in newspapers and magazines that pertained to the subject of child/youth sexuality, pleasure and abuse and then discussed these pieces and their meaning. We were not fearful of the child getting to know things without our knowing'.

Kyla says she has begun to talk about 'body changes, periods. My daughter wanted to buy a book for young girls—so I bought it'. Nina articulates something similar when she says that her daughter 'often comes to me with questions because she feels that I *up* her knowledge'. A woman I meet at a seminar talks wryly of the dangers of having too much information. As a researcher on sexuality, she has several books on sex and sexuality lying around. As her daughter grows up she is picking up these books, and it's becoming something of a problem for the mother.

The question of how much information and when is a tricky one. Sapna recounts a story that suggests that the concerns of a feminist parent may be diametrically opposite those who are not feminist. She says: 'My daughter shared some information she had got from me pretty openly with her friends and found, to her shock, that she was being labelled as "corrupt"—not just by the girls, but, apparently, by their mothers! A couple of years ago, the Hollywood film, *Juno*, was released and she watched it with me and her older cousin. Since the film deals with

---

[19] In 2009, in response to the Ministry of Human Resource Development's reported decision to provide sex education to students from class six in CBSE-affiliated schools, a Rajya Sabha committee wrote a report seeking a national debate on the introduction of sex education. The report stated: 'Message should appropriately be given to school children that there should be no sex before marriage which is immoral, unethical and unhealthy'. They suggested no sex education be given, but were willing to include appropriate chapters in the biology syllabus, but not before the plus two (classes eleven and twelve) stage. Further, chapters such as 'Physical and Mental Development in Adolescents' and 'HIV/AIDS and Other Sexually Transmitted Diseases' were to be removed from the existing curriculum and included in biology books at the plus two stage. As of November 2010, the AEP remains suspended in five states—Uttar Pradesh, Chhattisgarh, Madhya Pradesh, Maharashtra and Karnataka. Rajasthan, Gujarat and Kerala suspended the programme in 2007, but have recently started their own versions of AEP. See website of the AEP, National Campaign for Comprehensive Sexuality Education [http://knowyourbodyknowyourrights.com/fundamentals/adoloscence-education-program/, accessed 15 July 2012].

[20] A concern that came up in relation to sex education was sexual abuse, where many women talked of the dilemmas of first discussing sexuality in the language of danger. This is a theme I have been unable to engage with fully in this paper and I hope to be able to do so elsewhere.

teen pregnancy and abortion, I explained exactly what abortion was. When she relayed this knowledge to her friends, she was labelled "corrupt". Of course, when she came back home and told me this, I said to her, "Knowledge never corrupts. It is the misuse of knowledge that can corrupt...so don't worry about what your friends say". She was hurt, yes, but also felt her friends were stupid and ignorant. Now, when her friends want to know about something and feel they can't ask their parents, they ask her and even tell her to ask her mom!'

Priya articulates a sense of ambiguity when she says: 'I hesitate to teach my toddler words like vagina because I worry about what the playgroup will think if she uses them. I don't want her to be singled out. And then I wonder if by waiting for a little longer to teach her the correct names, I'm making a mistake. It's a tough call and sometimes you just have to go with your gut [instinct]'.

The politics of knowledge itself makes for a large part of the internal negotiations in which feminist mothers appear to engage. Knowledge about sex is coded with all manner of concerns about age appropriateness, context sensitivity, individual children, simple answers or open-ended ones. Here again, the women second-guess themselves, as Priya's comment suggests, and often wonder if they should be making a different choice. I would argue this lack of certainty is what gives their negotiations a more complex feminist edge, for they are far from convinced that they have all the answers.

Meera talks of the need for respecting her daughter's privacy: 'We talked about sex in the abstract, but never in the personal. For me, it was important to respect her sense of privacy and personhood. As a young woman, I wouldn't have wanted to discuss my own life and so I didn't ask my daughter either. We would talk about men—I would talk of such and such a man as hot or desirable, opening the window to seeing sex as something pleasurable and fun'. She says even when it came to a crucial issue, 'me being me and her being her, I could not talk face to face with her about contraception. I wrote her an email. In retrospect, we both laugh about it'.

Maya says she believes her children have the confidence that they can come to her when they need her, but 'otherwise, they are individuals and must have their space. I do worry whether they will come to me when they need me or [whether] my keeping [a] distance on a day-to-day basis makes them feel distant as a whole'.

One of the fundamental dilemmas of feminist mothering then is the question of how to expand one's child's boundaries even as one draws other kinds of boundaries—boundaries that will keep them from harm. What is the kind of information that one can share at various stages? What are the inevitable anxieties that this balancing act brings with it? All the women I speak to struggle with the question of how much to tell, when to tell and how best to tell. What does it mean to talk about sex as a feminist mother? How do our words transform the content of what we are talking about? As feminists, how do we convey information and also create the basis for our children to understand that both respect and fun are integral to sex and sexuality? What are the choices our daughters are going to be making and how can we facilitate them?

'I Already Know All This': Daughters Making Choices on Their Own

I struggle very hard not to call my daughter a 'good' girl. I never want her to think she has to be a good girl to get my approval. I know how loaded the term can be. I try to use substitutes: 'clever girl', 'creative girl', 'that was a nice thing to do'. But it's surprisingly hard. The word, 'good', is easy. Also further, even if I don't use it, many others around her do. I understand that I will have to struggle to let her know that she can be any kind of girl as far as I'm concerned, so long as she is a happy person.

Nina says: 'I was never a "goody-goody" girl myself and I don't expect my daughter to be one. I know how much fun it is not to be good, but I'd like my daughter to be careful'. Priya adds: 'I hope as our daughter grows, we will, as parents, be able to talk to her about taking calculated risks. Of making sure that she has a back-up. But I hope we won't be over-protective. I want my daughter to have fun'. Isha avers: 'I want my daughter to be street smart, I don't want some smooth-talking man to fool her'. Rose says: 'My daughter's biggest anxiety at the moment is that she doesn't have a boyfriend. I'd be really happy for her if she found a nice boyfriend. I don't want her to think of forevers or marriage, but I see no reason why she can't enjoy having a boyfriend'. Meera tells me she knew her young daughter was 'canoodling with boys' and she also knew that her daughter knew she knew. So, though it had never been discussed, she felt she offered her daughter implicit faith and support.[21]

As someone who has been engaged in thinking about the politics of fun, I am struck by how many of the women say they would like their daughters to have fun. There seems to be a tacit assumption that sex, sexuality and the various rituals and performances that these often entail can be enjoyable. When I ask the women when it would be okay for their daughters to have sex, most respond with a laugh. 'At least eighteen', says Kyla, smiling sheepishly. Vani agrees: 'I don't want my kid to be sexually active at twelve. In fact, I don't want her to even kiss till she's sixteen. But still, I am not worried so much about shame as I am about sexual exploitation. Shame can sometimes add to one's enjoyment—the taboo-ness of it, sexual exploration is fine, but not sexual exploitation'. Isha adds: 'I'd like my daughter to make any choices knowing fully well what she is getting into and, from my perspective, the older she is, the better equipped she will be to make these choices. In any case, whatever she decides, I want her to be safe'.

Priya brings another dimension to the question when she says: 'I am not sure when I think it would be okay for my daughter to have sex, but if she's having sex at sixteen, I'd hope it was safe sex. Also, I'd be much more okay if she was having sex with a sixteen-year-old boy than if she was having sex with a twenty-year-old. Age differences mean power differences and that's a no-no for me'.

Once again the theme of knowing and knowledge assumes centre stage. Many feminist mothers believe that the more their daughters know about sex, safe sex and contraception, the fewer risks they will take. On the one hand, they want their children to have a sense of sexual agency, while, on the other, they do not want them sexually active too early. They want them to know sex is fun, but they would rather they did not take risks. Yet, I would argue that these are not really contradictions, only the subtle nuances of feminist mothering.

Many of the other mothers also express anxieties related not so much to the choices their daughters are making, but to the outside environment and how this might impact upon their daughters. For Nina, it is not even so much about actual assault as the impact of that assault. Others also echo the anxiety of what an assault would mean. Priya says: 'There is a lot of victim blaming now. And it feels like parents don't have their daughters' backs[22] at all. In the case of, say, the Marine Drive rape, I felt like one way the policeman could have got the girl to stay is to threaten to call her parents.[23] It's scary that for this girl, it seemed like the stranger

---

[21] Meera's comment on the trust she implicitly offers her daughter raises several questions: How do we decide what questions to ask and when? What are the boundaries we draw and what is their impact? These concerns merit a much longer discussion than is possible here.

[22] 'Having your back' is a colloquial expression meaning being supported or being stood up for, and so having a sense of security.

[23] In 2005 a young college girl was raped in broad daylight by a police constable inside a police station at Marine Drive in Mumbai.

policeman was less frightening than her parents. I want my daughter to be able to say "Sure, call my parents. Call them now. *In fact, I will call them*"'. Kyla echoes Priya when she says: 'My hope is that if my child is in trouble, she would come first to me. If she had a backstreet abortion or even just an abortion without telling me, I would feel I had failed as a parent. It's not about the abortion, it's about being there for them. I would feel the same about sexual assault, how can I be there for my daughter for what comes afterwards?'

In a similar vein, a feminist academic with whom I was discussing my research told me this story about her nineteen-year-old daughter. 'My daughter called me from another city to say that she was going pubbing with her friends, though at least some of them, including her, were under 21. What could I say? I'd rather know about this than not. If I censure her, the next time I won't hear about it. If she lands up in jail, I want to be the first person she calls'.

Isha adds: 'I don't want to be the parent whose daughter has to hunt for a gynaecologist far away from her home for a prescription for oral contraceptives or worse, a medical termination of pregnancy. I want to know. I want to be there, holding her hand'. Isha's assumption that young women feel the need to hide their contraception is not unfounded. During research I conducted in 2010, I found that one reason young women were choosing not to use the oral contraceptive pill was because they feared it would be found in their possession by their parents, thus immediately marking them out as sexually active and, therefore, not 'good' girls.[24]

As I have argued elsewhere, the fear of giving consent sometimes leads young women to place themselves at physical risk.[25] If, as Priya suggests in her stark comment on the Marine Drive rape case, young women did not need to fear their parents more than random and possibly dangerous strangers, they might actually reduce their risk of assault.

The question of consent is an important and very relevant one, since the recently-passed Protection of Children from Sexual Offences Bill criminalises consensual sexual activity between consenting adolescents by raising the age of consent from sixteen to eighteen.[26] What distinguishes feminist mothers' reflections on their children's sexuality is the recognition that consent is very different from coercion. The risk posed by giving consent is certainly that one might be hurt or, as Isha suggests, 'taken for a ride', but it is different from the risk of assault. Also, in a context where 'giving consent' is not fraught with peril from one's own mother, young women may give consent and/or change their minds, knowing that they will not be blamed for their choices.

There is another important choice that some young women are making—that of choosing other women as romantic partners. What if your daughter were lesbian? Vani responds: 'In general, I'd hope she has a happy, healthy, fulfilling life—everything else that happens, choices, non-choices, decisions, are hers to make and mine to get used to'. Kyla echoes this: 'I think I would be okay…maybe worry about whether she has a supportive enough

---

[24] Shilpa Phadke, 'But I Can't Carry a Condom! Young Women, Risk and Sexuality in the Time of Globalisation', in Sanjay Srivastava (ed.), *The Sexualities Reader. Oxford India Studies on Contemporary Society* (Delhi: Oxford University Press, forthcoming).

[25] Shilpa Phadke, 'Dangerous Liaisons: Women and Men; Risk and Reputation in Mumbai', in 'Review of Women's Studies', in *Economic & Political Weekly*, Vol.42, no.17 (2007), pp.1510–8.

[26] Flavia Agnes points out that women's consent is rarely the premise on which decisions are made. She writes: '[C]hoice, or desire, as expressed by a woman, is somehow intrinsically illicit when it is against parental diktat and caste or community norms, and therefore needs to be contained and controlled. Girls who exercise active agency to defy convention pose a threat to the established social order, and are confined by reframing consent itself'. This is yet another area that merits a much longer discussion. See Flavia Agnes, 'Consent and Controversy', in *Indian Express* (12 May 2012) [http://www.indianexpress.com/news/consent-and-controversy/948277/, accessed 1 June 2012].

environment and friends and community to feel accepted in, otherwise I really want her to be fulfilled and happy whatever her sexual preference'.

Suggesting a similar awareness of how society still views same-sex love, Sapna says: 'I don't know. I hope I am supportive and can strengthen her for what is still a difficult choice'. Meera says: 'If she was queer, I honestly don't know how I would have dealt with it. I obviously would have had no problems with it, but frankly, that's a facile response. I am sure it would have been difficult, primarily because of anxieties about social responses, whether she could be "happy" in a heterosexist world'. However, she adds that her daughter once told her: 'You would probably have been happy if I was lesbian, with your politics'. She says: 'I was a little stunned by this and do wonder whether I used to lay on my anti-patriarchal ideologies too hard so [that] I was understood as being anti-male. I guess jokes about men and their ways have to be dealt with more sensitively with young women!' What these responses seem to suggest is not so much a concern with the choice itself, but with the thought that this is one choice that is likely to make their daughters' lives much more difficult.

Meera talks of 'the ambivalence and ambiguity around sex and how it's likely to remain and that's okay. Whatever we do or think, this greyness is not going away'. She says: 'As feminist mothers, we are constantly wearing analytical hats and thinking all the time, second-guessing ourselves. One of my fears was that there would be a negative reaction to our progressive/feminist politics as some parents have seen'.

Kyla echoes this: 'I'm keen that they don't believe that if you are born a girl, you will have a particular life...the idea that girls do this and that, the idea that marriage and babies are compulsory; the scary thing for me would be if my daughters want to be housewives. They could also reject gender politics, that's a major fear. But so far, I think my older daughter is getting it'. This anxiety that their daughters would 'reject' feminism is one I heard several times, often accompanied by stories of friends' daughters who had done so.

Feminist scholarship has long since understood that, especially for adolescent girls, growing up in modern societies is fraught with peculiar kinds of risks, anxieties and pressures. Joan Jacobs Brumburg suggests that for American girls in the late twentieth century, the body was the 'central personal project' in a context where they believed that their bodies were 'the ultimate expression of the self'. She writes: 'Contemporary girls *seem* to have more autonomy, but their freedom is laced with peril'.[27] In 1994, Mary Piper wrote of American girls that they were coming of age in a culture that was dangerous, sexualised, media-saturated and girl-poisoning. As a clinical psychologist, she attempted to build a case for a different culture that would support and nurture girls while giving them choices and freedoms.[28] More than a decade later, Evelyn Resh wrote a very different kind of book on how to parent girls on the threshold of discovering their sexuality, suggesting that girls were/are being left to develop their sexual identities without any guidance from their parents. She argues that sending out messages on the dangers of sexuality, in the form of diseases and unwanted pregnancies, does not enable girls to think of sexuality in terms of pleasure.[29] Naomi Wolf shares Brumburg's concerns, pointing to the destabilising effects of a lack of boundaries for young girls, which makes them more vulnerable. Wolf suggests that the lack of any sense of initiation into erotic sexuality or womanhood for American girls meant that young girls were somehow adrift in a

---

[27] Joan Jacobs Brumburg, *The Body Project: An Intimate History of American Girls* (New York: Vintage Books, 1997), pp.97, 197 (emphasis in original).
[28] Mary Piper, *Reviving Ophelia: Saving the Selves of Adolescent Girls* (New York: Ballantine Books, 1994), p.12.
[29] Evelyn Resh, *The Secret Lives of Teen Girls: What Your Mother Wouldn't Talk About But Your Daughter Needs to Know* (New Delhi: Hay House Publishers, 2009).

world where they were expected to make sexual choices. She argues that girls often have sexual intercourse without an understanding of their own bodies or desire.[30]

Both Brumburg and Wolf seem to suggest that there is a way of co-parenting or producing strong women models for young girls and a space where questions might be asked and answered without judgement being passed. Wolf writes: 'Can we imagine for our own daughters something better than what we had—better information that can shape a better sexual culture?'[31] As a possible solution, she suggests that groups of friends with children sign up for the responsibility of providing a kind of initiation into womanhood, to teach girls what they have learnt about being women, doing this through retreats and hiking camps or other activities. A feminist mother in Mumbai told me that she and some friends have started an initiative. They gather a group of children and attempt to both raise questions and answer questions asked of them in an effort to raise gender consciousness and address dilemmas.

My still preliminary research suggests the need to keep the conversation on sex going—to open up questions on both pleasure and risk for discussion and negotiation. There is a need to reflect on re-thinking the definition of assault itself, not just in terms of the dangers, but how we might transform its outcomes from being something that is impossible to recover from, to something that is difficult but can, if it were to happen, be negotiated. In the same way, significantly feminist mothers who acknowledge the pleasures of the body may be able to create an environment in which their daughters are better able to make choices and exercise informed consent.

The difficult question here is: what are these conversations feminist mothers envisage with their daughters and how will they texture them? What is the content they imagine them to have? How do they articulate a politics of not just gender, but also class, caste, race and other kinds of justice? Will they be able to find, as Wolf suggests, a cohort of similar like-minded mothers/women? If their daughters indeed need a village of feminist/progressive women to raise them, how easy will it be to provide these spaces and individuals?

Concluding Thoughts

Even as we reflect on feminist mothering, it is important to think about how feminists and feminist ideas are themselves perceived. Gill uses the term 'unspeakable inequalities' to point towards the operation of sexism in a '"postfeminist" climate in which equality is assumed, yet in which men are privileged'. She argues that sexism operates 'through the invalidation and annihilation of any language for talking about structural inequalities'.[32]

I want to reflect on this term, 'unspeakable inequalities', when it comes to feminist mothering. As someone who went to school in urban India in the 1980s and grew to feminist consciousness through classroom discussions on dowry and sati, the early twenty-first century is palpably different. It is not that there were no sexual risks then, they were simply cast differently. The 1980s were the high point of the Indian women's movement and the media was extremely supportive in its reporting. Today, in the post-globalisation scenario, not only is the media reporting differently, feminism itself has become in some ways 'unspeakable' and subject to the worst kind of stereotyping.

Increasingly, I find young women articulating variations on the theme of 'I'm independent, but I'm not a feminist' because being a feminist, saying these 'unspeakable' things, makes one a social pariah. In this environment, it has become ever more important to discuss a politics of

---

[30] Naomi Wolf, *Promiscuities: A Secret History of Female Desire* (London: Vintage, 1998).
[31] *Ibid.*, p.239.
[32] Gill, 'Sexism Reloaded, or, It's Time to Get Angry Again!', pp.62, 63.

gender and to make this part of the more taken-for-granted realities of our daughters' worlds even as we grapple with the reality that they are unfortunately not taken for granted at all. In doing so, we have to confront the fear, which many have articulated, that our daughters will reject our feminist politics. For many feminists, our politics is something we believe we 'gift' to our daughters, both in terms of an egalitarian upbringing and also as a way of leading a more fulfilling life.

It has become more important than ever to bring up our daughters in ways we believe promote a sense of self, in the hope that our daughters will become well-informed young women who are able to exercise important choices with a degree of freedom. This is a tall order and perhaps a utopian dream. Not now, perhaps not ever, will there be easy answers, only a minefield of possibilities that we must negotiate with our daughters, trying to teach and learn from each other.

My Brother's Keeper: Regulation of the Brother–Sister Relationship in the Religious Personal Laws of India

ARCHANA PARASHAR and VIJAYA NAGARAJAN

This article analyses the continued denial of equality to women in India's religious personal laws by focusing on the rights of brothers and sisters to illustrate the repeated failures of law. Although this failure has been normalised by deploying various conceptual tools, these theoretical trends need to be challenged. This article examines the 2005 amendment to the Hindu Succession Act which, although giving women extensive property rights, still gave sisters lesser rights than their brothers. It demonstrates that the concept of religious personal laws is a construct which is often used uncritically, and that it legitimises the denial of equal rights to women. The paper combines critical geography scholarship and legal feminist insights to argue that the law must be aware of spatial practices and that it is essential for legal thinkers to engage with the law in more than an instrumental sense. It analyses the processes of knowledge production and explores how the constitutive aspects of legal knowledge can be better integrated into legal scholarship. It thus aims to make visible the many spaces of the law: where laws are made; where ideas about men and women as owners of property are normalised; and where the law is expected to be implemented. It argues for legal scholars to be present and engaged in the contestation of meanings of the law.

Religious personal laws are a ubiquitous feature of the Indian legal system, which while recognising numerous religious practices generally, give women fewer rights than men. These laws straddle the divide between state and non-state legal rules because the Indian state enforces these rules, and to varying extents modifies them. Yet even when the state has introduced legislation to promote gender equality, not much has changed. The example of recent legislative changes in Hindu law, which deal with the relationship of siblings, demonstrates that merely changing legal norms will not create gender parity for women. In fact, in many instances, neither legislative inaction nor legislative reform impacts on women's lived-in spaces. However, this is not an argument for disengaging with the law. Instead we wish to emphasise the importance of creating nuanced legal knowledge to enable a better understanding of the repeated failures of the law to introduce equality. Combining the insights of critical legal geography and legal feminist scholarship, we seek to explore how and if the law can deliver a fairer society.

This article focuses on the specific aspect of religious personal laws dealing with the inheritance rights of brothers and sisters in order to study the multi-spatial dimensions that the law and regulations ought to consider. The discussion is divided into three sections. The first part offers a brief overview of the history of the concept of religious personal laws (RPLs) and their ambiguous status in post-colonial India. This is followed by a discussion of the scope of RPLs in determining the rules of marriage, divorce, succession and inheritance. These rules primarily determine the claims of men and women as sons and daughters qua their parents rather than as sisters and brothers. However, the respective inheritance shares of sons and daughters are often different, thus creating disparities between the positions of sisters and brothers.

The second section details examples of RPLs in communities that give unequal shares to sons and daughters. It critically assesses the Hindu Succession Act 1956 (HSA) and its efforts to create gender parity between sisters and brothers. We begin by tracing these legislative developments to illustrate that legislating for equal rights has not always reached the spaces where women live, although this may not necessarily be an inherent limitation of the law itself. Taking seriously the constitutive role of legal knowledge, we explore the possibility of alternative knowledge production.

In the final section we rely on critical geography scholarship to argue that to be effective, any law must be aware of spatial practices and that it is essential for legal thinkers to engage with the law in more than an instrumental sense. Legislators aiming at creating gender parity have to be aware of the gender hierarchies that inform cultural and social relations. However this is not an argument against engaging with laws; rather it is our aim to explore how the constitutive aspects of legal knowledge can be better integrated in legal scholarship. The insights of critical geographers need to be supplemented by those from feminist jurisprudence to make visible the many spaces of the law: where laws are made; where ideas about men and women as owners of property are normalised; and where the law is expected to be implemented and enforced.

Religious Personal Laws and the Rights of Siblings

Religious Personal Laws in India

Religious Personal Laws (RPLs) are one of colonialism's peculiar bequests to India. The history of how the concept of RPLs was formulated, and its continued operation in post-colonial India, have been the source of much discussion.[1] For our present purposes, a broad account of these historical developments will suffice to contextualise contemporary debates.

The idea of laws as personal or territorial is an old European idea, originally used to inform the choice of law applicable to an individual. Personal laws were carried by a person wherever he went, and in this sense extended the reach of certain laws beyond territorial boundaries. Additionally, ecclesiastical laws in Christian Europe governed personal relations, and the two ideas combined to form the concept of religious personal laws.[2] In India, Muslim rule from the eighth to the thirteenth century led to the establishment of Shariat as the law, although the extent of its application in the Indian subcontinent remains a subject of academic debate. Even though many Indian rulers were Muslims, the population was identified by religion. However, no distinction was made between religious and non-religious laws and the various religious laws regulated all aspects of life.[3]

---

[1] For an introduction to the extensive literature on this topic see Archana Parashar, *Women and Family Law Reform in India* (New Delhi: Sage Publications, 1992); Vasudha Dhagamwar, *Towards the Uniform Civil Code* (Bombay: N.M. Tripathi, 1989); and Flavia Agnes, *State, Gender and the Rhetoric of Law Reform* (Mumbai: SNDT Women's University, 1995).

[2] Duncan Derrett, *Religion, Law and the State in India* (New Delhi: Oxford University Press, 1999), p.53.

[3] David Pearl, *A Text Book on Muslim Law* (London: Croom Helm, 1979), p.21; and J. Sarkar, *Mughal Administration* (Calcutta: M.C. Sarkar, 4th ed. 1959).

Early British contact with Indian society was more commercial than political. The British only gradually became interested in administration when their commercial activities required political certainty. For various reasons they decided that the religious customs of the people should be left unchanged as far as possible, and to this effect the early ordinances directed that judicial bodies should resolve disputes between people by reference to their religious laws. However there was no clear articulation of what constituted these religious laws and the areas of conduct that would be governed by them. Inevitably, though, judicial pronouncements set the parameters for both these issues, and this may be considered as the beginning of RPLs in India. Over time the RPLs were modified both legislatively and by virtue of being administered through courts that used procedures and concepts derived from the principles of English common law and equity.[4]

The Constitution adopted by India at Independence did not take an unambiguous stand about the relationship between the Constitution and the RPLs. The status of RPLs vis-à-vis the state legal system and the Constitution raises issues of *inter alia* the respective jurisdictions of religion and the law, legal pluralism and gender justice. The major area of contention is whether the state can reform the RPLs to make them conform to the constitutional mandate of equality. The history of legislative action in this regard has been uneven.[5] The judiciary has also not taken a consistent stand and even though the constitutional validity of the RPLs has been challenged in higher courts on many occasions, the courts have not declared them to be unconstitutional.[6] As a result, women in different communities and even in different parts of the country have varying rights to property and in other personal matters.[7] The issue of creating legislative equality for women has been so politicised that most feminist legal scholars have retreated from even academic commentary on the subject. Thus the aim of gaining gender parity in legal rights in and across various RPLs is no longer a topic of legal scholarship. For us, this raises the wider issue of the suitability of law reform as a means of changing social practices. We respond to this issue in the next section by arguing that pragmatic engagements with law reform must be informed by critical ideas about the constitutive nature of the law. We shall develop our argument with the specific example of the sibling relations in the personal laws, which is a relatively ignored area in the literature. However, our argument has wider application and extends to gender parity in all aspects of RPLs.

---

[4] For the details of these developments see Parashar, *Women and Family Law Reform in India*; and Flavia Agnes, *Family Law Vol.I: Family Laws and Constitutional Claims* (New Delhi: Oxford University Press, 2011), pp.1–9.

[5] For legislative history see Parashar, *Women and Family Law Reform in India*.

[6] See for example *State of Bombay v Narasu Appa Mali* AIR 1952 Bom 84 (a Hindu male's claim that a law prohibiting polygamy for Hindu men and not Muslim men contravenes article 14 was rejected by the court. It said personal laws are not 'laws in force' under Art 12 of the Constitution); *C. Masilamani Mudaliar v Idol of Sri Swaminathaswami Thirukoil* (1996) 8 SCC 525 (personal laws are laws in force and must conform to the Constitution); *Mary Roy v State of Kerala* AIR 1986 SC 1011 (federal law prevailed over state succession laws for Christians); and *Daniel Latifi v Union of India* (2001) 7 SCC 125 (SC upheld the Constitutional validity of the Muslim Women's Act, 1996).

[7] The immense diversity of applicable laws results from various exemption clauses in the laws that make the RPLs applicable. These exemptions can be for legislation by the states, colonial arrangements that have not been superseded, terms of agreement in the instruments of accession to the Union of India, saving the applicability of customs etc. See Poonam Pradhan Saxena, *Family Law II* (Delhi: Lexis-Nexis Butterworths, 3rd ed. 2011), pp.3–24.

Scope of the RPLs and the Regulation of the Relationships among Siblings

Generally the reach of the RPLs in personal relations extends to the formation and dissolution of marriage with the attendant rules of succession.[8] It is the latter that is our main concern here. The discussion of the Hindu Succession Law below has wider application and can extend to a study of state interaction with all religious personal laws.[9] Succession rules by their nature deal with intergenerational transmission of property, and at first glance the relationship of brother and sister is not a relevant relationship in this regard. Generally speaking, the relevance of being siblings is manifest in the rules of succession that determine the shares available to the son and daughter. Once succession opens and a share is granted, the legal relevance of being a sibling comes to an end.[10] However succession rules are also a means to provide for the needs of family members.[11] In these provisions one can see the operation of a combination of societal ideas about family obligations and state imperatives to ensure that destitution is avoided for vulnerable members of society. In the absence of social welfare measures, India has typically (but selectively) relied on the laws of succession to prevent destitution.[12] For example, under the provisions of Hindu law, adult children are responsible for maintaining their aged parents.[13] There are other provisions in the state-enacted Hindu Succession Act 1956 (HSA) that assume special significance in light of the fact that there is very little social welfare available for most people in India.[14]

The Shares of Sons and Daughters in Succession Rules

Even though the family relations of different communities are governed by the RPLs, the applicability of these laws is generally premised on state-enacted legislative provisions.[15] However the substantive rules of succession differ from religious community to religious community, and even though they are invariably claimed to be religious in nature, they are modified by state legislation to varying degrees. At one end of the spectrum are the Islamic rules of succession that are not modified at all by state legislation. In the middle are the laws enacted under colonisation, and sometimes modified since Independence, which govern the

---

[8] See also John H. Mansfield, 'Religious and Charitable Endowments and a Uniform Civil Code', in Gerald James Larson (ed.), *Religion and Personal Law in Secular India: A Call to Judgment* (Bloomington: University of Indiana Press, 2001), pp.69–103.

[9] We make this assertion being fully mindful of the different trajectories of various RPLs. Rules of inheritance for the four communities are different and found in legislation enacted by the states as well as uncodified Islamic law; see Saxena, *Family Law II*.

[10] The other major area where sibling relationship is relevant is in regard to the capacity to marry. All RPLs provide a list of prohibited relationships and declare marriages in contravention of such rules to be invalid; see Flavia Agnes, *Family Law Vol.II: Marriage, Divorce and Matrimonial Litigation* (New Delhi: Oxford University Press, 2011), p.10.

[11] For example Australian law provides for the possibility of overriding a will if claims are made by dependents of the deceased under the provisions of the succession laws. In New South Wales the amended Succession Act 2006, NSW, now incorporates the former Family Provision Act, 1982 NSW.

[12] See A.B. Bose and K.D. Gangrade, *The Aging in India, Problems and Potentialities* (New Delhi: Abhinav, 1988).

[13] See the Hindu Maintenance and Adoption Act 1956 s.20; the laws of Muslims, Christians and Parsis do not impose such obligations.

[14] An example of state law trying to provide for the maintenance needs of vulnerable family members is the Code of Criminal Procedure, 1973 s.125.

[15] In practice the numerous exception clauses in these Acts introduce immense diversity. The variability is due to the operation of customs or different state laws or even the laws of former colonisers. See Saxena, *Family Law II*, pp.3–24.

Christian and Parsi communities. At the other end is Hindu law which has been modified most extensively by state legislation.

Under Islamic rules of succession the shares of those entitled to inherit are determined as precise proportions of the total. The respective shares of the inheritors are calculated on the basis of who all the inheritors are. The relevant information for our purposes is that in the presence of a son, the daughter's share is half that of the son's. Where a sister and brother take a share, the share of the sister is half that of the brother.[16]

The rules in the Indian Succession Act 1925 (ISA) govern succession for Christians and Parsis.[17] The ISA was first enacted in 1865 and re-enacted in 1925. It governed succession for Christians but was primarily meant to regulate these matters for Europeans, because it allowed the various states to exclude Indian Christians governed by their customary laws.[18] The Christian son and daughter are entitled to an equal share of parental property. The brother and sister, when entitled to inherit, also take an equal share.[19] For Parsis, after amendments to the relevant sections of the ISA in 1991, the daughter and son now take an equal share.[20]

Hindu law was most comprehensively reformed by the state shortly after Independence. It is in Hindu law reform that the state has gone the farthest in trying to create legislative gender parity; as one aspect of these changes, the HSA granted Hindu women extensive property rights. This is discussed below in relation to efforts at creating gender parity between sisters and brothers.

Property Rights for Hindu Women

Hindu law in India has the distinction of being the RPL most extensively modified by legislation. One feature of these legislative reforms was that women gained extensive property rights. The Hindu Succession Act modified aspects of the Hindu undivided family and rules of property ownership, and *inter alia* gave sons and daughters an equal share in the father's property.[21] However, initially it did not make daughters coparceners[22] in the joint family property;[23] only after amendments in 2005 were daughters made coparceners.[24]

It is worthwhile examining the law prior to the 2005 amendments. While it attempted to grant brothers and sisters equal rights to their father's property, it still gave priority to the brothers' rights. Originally the HSA retained the institution of Mitakshara joint family and the

---

[16] *Ibid.*, pp.437–555.
[17] Indian Succession Act, 1925 part V, chapters II and III, respectively.
[18] As a consequence there was great variance in succession laws applicable to Christians in different parts of India and commonly daughters took a lesser share than sons. See Agnes, *Family Law Vol.I*, pp.73–5; and Saxena, *Family Law II*, pp.10–12
[19] This parity was, however, only achieved through Supreme Court decision *Mary Roy v State of Kerala* AIR 1986 SC 1011.
[20] For details see Agnes, *Family Law Vol.I*, pp.65–84.
[21] For a discussion of how sisters and brothers had very different rights in the Hindu joint family property see Lucy Carroll, 'Daughter's Right of Inheritance in India: A Perspective on the Problem of Dowry', in *Modern Asian Studies*, Vol.25, no.4 (1991), pp.791–809.
[22] Coparceners receive equal portions of an inheritance.
[23] Daughters and sons took an equal share in the father's property and even if the father was a member of an undivided Hindu joint family, on his death it was assumed that he had separated. He could will away the entire property but if he died intestate his separate share was divisible among his heirs specified in the HSA. Daughters were classified as class I heirs and took an equal share with the other class I heirs.
[24] The Hindu Succession (Amendment) Act, 2005.

right of sons only to be coparceners in the Hindu joint family.[25] Although technically it did not abolish coparcenary, it did modify aspects of it. One important modification was that at the death of an intestate Hindu male who was a member of a Hindu undivided family, his interest in the joint family property went to his class I heirs who now included his daughter. The incidents of traditional law that the HSA did not alter included the right of a daughter to have her marriage expenses paid, to be maintained through the joint family property if she was unmarried, and the right to live in the joint family home.[26]

This right of residence in the family home was not available to the daughter if she was married, but she could stay in the house if she had been deserted by her husband, was separated from him or was a widow. Moreover, under the legislation she could not ask for the house to be partitioned even though, as a class I heir, she had a legal share in the ownership of the house.[27] This restriction on partitioning the house was considered necessary only for daughters and not for sons, as any son could ask for a partition at any time. The clear assumption behind this restriction of the daughter's property rights was that a married daughter should not be able to disturb the dwelling house arrangements of her father's family. Two main reasons have been advanced for this: firstly, if a married daughter could claim a right of residence in the natal family home it would introduce strangers (sons-in-law) into the family; and secondly, it would cause dissension between brother and sister—the married daughter does not belong in her father's family, and if the sister can ask for a partition it could result in gross injustice to the brother.[28]

The significant issue here is that this legislative initiative subscribed to the unstated societal assumptions about the respective roles of sisters and brothers. This is especially relevant because the same legislation that had given to the daughter a 'new' inheritance right to an equal share with her brother, still treated their rights differently. Although this initiative had transgressed many dominant understandings of the entitlements of daughters and sons *vis-à-vis* the property of the father, it nevertheless made the daughter's right of ownership subject to the greater imperative of maintaining a joint family home. More precisely it gave only the son the prerogative as 'primary' owner to decide when to partition the house. Brothers were expected, as before, to look after the wedding and maintenance expenses of presumably 'needy' unmarried sisters.[29] Thus the radical change of granting daughters an equal share of

---

[25] Mitakshara and Dayabhaga are the two main schools for organising the Hindu joint family. The Mitakshara system was prevalent in most of India and its most distinctive feature was that the three generations of males were joint owners of property and the rule of survivorship applied: that is, at the death or birth of any coparcener, the remaining members' shares increased or decreased proportionally. Under traditional rules women did not become coparceners and did not own a share of Hindu joint family property. In the Dayabhaga school, the father had greater rights and women were owners of property along with men. For further details see Paras Diwan and Peeyushi Diwan, *Modern Hindu Law* (Allahabad: Allahabad Law Agency, 10th ed., 1995).

[26] See s.23 of the HSA. We will use this example to illustrate our argument in the following discussion. In choosing this focus we do not wish to underplay the very substantial gains made by Hindu women with respect to property rights in the HSA. However the law still carries enormous normative power, which is manifested in more ways than simply the formulation of legal rights.

[27] The section actually prevented any female class I heir from asking for partition of the dwelling house, provided that the house was wholly occupied by members of the family of the intestate.

[28] For details including the comments made by parliamentarians and judicial observations see Saxena, *Family Law II*, pp.425–32.

[29] Since the 2005 amendment of HSA daughters are coparceners; as well their claim for marriage expenses or maintenance now would be subsumed under their legal status of joint owners of the coparcenary property.

property was still accompanied by ideas of the primacy of property rights of sons and brothers.[30] Legal reforms, while bowing to societal expectations, were not bringing about any real change in rights. Any legal reform requires not only the clear articulation of goals but also a clear commitment to pragmatic engagement with the people affected. This involves an awareness of the spaces where laws are made, adopted, applied and enforced.

In 2005 the HSA was amended so that when a male member of an undivided Mitakshara coparcenary dies, the doctrine of survivorship does not operate. The daughters are now entitled to be coparceners with their father and brothers.[31] Furthermore the provision that denied the sister a right to ask for partition of the dwelling house if the brothers were living in it was deleted. By any measure these are radical changes,[32] but several problematic assumptions persist. The most obvious is the provision denying daughters the right to question the validity of a partition that had already taken place.[33] The 2005 amendment included a proviso that nothing in the Act should affect or invalidate a partition or other alienation of property that had taken place prior to 20 December 2004. Two separate consequences follow, which may have been unintended, but which have gendered implications nonetheless. Legislation by the states conflicts with this proviso, and the prohibition applies only to daughters and not to sons. The state laws do not include any such limitation, but they are superseded by federal law.[34] The effect of this interaction between state and federal laws is that some women have lost a right (to question the validity of a partition or alienation of property) that they had before the federal law was enacted. Thus a law enacted as a beneficial measure for daughters has worked to the disadvantage of some women. Secondly, among brothers and sisters, the limitation only applies to sisters. If a brother wishes to question the validity of a partition or alienation of property, nothing in the 2005 amendment prevents him from doing so, no matter when the partition had taken place.[35]

It could be argued that in the amendment Act the legislators had granted sisters the right to be coparceners with their brothers and, it being a 'new' right, that they were being cautious to not disturb existing property transactions. However the same legislators did have before them the example of state laws that had granted daughters and sisters similar rights to be coparceners, and there was no evidence of past property transactions being challenged *en masse* by the new coparceners. As well, the legislators did not restrict the right to question a

---

[30] The tension between conceptualising men and women as equal owners of property and according primacy to the rights of men surfaces in many provisions of the HSA. For example the equality principle did not apply to agricultural land s.4(2); only men were coparceners; and different schemes of succession for Hindu men and women were stipulated (ss.8 and 16).

[31] Moreover, the HSA has deleted the provision that exempted agricultural land from the application of this Act. Prior to this amendment a number of states had enacted legislation to either abolish the Hindu undivided family or make the daughter an equal coparcener with the son. See The Kerala Joint Hindu Family System (Abolition) Act, 1975, The Andhra Pradesh Hindu Succession (Amendment) Act, 1985, The Tamil Nadu Hindu Succession Amendment Act 1989, The Maharashtra Hindu Succession (Amendment) Act, 1994, and The Karnataka Hindu Succession (Amendment) Act, 1994.

[32] For empirical evidence that the legal change making Hindu women coparceners had a positive effect, see K. Deininger, A. Goyal and H. Nagarajan, 'Inheritance Law Reform and Women's Access to Capital: Evidence from India's Hindu Succession Act', The World Bank Development Research Group, Policy Research Working Paper 5338, June 2010 [http://works.bepress.com/aparajita_goyal/subject_areas.html, accessed 24 Nov. 2011].

[33] The other two provisions deal with the ambiguity about the application of the HSA to agricultural land, and the retention of the concept of coparcenary.

[34] The central amendment Act makes all daughters, whether married or unmarried, coparceners. The state Acts had done so only for unmarried daughters.

[35] This provision was declared unconstitutional as it differentiated between the rights of coparceners on the ground of their gender in *R. Kantha v Union of India* AIR 2010 Karn 27.

partition by anyone but daughters. As a result of this provision any other coparcener including a brother remained capable of questioning a partition, but not the sister.

It is clear from the above analysis that even when legislators extensively reformed Hindu law to prioritise equal rights, they did not manage to achieve gender parity. The lawmakers seem to be pursuing simultaneously the aims of granting gender parity in rights while trying not to disturb prevailing societal expectations about gender roles. It is reasonable to ask why the lawmakers were reluctant to push for genuine gender parity. How did they determine whether a change would be accepted or whether it would be seen to transgress some unstated but real boundaries? In defining rights, lawmakers work under certain assumptions and it is these assumptions that need to be carefully scrutinised. However, this analysis is not about identifying *mala fides* on the part of lawmakers. Rather we aim to examine how the many spaces of law construct gender specific consequences.

The Multiple Spaces of Law and the Construction of Legal Knowledge

Diversity in the existing RPLs and the consequent lesser rights of women in many instances result both from state action and inaction in the form of legislative intervention. With or without legislative action, the position of women remains unchanged. Critical legal theorists, including feminist legal theorists, have analysed the continuation of gender hierarchies as a 'limit of law' argument with the implication that the law is simply incapable of doing certain things.[36] The failure of the law to achieve gender parity is normalised by critical scholarship through analyses that show up the law as force, violence and inherently pathological.[37]

However, this kind of analysis ends up being as deterministic as the ones it set out to refute.[38] And it conceptualises the law in the top-down manner of mainstream legal theory. Paradoxically, such analyses go against one of the central insights of post-structuralist theory, that all knowledge is socially constituted. If this idea is taken earnestly it follows that legal thinkers must deconstruct the claims of the law and better explain the complexity of any legal system. Accepted or authoritative legal knowledge is primarily the ideas that find acceptance in the legal and the wider community. Therefore, it is incumbent upon critical legal scholars to take on the responsibility for scrutinising all ideas about the nature of the law, its limits or its inherent shortcomings. This is not to say that only optimistic analyses of the law are acceptable, but that the agency and responsibility of those influential in discourse formation should be taken seriously.

Knowledge production is more complex than simply putting forth ideas, and it is this complexity that requires attention. We rely on the argument put forward by feminist geographers Pamela Moss and Karen Falconer Al-Hindi that the metaphor of rhizomatic thinking captures the complexity of knowledge formation.[39] Feminist thinking in geography,

---

[36] Such arguments are made by non-legal as well as legal scholars. See for example Nivedita Menon, *Recovering Subversion: Feminist Politics Beyond the Law* (Chicago: Permanent Black, 2004); and Maria Drakopoulou, 'Feminism, Governmentality and the Politics of Legal Reform', in *Griffith Law Review*, Vol.17 (2008), pp.330–56.

[37] For an introduction to this literature see Ian Ward, *An Introduction to Critical Legal Theory* (New York: Routledge Cavendish, 2nd ed. 2004).

[38] See the review article by Rosi Braidotti, 'A Critical Cartography of Feminist Post-Postmodernism', in *Australian Feminist Studies*, Vol.20, no.47 (2005), pp.169–80.

[39] See Pamela Moss and Karen Falconer Al-Hindi (eds), *Feminisms in Geography: Rethinking Space, Place, and Knowledges* (Lanham, MA: Rowman and Littlefield Publishers, 2008), pp.12–15. The following account is based on their use of Deleuze and Guattari's concepts of rhizomatic thinking, positive ontology and segmentarity. A rhizome is an underground root system made up of nodes and internodes that spread horizontally. Even if a rhizome is destroyed, other nodes keep growing and reproduce.

they argue, is rhizomatic in the sense that '[i]deas are introduced, discussed, picked up, transferred, engaged, rejected, contested, reworked, transformed, and reintroduced yet again'.[40] The metaphor of rhizome then reflects how thinking materialises in feminist discussions at the same time at it prevents any one form of thinking from becoming an orthodoxy.[41] These ways of thinking about knowledge production can explain how new approaches exist alongside more established ways of thinking. However, they argue that such diverse declarations of authority cannot go unchallenged. It is important to continually contest discursive authority so that conformist orthodoxies, even in critical and progressive thinking, are not allowed to take hold.

These ways of thinking about knowledge production can and ought to be extended to critical legal knowledge as well. It is our objective to analyse the processes of knowledge production to better understand why and how the RPLs manage to maintain gender disadvantage and yet retain legitimacy even with some feminists. In order to do that we use the insights of legal geography literature to bring into sharper focus the multi-spatiality of the law. The insights of legal geographers, when supplemented by those of legal feminists, make visible the many spaces of the law where ideas about men and women as owners of property are normalised. The failure of the law to achieve gender parity is normalised by deploying various conceptual tools, and these contemporary trends in critical legal theory need to be revisited.

The Contributions of Legal Geographers and Legal Feminists

Critical legal scholars and critical geographers both aim to illustrate the discourses within and outside accepted boundaries.[42] They point out that legal thought and practice conceal many geographies of the spaces of political, social and economic life.[43] For example, these writers have challenged our understandings of property and questioned the adequacy of legal definitions that see it as a right to exclude others. Instead these authors have demonstrated how property is a set of relationships of belonging upheld by the surrounding space.[44] Law and space scholarship is distinct both from critical geography and critical legal analyses. While critical geographers reconceptualise space, law and space scholars focus on legal spaces. Similarly critical legal scholars question the self-acclaimed rationality of the law but do not focus on geographical questions.[45] It has been argued that the focus of a great deal of critical legal scholarship is on histories, but there is much to be gained from combining spatiality with

---

[40] *Ibid.*, p.12.

[41] *Ibid.* They also use the concepts of positive ontology and segmentarity. The concept of positive ontology invokes the definition of something in terms of what it is rather than what it is not. For example feminism becomes what it is depending on how it is taken up in one's practices rather than being defined against another type of thinking. Positivity as an ontological orientation thus means feminisms can be understood as both constituting and constitutive of various ideas rather than being told to conform to dominant definitions.

[42] Chris Butler, 'Critical Legal Studies and the Politics of Space', in *Social and Legal Studies*, Vol.18, no.3 (2009), p.314; and Alexandre Kedar, 'On the Legal Geography of Ethnocratic Settler States: Notes Towards a Research Agenda', in *Current Legal Issues*, Vol.5 (2003), pp.401–41. See Kedar pp.405–7 for a succinct account of how the critical geography literature has reconceptualised space among other categories of analysis and this is in turn reflected in the changing relationship between law and geography over time.

[43] N. Blomley, *Law, Space and the Geographies of Power* (London: Guilford Press, 1994), p.xiii; and D. Harvey, *Social Justice and the City* (Athens: University of Georgia Press, 2009).

[44] See Sarah Keenan, 'Subversive Property: Reshaping Malleable Spaces of Belonging', in *Social and Legal Studies*, Vol.19, no.4 (2010), p.427; and Fleur Johns, 'Private Law, Public Landscape: Troubling the Grid', in *Law Text Culture*, Vol.9 (2005), pp.60–90.

[45] See Blomley, *Law, Space and the Geographies of Power*, p.25.

histories and thus interweaving both *law* and *space*, resulting in a horizontal enquiry into spatial settings and a concurrent vertical enquiry into legal histories.[46] Legal geographers alert us to the spaces that the state must be aware of in its reflexive role. The examination the RPLs, their modification by legislation and specific analysis of the 2005 HSA amendments illustrate the importance of considering all these spaces.

Legal feminist and post-colonial scholarship[47] is often aimed at illustrating how legal spaces are embedded in or are embedding broader political and social values. This is particularly relevant to understanding the RPLs and the connected legislation and law reform efforts. Rachel Silvey says that feminist geographers address 'the question of who has the power to define a place as accessible to whom, how various social groups experience places as inclusive or exclusive of them and others, and how the regulation of space reflects and reinforces the privileges and interests of some groups over others'.[48] As explained above, the discourse around the RPLs has been constructed with the help of a number of concepts and it is important to analyse how these discourses create the spaces for the law to maintain gender hierarchies. We seek to examine three such spaces: firstly, the shape of the rule and the spaces where it will apply; secondly, the source of the rule which will determine the spaces that are prioritised; and thirdly, the manner of enforcement and whether this space is accessible to the women for whom it is created. Each of these three spaces is examined below with the overlapping deployment of concepts of state rules or non-state rules and universal rules or diversity.

There is support for rules that respect diversity over uniformity and this support comes from many quarters. Post-structuralist theory celebrates difference as non-essentialising and it seems to follow that the diversity of the RPLs is more desirable than replacing them with a single uniform law. When combined with critical scholars' disenchantment with law reform,[49] it seems almost inevitable that this diversity should remain undisturbed.[50] Further, the fact that India as a secular state guarantees freedom of religion as a fundamental right, would seem to make any state interference with the RPLs problematic, while favouring reliance on non-state laws. It is also true that differences between the religious communities of India are markers of identity and more significantly markers of minority identity. Arguments about both minority

---

[46] *Ibid.*, p.26.

[47] For legal feminist scholarship see Jane Conaghan, 'Reassessing the Feminist Project in Law', in *Journal of Law and Society*, Vol.27 (2000), pp.351–85; J. Richardson and R. Sandland (eds), *Feminist Perspectives on Law and Theory* (London: Cavendish Press, 2000); and Anne Bottomley 'Shock to Thought: An Encounter (of a Third Kind) with Legal Feminism', in *Feminist Legal Studies*, Vol.12, no.2 (2004), pp.29–65. For post-colonial scholarship see Boaventura De Sousa Santos, '"Law": A Map of Misreadings: Towards a Postmodern Conception of Law', in *Journal of Law and Society*, Vol.14, no.3 (1987), pp.297–302; Judith Butler, *Gender Trouble: Feminism and the Subversion of Identity* (New York: Routledge, 1990); Elizabeth Grosz, 'Becoming: An Introduction', in Elizabeth Grosz (ed.), *Becomings: Explorations in Time, Memory and Futures* (Ithaca: Cornell University Press, 1999), pp.1–14; and Drucilla Cornell, *Beyond Accommodation: Ethical Feminism, Deconstruction, and the Law* (New York: Routledge, 1991).

[48] Rachel Silvey, 'Geographies of Gender and Migration: Spatializing Social Difference', in *International Migration Review*, Vol.40, no.1 (2006), p.70.

[49] Critical legal feminist analyses amply demonstrate that law reform can be implicated in the perpetration of social hierarchies constructed around gender, race, and sexuality. See Martha Albertson Fineman (ed.), *Transcending the Boundaries of Law: Generations of Feminism and Legal Theory* (London: Cavendish-Routledge, 2011); Margaret Thornton (ed.), *Public and Private: Feminist Legal Debates* (Melbourne: Oxford University Press, 1995); and Ngaire Naffine (ed.), *Gender and Justice* (Aldershot: Ashgate, 2002).

[50] It is partly a function of different disciplinary affiliations that anthropologists and legal analysts see the existence of diversity in very different ways. See for example Livia Holden, *Hindu Divorce* (Aldershot: Ashgate, 2008); and Sylvia Vatuk, 'Muslim Women and Personal Law', in Zoya Hasan and Ritu Menon (eds), *In a Minority: Essays on Muslim Women in India* (New Delhi: Oxford University Press, 2005), pp.18–68.

identity, as well as the fundamental right to freedom of religion, may be deployed to create spaces where state law becomes an intruder.

Minority identities are constituted in multiple sites, but Bruce Lawrence articulates a common sentiment when he says: '[l]aws governing women have provided the touch-stone for Islamist identity in the maelstrom of Indian politics'.[51] Significantly, when some Islamic feminists claim that the question of whether any change for them is possible or even desirable and moreover it is for no one else to decide, a space is cordoned off.[52] This is a complex issue that requires a reflexive sensitivity to many issues of minority identity,[53] the communalisation of politics,[54] and global discourse over events since 11 September 2001. Without going into these controversies, we use this insistence by some prominent Muslim feminists to illustrate how the privileged voice contributes to discourse formation and for that reason they must also accept responsibility for the outcomes. Of course these arguments come from Muslim scholars, but this should not be read as a particular characteristic of this community. Thus in the case of Islamic law, the arguments invoking the fragility of minority identity function to insulate from scrutiny any practices labeled as religious. This stance invokes the problematic concept of public and private spheres to deny entry to legislature in matters of religion and culture that are equated to RPLs.[55] Feminist voices lend credence to this claim in a manner that is perhaps not available to members of other communities.[56]

A significant consequence of this stance is that the academic discourse focuses on minority versus majority identities to the exclusion of every other consideration. Zoya Hasan argues persuasively that the political movements of the 1920s used religious and cultural symbols that were relevant to all strata of community to foster unity among believers and so enhance their bargaining power. However after Independence this symbolism has been embodied exclusively in laws about women and families. This cultural distinction becomes a burden for women because community identity is defined almost entirely in terms of family laws, which tend to subordinate women.[57] When feminists focus primarily on minority identities they miss the opportunity for creating spaces for articulating genuinely fair, gendered conceptions of

---

[51] Bruce B. Lawrence, 'Woman as Subject/Woman as Symbol: Islamic Fundamentalism and the Status of Women', in *Journal of Religious Ethics*, Vol.22, no.1 (1994), pp.163–85.

[52] See for example Gail Minault, 'Women, Legal Reform, and Muslim Identity', in *Comparative Studies of South Asia, Africa and the Middle East*, Vol.17, no.2 (1997), pp.1–10; Sylvia Vatuk, 'Islamic Feminism in India: Indian Muslim Women Activists and the Reform of Muslim Personal Law', in *Modern Asian Studies*, Vol.42 (2008), pp.489–518; and Agnes, *Family Law Vol.I.* For an analysis of how 'voice' is constructed see Mrinalini Sinha, 'Gender in the Critiques of Colonialism and Nationalism: Locating the "Indian Woman"', in Joan Scott (ed.), *Feminism and History* (New York: Oxford University Press, 1996), pp.477–504.

[53] For a very incisive discussion of the difficulties moderate Muslims feel in articulating a reform agenda for Islam, see Akeel Bilgrami, 'What Is a Muslim? Fundamental Commitment and Cultural Identity', in *Economic and Political Weekly*, Vol.27, no.20/21 (1992), pp.1071–8. See Erin P. Moore, *Gender, Law and Resistance in India* (Tucson: University of Arizona Press, 1998), for a study of how some Muslim women have resisted the modern state institutions and practices that reinforce traditional arrangements by which women are subjected to patriarchal control and deprived of equal rights before the law.

[54] Ratna Kapur and Brenda Cossman, 'Communalising Gender/Engendering Community: Women, Legal Discourse and Saffron Agenda', in *Economic and Political Weekly*, Vol.28, no.17 (1993), pp.WS35–WS44.

[55] See also Susan Moller Okin, Joshua Cohen, Matthew Howard, and Martha C. Nussbaum, *Is Multiculturalism Bad for Women?* (Princeton: Princeton University Press, 1999).

[56] See Sherene Razack, 'The Sharia Law Debate in Ontario: The Modernity/Premodernity Distinction in Legal Efforts to Protect Women from Culture', in *Feminist Legal Studies*, Vol.15 (2007), pp.3–32, who criticises Western writers, including feminists, who critique Islamic rules as a manifestation of continuing colonial dominance.

[57] Zoya Hasan, 'Minority Identity, Muslim Women Bill Campaign and the Political Process', in *Economic and Political Weekly*, Vol.24, no.1 (1989), pp.44–5.

property rights for women.⁵⁸ If the discourse of the RPLs and gender justice is to move forward, at the very least it is necessary that all arguments be scrutinised for how they function to create silences and draw boundaries that are then claimed to be inevitable. Therefore, the claims about the inevitability of the RPLs need to be examined to ask who is making the claim, what is its basis, and who would be disadvantaged if it is upheld.⁵⁹ The objective of critique should be to create discursive spaces for articulating what a fair or gender-just family law might look like.

Restricting the state's role in guaranteeing women's fundamental rights can reinforce gender disadvantage in other ways as well. Vasudha Dhagamwar provides a good illustration of the second space for the source of rules that helps prioritise certain spaces. She says that family law governs matters of social conduct and generally makes up the non-formal aspect of the legal system.⁶⁰ Informal bodies like caste *panchayat*s impose these rules,⁶¹ which are a combination of religious and customary rules. However in the process, the formal rights of women, whether given by the RPLs or other state laws, risk being overlooked. The issue is that in this process of informal/community dispute resolution, women are disadvantaged. Both state laws and the RPLs, however, leave enough scope for the application of customary practices. For example, in the extensively codified Hindu law, the *Shastras* have been virtually replaced by state legislation but custom has not. The Hindu Marriage Act of 1955 sets out the procedure for marriage and the capacity to marry, as well as the grounds and procedure for divorce. However in each instance it leaves open the option for the parties to follow custom if they have such community customs.⁶² Thus not only does state law make space for customs to operate in matters of substantive rights, but it also permits a second set of rules that determine what may constitute transgression.

Furthermore, customary rules deal with transgressions as well insofar as they decide what would constitute evidence or proof, and determine the quantum and mode of punishment. These rules have to be applied by some body or organisation, and in India that very often happens to be the caste *panchayat*. Dhagamwar says that these mainly operate for lower and middle castes, for tribes and for nomads. For the most part these customs and practices are not widely known or documented, but 'punishments in the non-formal system fall heaviest on women of any age whether she be a toddler or a grandmother'.⁶³ She also describes how most of these punishments would be considered criminal offences under the formal legal system, yet they continue to operate with the 'permission' of the formal system. However from this

---

⁵⁸ Examples of scholars articulating such conceptions of a fair family law are nonetheless present even if not widely discussed. See for example B. Sivarammayya, *Matrimonial Property Law in India* (Delhi: Oxford University Press, 1999); and Kamala Sankaran, 'Family, Work and Matrimonial Property: Implications for Women and Children', in Archana Parashar and Amita Dhanda (eds), *Redefining Family Law in India* (New Delhi: Routledge, 2008), pp.258–81.

⁵⁹ For an argument that assertion of religious identity should not only be seen as a manifestation of religious fundamentalism, see Asghar Ali Engineer, 'Remaking Indian Muslim Identity', in *Economic and Political Weekly*, Vol.26, no.16 (1991), pp.1036–8.

⁶⁰ Vasudha Dhagamwar, 'Invasion of Criminal Law by Religion, Custom and Family Law', in *Economic and Political Weekly*, Vol.38, no.15 (2003), pp.1483–92.

⁶¹ The caste *panchayat*s are different from the Nyaya Panchayats instituted by the state as an alternative to the courts. See Marc Galanter and Upendra Baxi, 'Panchayati Justice: An Indian Experiment in Legal Access', in M. Galanter (ed.), *Law and Society in Modern India* (Delhi: Oxford University Press, 1989), pp. 54–92.

⁶² For a study of some of these practices see Holden, *Hindu Divorce*.

⁶³ Dhagamwar gives examples of horrific punishments in the non-formal system, sometimes carried out on the spot by those present. More troubling are the examples where the state criminal system, through the courts, condones such ad hoc and inhumane punishments. See Dhagamwar, 'Invasion of Criminal Law by Religion, Custom and Family Law', p.1489. Cf Nandita Haksar, 'The Political Issues', in *Seminar*, Vol.39 (1996), p.441.

analysis it does not follow unproblematically that when formal laws do apply, women gain gender parity. We will return to this issue later.

The third space concerns the manner of enforcement of legislation and the issue is whether this space is accessible by the women at whom it is aimed. In the case of Hindu law, the history of reforms shows that the impetus for reform did not come from women.[64] Rather it was the state which pursued gender equality through legislation, albeit in half measures as discussed above. Although it is clear that women have not benefited widely from these reforms, such recognition is preferable to no recognition at all, and the critique of state-enacted reforms must continue apace. It is important to separate the two issues of granting legislative equality and the realisation of those rights in the lived-in spaces.

Decisions on the manner of enforcement require reflection about the lived-in spaces of women, including how they are likely to respond to different modes of enforcement. There is ample evidence that Hindu women have not taken recourse to litigation to realise their property rights,[65] but there is disagreement about why Hindu women, in their capacity as daughters/sisters, have not exercised their legal rights.[66] Often the answers are found in the mismatch between legal and social mores.[67] Thus a common argument is that the law is so distant from accepted ethical behavior that it cannot have any real effect on people's actual practices. In Hindu (and even Indian) society a sister would sacrifice her right to property in her father's estate rather than disrupt social expectations of how she should behave towards her brothers, which is how Reena Patel explains why the grant of legislative and constitutional rights to Indian (Hindu) women has failed to enable them to access their property.[68] She argues that the rights legitimised through legal norms must take account of historical, political and cultural contexts, and that only laws that reflect and substantiate wider social relations are likely to be successful.

Significantly she directs her argument at legal analyses and says that these need to move beyond positive laws and take into account women's particular locations and the constitutive realities of their lives. We agree that the analyses of explanations for the success or failure of law reforms are important, as otherwise the discussion becomes a simplistic argument for or against law reform as a strategy of change. Rather than adopt an instrumental view of the law, it is more important to understand the mutually-constitutive relationship between the law and society. It is important to focus on the fact that the legislation itself makes an assumption

---

[64] See Parashar, *Women and Family Law Reform in India*; Jana Everett, 'All the Women Were Hindu and All the Muslims Were Men: State, Identity Politics and Gender', in *Economic and Political Weekly*, Vol.36, no.23 (2001), pp.2071–80; and Mytheli Sreenivas, 'Conjugality and Capital: Gender, Families and Property Under Colonial Law in India', in *Journal of Asian Studies*, Vol.63, no.4 (2004), pp.937–60.

[65] Bina Agarwal, *A Field of One's Own: Gender and Land Rights in South Asia* (Cambridge: Cambridge University Press, 1994); and Shrimati Basu, *She Comes to Take Her Rights* (New Delhi: Kali for Women, 2001). See also Rochona Majumdar, 'History of Women's Rights: A Non-Historicist Reading', in *Economic and Political Weekly*, Vol.38, no.22 (2003), pp.2130–4 for the argument that women gaining increasing property rights but then not claiming them are not contradictory developments but two versions of modernity.

[66] Basu, *She Comes to Take Her Rights*; and U. Sharma, *Women, Work and Property in North-West India* (London: Tavistock, 1980).

[67] This is another site where anthropologists, sociologists and legal writers attribute very different significance to the existing diversity of community practices. It is one of the areas where much more inter-disciplinary dialogues need to take place. See S. Basu, 'Judges of Normality: Mediating Marriage in the Family Courts of Kolkata, India', in *Signs*, Vol.37, no.2 (2012), pp.469–92 for a critique of the feminist move to alternative dispute resolution. She argues that feminists must establish substantive rather than innovative gender justice.

[68] Reena Patel, 'Hindu Women's Property Rights in India: A Critical Appraisal', in *Third World Quarterly*, Vol.27, no.7 (2006), pp.1255–68; see also Reena Patel, *Hindu Women's Property Rights in Rural India, Law, Labour and Culture in Action* (Aldershot: Ashgate, 2007).

about men being primarily property owners and thereby plays a double role of setting new norms of gender equality as well as bolstering traditional patterns of property ownership. Again it requires engaging with the lived-in spaces of women and reflecting upon these before decisions can be made about the design of future law reforms.

It is salutary to remind ourselves that family laws are not necessarily religious laws, as discussed above. The RPLs are very much laws enforced by the state. Moreover both the formal laws and the RPLs are complicit in allowing customary practices to operate. The existence of customary practices restricts the domain of state law (e.g. criminal law) but these customary practices are neither religious nor legal. Customs are a category of their own and it is always the case that state law chooses whether to recognise or not recognise customs. Dhagamwar has demonstrated how the idea of family law as a special kind of law creates the space for imposing on some women customs and penalties that are criminal in a literal sense. To call the resulting diversity of practices post-modern diversity,[69] or legal pluralism,[70] does not yield any analytical advantage, especially since the very existence of customs is allowed by the country's legal system. In view of this lived-in reality of women, when scholars deploy the concept of the RPLs they are necessarily complicit in maintaining gender disadvantages for women.[71] To counter this assertion by pointing out that sometimes customs better serve women's interests is a red herring.[72] The point is that such lauding of customs deflects attention from the fact that the state is maintaining its prerogative to decide when and how to legislatively modify these rules. Moreover, the main issue of what might constitute gender justice for women, independent of the discourse of the RPLs, once again fails to gain serious attention. The task of legal scholars is to interrogate any argument that perpetuates the hierarchical status quo.

In the slightly different context of colonial India, Mytheli Sreenivas demonstrates that the demands for property rights for women were shaped by discourses that linked conjugality, capitalist development and modernity. Legal reformers strongly supported the modernity of male individual property rights while failing to challenge the 'tradition' of joint ownership when discussing the property rights of women.[73] The same selective respect for tradition could be the explanation for not abolishing the institution of the Hindu joint family in the 2005 amendment to the HSA. It is important to remember, however, that this example is not an illustration of the inherent incapacity of the law to deliver gender parity, or even that the 'cost'

---

[69] Menski describes the existence of a multiplicity of practices under the banner of Hindu Law as post-modern Hindu Law. See Werner Menski, 'Postmodern Hindu Law', Centre for Applied South Asian Studies [www.casas.org.uk/papers/pdfpapers/pomolaw.pdf, accessed 24 Nov. 2011]; see also Prakash Shah, *Legal Pluralism in Conflict: Coping with Cultural Diversity in Law* (London: Glass House, 2005).

[70] There is a developing trend for writers to describe the existence of formal and informal rules in the area of personal relations as an example of legal pluralism, but this loose characterisation of any set of rules as legal pluralism yields no analytical advantage. See Karin Bates, 'The Hindu Succession Act: One Law, Plural Identities', in *Journal of Legal Pluralism and Unofficial Law*, Vol.50 (2004), pp.119–44; and Christoph Eberhard and Nidhi Gupta, 'Legal Pluralism in India; An Introduction', in *Indian Socio-Legal Journal*, Vol.31 (2005), pp.1–10.

[71] See also Everett, 'All the Women Were Hindu and All the Muslims Were Men', p.2079, where she says that when women's organisations agreed to a religiously-based identity, both Hindu (AIWC advocated the Hindu Code Bill) and Muslim (support for the application of the Shariat Act and separate electorates) organisations became more vulnerable to patriarchal domination.

[72] See for example Gopika Solanki, *Adjudication in Religious Family Laws: Cultural Accommodation, Legal Pluralism and Gender Equality in India* (Cambridge: Cambridge University Press, 2011), for an argument that by the state sharing adjudicative functions and authority with other societal sources, it can potentially balance cultural rights and gender equality.

[73] See also Sreenivas, 'Conjugality and Capital'.

of such interference in Hindu tradition is too high a price to pay. Rather it is an illustration of the need for legal scholars to recognise legal reform as a site for contesting the meanings of the law, and for that reason a site where they must be engaged.[74]

This involves seeing the law as a process, and recognising that the law constitutes, and is in turn constituted by, social practices. The enunciation of legal norms and concepts in turn affects women's lived-in spaces. For example, mandating gender quotas in parliament or on corporate boards will be most effective where there is societal support for the idea, because it is this support that induced legal reform in the first place. In such instances the state is using its power to create top-down law while acknowledging support for such laws within spatial settings. However where the law does not reflect custom and norms, the challenge for the state is to consider carefully not only the space of law-making, but also the multiple spaces whereby knowledge of the law, commitment to the law and enforcement of the law can be increased. Ideally such consideration will be a continuous process, whereby the state can engage with the law in its multiple spaces. Where the law is based on custom, the state can add its weight to enforcement of the practice, contributing to the effective enforcement of the law. On the other hand, where the practice is reprehensible, the state will have a role in how it can use its normative force to discourage such practices. We see the role of the state as the important one of steering other actors and institutions, the direction of which will change depending on the spaces being considered. On the one hand this may be asking too much of the state—to be reflexive and selectively directing institutions towards universal norms in a pluralist legal environment, while at the same time being respectful of difference.[75] However on the other hand we see this role as necessary for dealing with the multiple challenges of a globalising world, such as ensuring religious freedom, providing security, enabling environmental protections and recognising same-sex relationships and so on.[76]

Legal feminists need to take on board the insight of critical geographers that spatial dimensions matter, and that the spaces in which women exist is the context that any legal initiative has to consider. Where necessary, policies and incentives that encourage commitment to the law and increase the capacity for enforcement should be negotiated as part of the package of law reform. So too, the argument invoking the fragility of minority identity requires closer scrutiny to enquire how this argument functions to insulate practices from being judged. In every instance, the objective of critique should be to create discursive spaces for articulating what a fair or gender-just family law might look like. We see the state as having an important role here, one which is observant of these spaces and can be reflexive in moving towards gender justice. While this does not mean that the state has to resort in all instances to top-down universal laws, it does require a nuanced approach where the normative force of the state can support customary practices where appropriate and steer these practices towards fairer ones where they are not.

---

[74] Feminist scholars are increasingly moving beyond the relativism of post-structural thought and exploring the transformative potential of discourse. See the review article by Linda Alcoff, 'Philosophy Matters: A Review of Recent Work in Feminist Philosophy', in *Signs*, Vol.25, no.3 (2000), pp.841–2. Basu makes the same point in her 'Judges of Normality' about the need to focus on substantive rather than innovative justice.

[75] Gunther Teubner, 'Substantive and Reflexive Elements in Modern Law', in *Law & Society Review*, Vol.17 (1983), p.239.

[76] Jean L. Cohen, *Regulating Intimacy: A New Legal Paradigm* (Princeton: Princeton University Press, 2002); Peer Zumbansen, 'Law After the Welfare State: Formalism, Functionalism and Ironic Turn of Reflexive Law', in *The American Journal of Comparative Law*, Vol.56, no.3 (2008), pp.769–808; and Charles Sabel and Jonathan Zeitlin, 'Learning from Difference: The New Architecture of Experimentalist Governance in the EU', in *European Law Journal*, Vol.14, no.3 (2008), p.271.

In conclusion we argue that it is the responsibility of all legal feminists and other scholars to be conscious of their role in either legitimising the status quo, or creating discursive possibilities for change. As discussed above, the state has introduced legislative changes in the relative rights of brothers and sisters in the Hindu law of succession and society has not become dysfunctional as a result. The main issue, therefore, is not a choice between the two questions of whether it is worthwhile to pursue equal property rights for all women, or whether religious diversity prevails in the form of the RPLs with the possibility of consequent gender inequalities. Even while accepting that formulating perfect laws may be an impossible task, it is time for Indian legal feminists to re-engage with the task of creating a discursive space for articulating what may constitute fair family laws for everyone.

Desirable or Dysfunctional? Family in Recent Indian English-Language Fiction

PAUL SHARRAD

Contemporary Indian English-language fiction marks both a continuous focus on the Indian family as central to society, and also a break from the traditional socialisations of family life. Shifting away from the former calls for reform of marital conventions to accommodate individual needs and many recent novels show families to be dysfunctional sites of domestic violence, incest, extramarital affairs and divorce. Moreover, under the impact of better levels of education, urbanisation and expatriation, the novels of young professional experience tend to portray one's peers as a surrogate family. The idea of family, however, persists.

In the period when Commonwealth literature was attempting to establish the difference of national cultures from the British canon, Meenakshi Mukherjee pointed to the perception of early Indian novelists that South Asian family structures mitigated against working in a form based around individual characters.[1] Where arranged marriage, the greater importance of the extended family unit, and caste affiliations had more social force, stories and their resolutions would have to look different from those of Thomas Hardy, George Eliot or Henry James. If we think of the world of Jane Austen, this is evidently a difference of degree rather than an absolute distinction, but Sudhir Kakar has also elaborated upon the strength of ties in India between child and parent that moderate teenage rebellion and the radical break of adult individuation that the West has come to see as normal.[2] The stress on cultural specificity and local aesthetics of Commonwealth literature and its variants, matched at the local end of the critical scale by nationalistic insistence on authenticity and tradition, kept literary treatments of the Indian family more or less centre stage, but also, perhaps, under-examined in that they took for granted the general social grounding of particular fictions.

In recent times, however, we find what appears to be a major shift in outlook. Aravind Adiga's *The White Tiger*, to take the most striking example, shows the rise of a new kind of entrepreneur, breaking caste and class bounds through acts of violence that include the sacrifice of almost his entire family.[3] Its protagonist, Balram, is the modern individual par excellence, and for all his extreme facets, is perhaps indicative of a new move away from the family-based novels of the past. Critics might well argue that Adiga is an expatriate freshly returned to his homeland and, therefore, he constitutes an exceptional case. However, if we

---

[1] Meenakshi Mukherjee, *Realism and Reality: The Novel and Society in India* (Delhi: Oxford University Press, 1985), pp.7–9.
[2] Sudhir Kakar, *The Inner World: A Psychoanalytic Study of Childhood and Society in India* (Delhi: Oxford University Press, 2nd ed., 1981).
[3] Aravind Adiga, *The White Tiger* (London: Atlantic Books, 2008).

look around, it is evident that the Indian English novel reflects a significant change of outlook when it comes to family life and depictions of how it socialises its members. Vikram Chandra's 'Kama' depicts the emotional complexities of divorce and swinging couples in *Love and Longing in Bombay*, while Arundhati Roy reveals the viciously dysfunctional claustrophobia of family life in a minority community in *The God of Small Things*. There is incest at the heart of a number of recent novels (Raj Kamal Jha's *The Blue Bedspread*, Akhil Sharma's *An Obedient Father*),[4] and extramarital affairs abound (Ammu's transgressive affair with the low-caste Velu in *The God of Small Things* is merely a dramatic highlight in a range of books, including Nilita Vachani's *HomeSpun*, Manju Kapur's *Difficult Daughters*, Namita Gokhale's *The Book of Shadows*, going back to Anita Desai's *Fire on the Mountain*).[5]

Conservative critics no doubt fulminate against this trend, seeing it as symptomatic of the decline in morality, loss of nationalist ideals enshrined in Gandhi's principles of selfless service, godless Western influence, and so on. However, as the early criticism of 'feminist' writing shows, this has been a complaint levelled at anyone daring to write about things that orthodoxy hypocritically will not discuss: female dissatisfaction within marriage, for example. Subaltern historians and novels such as *Difficult Daughters*, *HomeSpun* and even the tame humour of R.K. Narayan, also reveal that a good deal of obfuscation, self-delusion and moral failing was in play amongst individuals supporting the Gandhian movement, just as films like *Rang de Basanti* show the cynical perversion of those principles in more recent times by people in power.[6] In all of these works, however, the stage on which the conflicts of communities, history, gender interests and morality are enacted is the family. And insofar as the novel remains linked to realistic depictions of society and human existence, it continues to set cultural ideals against actual engagements with them shaped by social movements nationally and globally.

Perhaps, we could set up alongside the old critical models of Indian fiction that divide *bhasa* (vernacular) and Anglophone, *desi* (local) and diasporic, another in which novels conveying continuity between individual, family, clan and nation are distinguished from those in which the seams of such a social fabric stretch and split. Like other binaries, this one is an untidy one, allowing some crossover, but it comes down as a contrast between work in which the family remains a primary vehicle for socialisation and finding identity on the one hand, and work in which the family is a prison, something obsolete or, more significantly, an irrelevance on the other. The division is not an historical one: some of the earliest work in Indian fiction protests against the failings of arranged marriage, the restrictions around widowhood, and sati.[7] Equally, modern urban novels, whether locally-produced or written by expatriate Indians, can still centre on the family as the site of all being (a work such as Manju

---

[4] Vikram Chandra, *Love and Longing in Bombay* (London: Faber and Faber, 1998); Arundhati Roy, *The God of Small Things* (London: Flamingo, 1997); Raj Kamal Jha, *The Blue Bedspread* (London: Picador, 1999); and Akhil Sharma, *An Obedient Father* (London: Faber and Faber, 2001).

[5] Namita Gokhale, *The Book of Shadows* (New Delhi: Penguin, 2001); and Anita Desai, *Fire on the Mountain* (Harmondsworth: Penguin, 1981).

[6] Manju Kapur, *Difficult Daughters* (New Delhi: Penguin, 1998); Nilita Vachani, *HomeSpun* (New Delhi: Penguin, 2005); R.K. Narayan, *The Vendor of Sweets* (Harmondsworth: Penguin, 1983); and *Rang de Basanti* (dir. Rakeysh Omprakash Mehra, UTV, 2006).

[7] Chandani Lokugé (ed.), *Saguna: The First Autobiographical Novel Written in English by an Indian Woman* (New Delhi: Oxford University Press, 1998); *India Calling, The Memories of Cornelia Sorabji, India's First Woman Barrister* (New Delhi: Oxford University Press, 2001); *Ratanbai: A High-Caste Hindu Child-Wife* (New Delhi: Oxford University Press, 2004).

Kapur's *Home*, for example, or Amulya Malladi's *Serving Crazy with Curry*), even when those families encompass divorce, suicide attempts, unhappy marriages and affairs.[8]

That said, it must be admitted that certain modernising trends in society have a direct correlation with those novels in which family is no longer central to people's formation. Education can be a contradictory element in shaping family members. Obviously, it played a major role in building the intelligentsia and merchant classes on which the management of independent India rests. We can clearly see the mutually-sustaining connection of family and politics in the Nehru/Gandhi dynasty, even when (especially when) a member of it like Nayantara Sahgal writes novels critiquing its power.[9] But educating one's children to improve the family's social prospects can also lead to their alienation from the family and to the restructuring of the family. When the elites of India began sending their sons to colleges to advance their prospects, the colleges started boarding facilities in part because the young men were often married by the time they reached senior school and lived in busy extended families and could not concentrate on their reading.[10] We can see this reflected in the out-of-kilter life of Jagan in Narayan's *The Vendor of Sweets*: Jagan's education is disrupted by his student activism against the Raj, and when his family marries him off to settle him down, he fails to gain his university degree because he is too distracted by connubial delights and family quarrels when his wife does not immediately conceive.

Jagan gives up and becomes a shop owner, whereas others go to college, acquire degrees, enter professions, demand educated wives who can mix openly in society and participate in social reform (as in Prem Chand's story, 'From Both Sides'), and so set in train a number of social changes to family life.[11] Educated families curbed the number of children they had so that they could afford to give them the same level of schooling, educated girls did not have to pay the large dowries demanded of other families, the age of marriage for educated women rose,[12] and so the cycle perpetuated itself to the point that families wanting to appear modern and liberal could show off by not demanding a dowry at all, while young educated people, increasingly mixing on co-educational campuses and spreading across the country and then overseas as they found work, could push for the right to choose their own partners.

This process is reflected in Gurcharan Das' conventional saga, *A Fine Family*, in which a senior judge has to persuade his daughter, Tara, to accept an arranged marriage rather than pursue an infatuation with her cousin.[13] Her father wryly notes that as soon as the young man's outgoing and outspoken nature leads him to jail as an independence fighter, his stakes in the marriage market fall, though his stocks with romantic girls go up: 'You admire heroes from a distance thought Bauji; you don't marry your daughters to them'. Accordingly, he finds a safer option for his own daughter.[14] The book seems to support the idea of the arranged marriage as more stable and superior to the modern love match, and though we see Tara becoming rather brittle and materialistic in reaction against her husband's non-worldliness,

---

[8] Manju Kapur, *Home* (New Delhi: Random House, 2006); and Amulya Malladi, *Serving Crazy with Curry* (London: Piatkus, 2004).

[9] Nayantara Sahgal, *Rich like Us* (London: Heinemann, 1985).

[10] David Baker, 'St. Stephen's College, Delhi, 1881–1997: An "Alexandria on the Banks of the Jamuna"?', in Mushirul Hassan (ed.), *Knowledge, Power and Politics: Educational Institutions in India* (New Delhi: Lotus/Roli, 1998), p.73.

[11] Prem Chand, *Deliverance and Other Stories* (trans. David Rubin) (New Delhi: Penguin, 1988).

[12] Narayani Gupta and Sheila Uttam Singh, 'The Interior and the Exterior: Indraprastha College for Women', in Mushirul Hassan (ed.), *Knowledge, Power and Politics: Educational Institutions in India* (New Delhi: Lotus/Roli, 1998), p.152.

[13] Gurcharan Das, *A Fine Family* (New Delhi: Penguin, 1990), pp.61–2.

[14] *Ibid.*, pp.83, 87–8.

they do manage moments of tenderness, especially when united in the beauty of Shimla's natural settings. Tara's husband, Seva Ram, though sharing a Punjabi male view of women as naturally weak and flighty (the author's words), admires his wife for her education and she, in turn, appreciates his earnest idealism.[15] Her education complements her husband's rise through the civil service and they eventually move to Delhi post-Independence. Tara's education comes back into focus when, as an enthusiastic supporter of Nehru's modernisation, she celebrates the passing of a bill allowing divorce and remarriage, abolishing dowry and requiring equal distribution of property amongst sons and daughters. Although he has raised her along principles of equity, her father is hurt that she protests when he attempts to give more of the family wealth to her brother.[16]

As the title of the book suggests, family supplies a strong binding support, backed up by education. Cousin Karan becomes the beloved uncle of Tara's son, Arjun, instructing him in all kinds of things. Karan has given up his politics for scholarly and artistic pursuits, including reading the *Upanishads* and giving sitar recitals. Arjun goes to a Jesuit school and is the typical offspring of an upwardly mobile intelligentsia. His mother, like a good citizen of the new national elite, wants him to go on to:

> a fine college in Delhi like St. Stephens, where he would acquire the necessary intellectual equipment, but not necessarily become a scholar. Then he would be ready to join the civil service or one of the professions, or industry or any of the pleasant niches for which the post-Independence Indian bourgeoisie groomed its young. After Arjun was settled she would marry him to a good Punjabi girl with the same background and education.... And she hoped he would want to repeat the same process with his children. It was important to her that he should have more money than they did, so he would be able to send his children to boarding schools like Mayo or Doon, and if possible to a good university abroad, such as the Ivy League colleges in America or Oxford and Cambridge in England. This was Tara's recipe for an enviably happy life.[17]

His father is less inclined to accept such a materialist vision and deplores Arjun's contact with the socialite Mehta family, who 'drink...smoke [and] eat meat'.[18] His grandfather is more of an indulgent sensualist, disinclined to withdraw from the world, even though he is now seventy. But he too worries that Arjun will be hurt by Priti, the *femme fatale* Mehta daughter who leads the young man on, but who also has a crush on the charismatic Karan. With his mother's emotional drive, his father's principled patience and his Jesuit schooling, Arjun eventually becomes a successful salesman for a Mumbai pharmaceutical company. There he eventually meets up again with Priti, who has come there to look for a job. They decide to marry (and their daughters do go to a boarding school).

Those daughters, however, are unlikely to produce the same kind of story as the older generations in *A Fine Family*. Arjun and Priti live in a Mumbai that is depicted as a positive energy source for progress and freedom.[19] India's rate of urbanisation suggests that this is a widespread view and, although the mega-cities have since provoked less positive representations (such as Vikram Chandra's or Vikas Swarup's depictions of the gangland

---

[15] *Ibid.*, pp.147–8.
[16] *Ibid.*, pp.168–70.
[17] *Ibid.*, pp.217–8.
[18] *Ibid.*, p.219.
[19] *Ibid.*, p.345.

violence that goes along with the real estate and IT boom and the movie industry)[20] and begun to tail off in growth, other cities are still pulling in rural youth wanting to improve their prospects and young educated men and women chasing start-up industries and cheaper accommodation.[21] Rohinton Mistry shows us (somewhat gloomily in *A Fine Balance*) how, in the metropolis, families can close themselves off against the world and also how people can create new modes of family to provide mutual support.[22] But if Arjun and Priti's children join this general push to the big cities, their socialisation is more likely to depend on their 'batch mates' in school and college, and if they become the yuppie urbanites now consuming books like Chetan Bhagat's *One Night @ the Call Centre*, they will rely more on their fellow professionals for solace, advice and potential partners than on their families. (Bhagat's call-centre gang still reproduces some of the socialisation patterns of old, particularly daughters warring with emotional blackmail from mothers wanting to marry them off or with domineering mothers-in-law, but the result is that those daughters break free with the support of their peers.)[23]

Karan Bajaj's *Keep Off the Grass* can be taken as a fair sample of the world of this 'Facebook generation'.[24] In a seemingly autobiographical picaresque philosophical comedy of stereotypical characters and situations, Samrat leaves his successful career on Wall Street and his American upbringing to seek his fortune in India. He joins the Indian Institute of Management in Bangalore to get an MBA, is blown away by the competitive culture of the higher education system, and hangs out with the cynical son of a minister and an ex-soldier burnt out after fighting in Kargil. They drink and smoke dope through their course, swapping superficial philosophies until the inevitable police bust, the predictable trip to an ashram, and Samrat finding satisfaction in selling toiletries to Varanasi traders. He goes back to his family roots in India to take a course on Indian society and learns some of the things that make him tick, including the importance of family and social connections.[25] At the same time, Samrat studiously avoids making contact with his relations in India, declines to go back to his family in the USA and, in the most successful moment of the book, goes on a pilgrimage to the mountains to find wisdom at the feet of—Ruskin Bond![26] We learn we must be who we are, belong where we feel we need to be and other such profundities. Samrat does discover his 'roots', but only through reading. Indian writing at first seems pretentious and unreal, but Narayan and Upamanyu Chatterjee's *English, August* speak to him.[27] Bond, as a foreign resident, offers him a model for anchoring his diasporic self. Rejecting the heady but alienating heights of the globalised corporate world, Samrat resolves to settle for a 'middle-brow' straightforwardness in which no one in the diasporic world will ask him when he is going back home, no one will mispronounce his name or oblige him to read 'confused

---

[20] Vikram Chandra, *Red Earth and Pouring Rain* (London: Faber and Faber, 1995); *Sacred Games* (London: Faber and Faber, 2006); and Vikas Swarup, *Slumdog Millionaire* (London: Doubleday, 2005; Black Swan, 2006); *Six Suspects* (London: Doubleday, 2008; Black Swan, 2009).

[21] R.B. Bhagat, 'Urbanisation in India: A Demographic Reappraisal' [http://www.iussp.org/Brazil2001/s80/S83_03_Bhagat.pdf, accessed 6 Dec. 2011]; and Chetan Chauhan, 'Urbanisation in India Faster than Rest of World', *Hindustan Times* (27 June 2007) [http://www.hindustantimes.com/News-Feed/India/Urbanisation-in-India-faster-than-restof-the-world/Article1-233279.aspx, accessed 6 Dec. 2011].

[22] Rohinton Mistry, *A Fine Balance* (London: Faber and Faber, 1995).

[23] Chetan Bhagat, *One Night @ the Call Centre* (New Delhi: Rupa, 2005).

[24] Karan Bajaj, *Keep Off the Grass* (Noida: Harper Collins, 2008).

[25] *Ibid.*, p.179.

[26] *Ibid.*, p.255.

[27] Upamanyu Chatterjee, *English, August* (Kolkata: Rupa, 1988).

immigrant fiction...about how much the author understood my dislocation in the US'.[28] *English, August* is a book to feel good about being Indian in which family seems not to feature, but in which the pulling together of alternative means of socialisation, the construction of a personalised 'family', is the key.

In such an atomised, urban, consumerist and corporate world, if one's marriage is unsatisfactory and one's social set too caught up in its own hip-ness, one might turn for help to the personal help industry of psychologists. Anupa Mehta's *The Waiting Room* is perhaps indicative of the new middle-class professional world's experience.[29] It centres on a cross-section of unhappy women who go to a psychologist for counselling and fall into a trap of sexual abuse. One of them, Maya Roy, conducts a series of interviews with fellow victims and writes her diaries as a means of working through her emotional trauma, complicated by her estranged husband's suspected abuse of their daughter. Beneath her determined journalistic objectification of her abuse, Maya is a troubled soul, and this finds an outlet in successive affairs coloured by 'new age' spiritual hunger, first in the form of Tantric practices and then in a more sublime access to Sufism. After her death (of a broken heart or, as the text puts it, 'acute melancholia' and a body worn out by her quest for serenity), Maya's story is pieced together from documents by her long-time admirer from a distance, Aniket (Ket) Nair. Ket not only conserves her memory, he also ends up with custody of her child.

The book would have been voyeuristic and pornographic if it had not been written so clinically and with such an air of personal therapy about it. Formula devices such as insistent adjectives and brand names with each noun are offset by the evident seriousness behind the story and the apt reproductions of different speech patterns from yuppie women, post-feminist cynics and so on. What is of interest in the context of this study is the total failure of family for nearly all these women. Although one of them does have an understanding husband, his task is merely to keep her psychosis under control with nurses and drugs.[30] Jaya Singh, a Delhi socialite, resigns herself to her fate to maintain material comfort within a marital relationship that includes her abuser, her husband's friend.[31] The young Tara has been used as a surrogate wife by her widower father and is totally cynical about all relationships. Maya's husband 'flogs' her, verbally if not also physically, Anahita's husband instantly divorces her. Maya's childhood is marred by a mentally-disturbed mother who never holds her and a cook who molests her at night.[32] If this book has anything to do with the socialisation process, it must be read, like *The God of Small Things*, as a 'terrible example' of how dysfunctional families reproduce themselves with minor differences across generations. Like Anahita, Maya's support comes from old friends such as Ket and from children. They are the break in the chain of family tyranny. Another means of re-socialisation for Maya (though, in her case, it ambiguously perpetuates some aspects of her neurosis) is the comfort of religious yearning.

Anupa Mehta's 'new age' spiritualism is a substitute mode of belonging that replaces her character's quest for alternative family via unhelpful bonding with a psychologist. One hesitates to read too much into this book, but Maya's name and the recurrent figure of the 'Ideal Beloved', Mir, suggests the longevity of the Bhakti/Sufi poetic conceit that we find earlier in Kamala Das' poetry of female anguish.[33] Paradoxically, the Hindu concepts and

---

[28] *Ibid.*, p.257.
[29] Anupa Mehta, *The Waiting Room* (New Delhi: Penguin, 2007).
[30] *Ibid.*, pp.82–4.
[31] *Ibid.*, pp.55–61.
[32] *Ibid.*, pp.84–6, 43, 78, 14–5, 18, respectively.
[33] Kamala Das, *Summer in Calcutta* (New Delhi: Rajinder Paul, 1965); *The Old Playhouse and other Poems* (Chennai: Orient Longman, 1973).

practices that tie the woman to either a secure or stultifying domestic life also provide the models for female liberation in Bhakti figures such as Mirabai and in transcendental symbols of fulfilled desire as in the Radha-Krishna relationship. Das flees a traumatic induction to marriage and subsequent neglect by her husband, then faces the melancholy aftermath of affairs. The bitter burning away of desire through physical indulgence is counterpointed with the unending hope for a fulfilling relationship in which the individual is sublimated into the ideal half of a spiritualised love figured as Radha-Krishna. We can note that such a personal consolation of non-carnal emotional union is adopted by women who are resolutely presenting themselves as modern and who inhabit a world of cities. Anupa Mehta's characters all move into and out of Mumbai, and Das was removed from her Kerala origins to spend most of her creative life in Kolkata and Delhi. In such a context, poetic religion offers a way to transcend the disruptions of time and space, the weaknesses of personality, and to find belonging and identity in cultural tradition. So when Priti, in Gurcharan Das' *A Fine Family*, seeks to resolve an inner restlessness that neither life experience, city living nor marriage can assuage, she turns to the guru her father-in-law has followed and retreats to his ashram. This particular guru is a modern thinker of multi-faith sympathies and Nehruvian practicalities, combining meditation with hard labour to promote a green revolution in the Punjab.[34] The novel approves of him because his way is compatible with its secular, humanist and democratic ideals. Such ideals, however, begin to displace the consolations of religion for the next generation, if we believe all the popular fiction of the 'chick lit' and 'IT lit' kind. (Again, Chetan Bhagat's book is almost entirely secular apart from the author's use of the divine as a self-aware narrative trick.) In the more literary work of Siddharth Dhanvant Shangvi, too, family for the younger Bombayite seems to be friends or nothing, and though *The Lost Flamingoes of Bombay* is haunted by longing, religion is not available as a surrogate family, nor is education a bulwark against misfortune or disappointment.[35]

The other option available to contemporary Indians is migration. Again, this is something a family might do to enhance its place in the world, either in terms of furthering education and career or making strategic marriages for children. But in the very act of 'going global', the family threatens itself with fragmentation and its individual members may face as much anomie as excitement. We have only to think of Jhumpa Lahiri's work and the break in communication in *The Namesake* that causes Gogol/Nikhil to wander aimlessly in search of an identity to see the cost to family and selfhood, quite apart from any hostility towards the migrant from the host population.[36] If there is a home-grown element of existentialist alienation, from Anita Desai and Arun Joshi[37] through to Upamanyu Chatterjee, in which family ceases to provide sustaining bonds, it is complemented, perhaps magnified, by diasporic writing (the central character in *Red Earth and Pouring Rain*, for example, is aimless in America and bored back home until the fantastic erupts into his world and he is progressively reinserted into his family, culture and community).[38]

When societies begin to pluralise and cross into transnational networks, the comfortable structures of class and family begin to take on new, flexible forms and there is often a political division between those benefiting from and celebrating the change, and those crying for a return to or preservation of 'family values'. Fiction can, wittingly or not, dramatise the splits, anxieties and freedoms of such a transition. Before he ceased being a globe-trotting

---

[34] Das, *A Fine Family*, pp.148, 292.
[35] Siddharth Dhanvant Shangvi, *The Lost Flamingoes of Bombay* (New Delhi: Viking/Penguin, 2009).
[36] Jhumpa Lahiri, *The Namesake* (London: Harper, 2004).
[37] Arun Joshi, *The Foreigner* (New York: Asia Publishing House, 1968).
[38] Chandra, *Red Earth and Pouring Rain*.

non-resident Indian (NRI), Shashi Tharoor mounted an apparently post-modern, but basically liberal, critique of Hindu fundamentalist sectarianism in his fictionalisation of communal violence. *Riot* deals with the Hindutva idea of nation as a close-knit cultural family crossing with nation as a multicultural space to produce communal warfare akin to inter-family vendettas.[39] There is little doubt that it scorns the self-seeking petit-bourgeois town politician who manipulates cultural differences to create a platform for his own career, but the characters set up as maintaining the state's authority are at best compromised by cynicism (in the figure of a foul-mouthed, hard-drinking Sikh police officer) and moral laxity (in the central male character, Lakshman, the district magistrate). The political events in Zalilgarh that result in riot and the seemingly-related death of an American aid worker are framed by a 'back-story' that charts how a dysfunctional foreign family indirectly comes to threaten the stability of the Indian governing class, and the novel ends with the secularised district magistrate closing down his 'modern' affair and suppressing the full story of his lover's death. Although shot through with ironies, such as the devout wife of the magistrate playing a part in the tragic denouement, the story's resolution seems to affirm traditional ideas about the sanctity of 'family values', which rest on stereotypical views of higher philosophical Hindu beliefs that the rest of the book seems to question.

A similar anxiety about letting go of old family structures can be found more overtly in Bharati Mukherjee's *Desirable Daughters*.[40] It is more apparent because the writer sets forth her own expatriation as the basis for a fictional quest for personal and family identity in Tara, a modern Indian divorcee resident in the USA. Mukherjee has celebrated the American idea of the melting pot, the adventure of migrant self-transformation through which American society is also transformed ('American Dreamer').[41] Tara, who continually takes on new personae, mocks her sister's 'ethnic exploitationism' in becoming a representative Indian media personality amongst the diasporic ghetto of Queens in New York, and criticises the barren lifestyle of Mumbai elite couples as represented by her other sister, but ultimately reconnects with them and with their parents' and grandparents' family story. That story is also part of the Indian national story and is itself subject to constant renewal and change, but the final vision of the novel seems to be an essentially conservative one, and the protagonist is reunited with her 'proper' Indian husband, and both are reconciled with their gay son. Like some of the other books mentioned here, traditional religious belief supplies the current that carries disparate elements towards a relatively harmonious ending. The Indian family can undergo all kinds of changes, but will accommodate them and spread to encompass the world. The same message comes through in the more popular American novel of diasporic family life, Malladi's *Serving Crazy with Curry*. This does not require reconnection with the homeland or even any mode of religious belief. Three generations are now resident in one place in the USA, all raised in professions such as medicine and the army, then IT and journalism, and all work out their personal angst with and against each other in a commendably reasoned way, albeit with dramatic outbursts of passion and the help of some therapeutic cooking (complete with recipes).

Most of the books mentioned so far, whether set at home or (at home) abroad, share one thing: class. As Mistry's *A Fine Balance* points out, belonging to a rich family, however oppressive that can be, provides more protection against the machineries of fate than even education. Coming to a big city as a lowly village artisan, on the other hand, for all the

---

[39] Shashi Tharoor, *Riot* (New Delhi: Viking/Penguin, 2001).
[40] Bharati Mukherjee, *Desirable Daughters* (Crows Nest, NSW: Allen and Unwin, 2002).
[41] Bharati Mukherjee, 'American Dreamer', in *Mother Jones* (1997) [MotherJones.com/commentary/columns/1997/01/mukherjee.html, accessed 29 April 2004].

opportunities a city can offer, can end in disaster and street beggary. Migrating overseas to the bright lights of America can be a happy experience for the professional, but it can also result in the sweated labour, crowded slum accommodation and uncertain fate of someone like Biju in Kiran Desai's *The Inheritance of Loss*.[42] In Rupa Bajwa's *The Sari Shop*, the orphaned Ramchand survives so long as he allies himself with his surrogate family of shop workers. He learns this when he witnesses drunkenness and death in a colleague's family because they lose employment. Class difference is highlighted by Bajwa when she has Ramchand selling saris to the rich, giving him dreams above his station without any sense of their effect on him.[43] The same kind of class contrast produces rather more self-questioning for the middle-class protagonist in Shashi Deshpande's *The Binding Vine*, in which she is confronted with helping to care for the raped daughter of a neighbour.[44] In line with these books, Thrity Umrigar tracks the relentless fall in the fortunes of Bhima and her granddaughter, Maya, contrasting and connecting this to the impervious comfort of a rich Parsi family in Mumbai.[45]

Thrity Umrigar's *The Space between Us* shuttles back and forth in time and to and fro between Parsi employer Sera Dubash and servant Bhima. They are friends of a kind since Bhima has comforted Sera during years of marriage in which she has been tormented by a manipulative, possibly deranged, mother-in-law and beaten by her outwardly-charming husband. (The book shows the distorting effect of the traditional socialisation of boys, where they stay spoiled by and tied to their mothers to the point of being blind to their wives' torment after they marry or being violent towards them when they complain.) Bhima has also helped raise Sera's daughter, Dinaz, now married to Viraf and expecting a baby. The Dubashes are criticised by their social circle for being too generous to Bhima. Sera is flexible about her punctuality and the family provide support for her husband when he is hospitalised after an industrial accident and then for her granddaughter's education. Bhima's husband later takes to drink and deserts her, and her daughter dies of AIDS contracted from marrying an unknowing HIV carrier, who also dies. Bhima and her granddaughter, Maya, are forced to live in a slum hut and now Maya, at sixteen, is pregnant and sullen.

The book captures well the mixed gratitude and resentment felt by the now 65-year-old woman towards her benefactors. She knows that their kindness is mixed with arrogance and carelessness and self-interest, just as her friendship with Sera is marked by different cups and different seating arrangements when they share a tea break. Dinaz's outspoken championing of the rights of the poor to respect and fair play comes from the privilege of being able to be charitable without any real cost. The Dubashes arrange an abortion for Maya without really consulting either Bhima or Maya herself. It is as though 'the family' asserts its rights over all individuals attached to it. But when Bhima reveals that Maya's pregnancy is the result of Viraf seducing her, the one extended family suddenly becomes two families: the rich close ranks, Viraf frames Bhima for petty theft, and they dismiss her with accusations of ingratitude. We are left with two distinct kinds of family dysfunction: one a tragic decline into destitution, the other a stasis of hypocrisy resting on the privilege of class, education, wealth and, in this case, ethnic enclosure. This is not the urban liberation of Arjun's Mumbai in Das' *A Fine Family*; it is closer to the mixed fortunes and messy lives in *A Fine Balance*. What unifies the two classes, though, is a common insistence on education as the way up in society. This is not just a reflection of the Parsi ethos; Hindu peasant Bhima is determined that somehow she will keep Maya at school so that she will not have to share her fate. Religion seems not to feature as any

---

[42] Kiran Desai, *The Inheritance of Loss* (London: Penguin, 2006).
[43] Rupa Bajwa, *The Sari Shop* (New Delhi: Penguin, 2004).
[44] Shashi Deshpande, *The Binding Vine* (New York: The Feminist Press CUNY, 2001).
[45] Thrity Umrigar, *The Space between Us* (New Delhi: Harper Collins, 2006).

more than a neurotic fixation on ritual amongst the older Parsi women or indifference on Bhima's part. Consolation comes from Umrigar choosing a more formulaic approach than Mistry did. This includes clinging to an improbably hopeful ending for Bhima that owes something to the sentimentality of Tagore's 'Cabuliwallah', but her book is nonetheless another story of the modern urban family under stress.[46]

Pranav Jani observes: 'In literary analysis, positing the nation as being always already inimical to women's progress and liberation sets up a false dichotomy in which nation-oriented writing is regarded as necessarily uncritical of women's oppression while texts that challenge gender norms are inevitably anti- or postnational'.[47] This can be argued, but certainly some of the more recent crop of 'women's' novels (such as Manju Kapur's *Home*) tend to centre on individual and family as though the politics of nation and state are extraneous. The link in all this is the concept of nation as family and India as mother, and Gurcharan Das' *A Fine Family* maps the progress of its characters against the historical emergence of an independent nation, matching family crisis with Indira's suspension of regular political process, as does Rohinton Mistry's *A Fine Balance*.

Woman-centred writing that exposes the inherent violence in traditional patriarchal families (often proxy-managed by oppressive mothers-in-law) may seem to put aside inspection of the national family. Githa Hariharan and Shashi Deshpande come to mind as well as Anita Desai, but their work is in part a statement that the personal *is* the political, the family *is* the nation, rather than the reverse (a point made clear in *Difficult Daughters* and *HomeSpun*).[48] But exposing disruption and dysfunction in one can require contrastive distinction between the two. The nation may need to remain an ideal guaranteeing the rights of citizens so that individuals can claim justice within families. Or families may need to remain the source of belonging, harmony and identity to compensate for the inadequacies of the modern state. *The White Tiger* takes the extreme position where state and family are both corrupt and each is so bound up with the other that both are rejected in a radical act of self-definition as defection and alienation.

Balram is beset by two families: his birth family, run by a venal and cunning grandmother, and his employer's family, urban businessmen involved in national politics, who are also the rural overlords of his grandmother's village. For a while, the latter provide him with a means of survival and a kind of education when he escapes to Delhi, but between them and his birth family, he is going to be kept poor and in service wherever he lives. His families socialise him to be a blindly compliant rooster in a crowded rooster coop. This is not unlike the situation in *The God of Small Things*, where we see a vicious family enclave of domestic violence, sexual exploitation of female workers and oppression of divorcees so mixed in with communal prejudices, caste discrimination, state politics and global economics that there seems to be no escape.

Balram's solution is to reject both families. He is able to do this because people from the edge and outside of each group (an inspector visiting his village school, the bus conductor who can 'see the world', then a USA-educated son returning to his *zamindari* clan with his Westernised wife) give him the ability to see his situation, until he himself moves to the edge and, in correspondence with the Chinese premier, can comment disparagingly on his national 'family' as well. His position parallels the love-hate relationship of Adiga as a returned

---

[46] Rabindranath Tagore, *Collected Stories* (Chennai: Macmillan, 1974).

[47] Pranav Jani, *Decentering Rushdie: Cosmopolitanism and the Indian Novel in English* (Columbus: Ohio State University Press, 2010), p.104.

[48] Githa Hariharan, *The Thousand Faces of Night* (Harmondsworth: Penguin, 1992); and Shashi Deshpande, *The Dark Holds No Terrors* (New Delhi: Vikas, 1980); *That Long Silence* (London: Virago, 1988).

expatriate with his strange/familiar nation/family. Balram ironically ends up as ruthless and corrupt as those he criticises. If he kills off his links with the family of mafia-like feudal India to become a rootless entrepreneur in a new city of migrants from everywhere else, he 'speaks the same language' as the Thakurs and the politicians—money—and he begins to construct a new family for himself. His workers become his children; he becomes the local powerbroker and consoler of the hurt. And although he remains isolated from social contacts in his chandelier-lit bunker with money as the only glue holding his 'family' together, he has kept his nephew with him and is, in good middle-class aspirational mode, trying to get the boy a good education. Balram's secessionist national family of one is already assuming the form of India's modern technocratic and capitalist family.

So although the early alliance in fiction between family, culture and nation noted by Mukherjee is seen to break open as the nation itself undergoes change, with increased emphasis on the individual in urban, commercial and diasporic contexts, this is not altogether a single narrative of progress away from the family as a central concern in Indian English fiction. Some elements (such as the prominence of the mother/mother-in-law/matriarch) remain important. Attitudes to the overall shift vary from nostalgic reconstructions of old communal ideals to satiric exposés of the realities behind them, from celebrations of individual liberty to laments about the alienation that can go with such freedom. Given the position of the writer in English, it is hardly surprising that the modern independent, educated individual is consistently the focus around which our sympathies are orchestrated, but somehow or other, it is a form of family, whether relatives, colleagues or religious communion, that is recuperated as a site in which meaning or solace can be found when the contemporary nation or modern globalised society can no longer be equated with the family.

White and Indian? Intermarriage and Narrative Authority in South Asian American Fiction

SHAMEEM BLACK

How does intermarriage affect a storyteller? In this essay, I seek to examine literary narratives of South Asian family formation that take late twentieth-century intermarriages—particularly between Indian men and white American women—as their central governing trope. This phenomenon raises two linked questions: first, how do South Asian families recruit or reject individuals within constructs of South Asian identity; and second, to what extent do individuals not of South Asian descent gain the authority to imagine and re-imagine the contours of their multiracial family? I here examine the work of the white American writer Robbie Clipper Sethi, whose novel-in-stories, The Bride Wore Red *(1996), tells the unfolding saga of a multiracial South Asian family in the United States and India. These narratives of white women socialised into ambivalent places within larger South Asian families, I argue, figure larger anxieties about imaginative representation across the mobile borders of what is considered one's culture. The family structure emerges as a contradictory space that empowers this border-crossing representational authority by simultaneously calling this authority into question.*

How does intermarriage affect a storyteller? In this essay, I seek to examine literary narratives of South Asian family formation that take late twentieth-century intermarriages—particularly between Indian men and white American women—as their central governing trope. This phenomenon raises two linked questions: first, how do South Asian families recruit or reject individuals from constructs of South Asian identity; and second, to what extent do individuals not of South Asian descent gain the authority to imagine and re-imagine the contours of their multiracial family?[1] As these marriage narratives raise pressing questions about how South Asian families socialise individuals of non-South Asian descent into their worlds, they invite us to think about who is afforded the authority to tell these multiethnic South Asian family stories. To think through these questions, I will turn to the work of the white American writer Robbie Clipper Sethi, whose novel-in-stories, *The Bride Wore Red* (1996), offers the

---

[1] A note on terms. Throughout this essay, I use, with some hesitation, the languages of race and ethnicity. My understanding of 'race' draws upon Omi and Winant's classic definition of it as '*a concept which signifies and symbolizes social conflicts and interests by referring to different types of human bodies*' (italics in the original), while my use of ethnicity signals an interest in dimensions of cultural practice. The history of racialisation of Indians in America has been a complex and contradictory one: Asian Indians have, legally and informally, been both evicted from and conscripted into categories of whiteness at different points in their history, while they have also been ambivalently located within the pan-ethnic racial category of Asian America. To acknowledge these legacies, in which socially perceived differences have sometimes been seen as racial, at other times as ethnic, I invoke both concepts. Michael Omi and Howard Winant, *Racial Formation in the United States: From the 1960s to the 1990s* (New York: Routledge, 2nd ed. 1994), p.55.

unfolding saga of a multiracial South Asian family in the United States and India. These narratives of white women socialised into an ambivalent space within larger South Asian families, I argue, figure larger anxieties about imaginative representation across the mobile borders of what is considered one's culture. The family structure emerges as a contradictory space that empowers this border-crossing representational authority, paradoxically, by simultaneously calling this authority into question.

I will explore intermarriage and narrative authority through one particular node in the South Asian diaspora: the imaginative terrain of Asian American studies. Within the last few years, Asian American studies has begun to experience a new unsettling of its contours (which have always been unstable, provisional, and sometimes even arbitrary) through the official sanctioning of texts not authored by writers of Asian descent. Jennifer Ann Ho describes the visceral shock she and others at the Association of Asian American Studies experienced in 2008 when the prize for the best work of Asian American fiction was awarded to a white American man. Asian American circles have often been loath to make space for white writers, since such productions raise crucial questions about the usurpation of narrative territory and the longstanding spectres of Orientalist constraint that Asian American writers have energetically sought to contest. Ho used this occasion to work through her discomfort, ultimately arguing that a proper commitment to an anti-essentialist, subjectless construction of Asian American studies requires moving beyond the racialised body of the author. 'The motivation to close the boundaries of the field around the body of the Asian American writer shares an impulse with a social justice agenda of creating a space for underrepresented voices, as well as safeguarding against Orientalist and racist depictions of Asians in America—ones that white writers have been generating about Asian Americans for over a century', she acknowledges.[2] But she goes on to contend that this social justice agenda is not the exclusive province of writers with bodies marked as Asian. Nor, as Sheng-mei Ma has shown, is an authorial body racialised as Asian any firm guarantee against the proliferation of Orientalist discourse.[3]

I want to take up some of the implications of such an opening: to discuss how narratives of multiracial families might create new spaces for narrative authority within Asian American writing. Doing so might allow us to perceive the workings of what Colleen Lye has theorised as 'racial form', or 'race as the construction that emerges out of our theorisation of the historically shifting relationship between these archives' of American Orientalism and Asian American literature. Severing bonds between Asian American identity and singular textual categories, such as 'author, narrator, character, thematic subject matter, and, less often, reception and interpretative community', Lye argues, allows us to re-theorise the ethnic subject as 'the product of the articulation of the links between two or more of these textual categories'.[4] These historically changing forms open up new possibilities for the meanings of racially embodied lives and literary representations.

Empirically, intermarriage has served as a catalyst for new historical forms of cultural expression. Timothy Yu has noted a contemporary boom in what he calls the 'I Married an Asian' genre, a form of fiction and memoir where non-racially Asian speakers use the trope of the interethnic marriage to establish the grounds for their reflections on the cultural politics of

---

[2] Jennifer Ann Ho, 'The Place of Transgressive Texts in Asian American Epistemology', in *MFS: Modern Fiction Studies*, Vol.56, no. 1 (Spring 2010), p.210.

[3] Sheng-mei Ma, *The Deathly Embrace: Orientalism and Asian American Identity* (Minneapolis: University of Minnesota Press, 2000).

[4] Colleen Lye, 'Racial Form', in *Representations*, No.104 (Fall 2008), p.96.

race.[5] Such works include Chang-rae Lee's novel *Aloft* (2004), narrated by a white man with an Asian American family; Ben Ryder Howe's *My Korean Deli* (2010), featuring a life divided between his work at the *Paris Review* and his Korean wife's convenience store in New York; and Diane Farr's *Kissing Outside the Lines* (2011), an exposé of the politics of Farr's intermarriage to a Korean man. These memoirs of multiracial Asian families have been accompanied by a range of digital texts. Marriage and family blogs have become a fast-growing phenomenon that affords a new place for interracial couples to make the politics of their pairings visible to global audiences.[6] With titles such as 'My Chinese Wife', 'I Married an Alien', or 'Indian Ties: East Marries West', these blogs often both inhabit longstanding stereotypes *and* forge new imaginative terrain. South Asian families have a growing presence within this new digital landscape. A network called DesiLink Blogs, for instance, lists 48 websites that all feature 'intercultural relationship blogs with a South Asian twist'.[7]

The experiences of raced bodies and ethnic practices most visible within this emerging genre often focus attention on majority–minority bonds within relatively homogenous class structures. While the history of Asian intermarriage is by no means confined to intermarriage with whites,[8] most of the dyads featured in these memoirs and blogs are white-Asian. By and large, these contemporary interracial narratives also remain within the confines of middle- and upper-middle-class development, especially in digital form. This linkage may attest to the ways in which marriage has been central to a bourgeois middle class's sense of itself. Arguably more for the middle class than for other social strata, marriage rites have often instantiated particular norms of family stability and authorised familial reproduction. Marriages that look different from historical patterns or from idealised norms have tended to evoke particularly middle-class anxieties about a family's ability to reproduce particular cultural values of respectability, responsibility, and continuity with tradition. This new genre thus tends to remain anchored within particular social parameters.

Classic theories of interracial romance often draw strength from Franz Fanon's celebrated description of black-white desire in *Black Skin, White Masks* (1952), which offers an influential reading of interracial desire from a colonised black man's perspective: 'I wish to be acknowledged not as *black* but as *white*', Fanon's narrator confides. 'When my restless hands caress those white breasts, they grasp white civilisation and dignity and make them mine'.[9] Such border-crossing relationships have traditionally been read as spaces where larger cultural scripts play themselves out: individuals of colour are seen to crave power and acceptance within mainstream white culture, while white individuals are understood to indulge in primitivist and exoticist longings for embodied otherness. Read through Fanon, interracial pairings tend to bespeak the pathologies of the imperial body politic, all the more wedded to hegemonic cultural power for their role in the private domain of longing and domesticity. Such pairings do not fundamentally challenge hierarchies of race; instead, they reflect how these hierarchies inscribe themselves within intimacies of desire.

---

[5] Timothy Yu, personal correspondence with author, 10 July 2011.

[6] See, for example, 'Indian Ties: East Marries West' [www.indianties.blogspot.com]; 'My Chinese Wife' [interacialmarriage.blogspot.com]; 'I Married An Alien' [www.imarriedanalien.co]; 'On My Mind' [foreverloyal.wordpress.com]; 'My Sky—Multiracial Family Life' [multiracialsky.wordpress.com]; 'My American Meltingpot' [myamericanmeltingpot.blogspot.com]; and 'Honeysmoke' [www.honeysmoke.com].

[7] 'Indian Ties: East Marries West' (17 June 2011) [www.indianties.blogspot.com, accessed 19 July 2011].

[8] See, for example, Karen Isaksen Leonard, *Making Ethnic Choices: California's Punjabi Mexican Americans* (Philadelphia: Temple University Press, 1992).

[9] Frantz Fanon, *Black Skin, White Masks* (trans. Charles Lam Markmann) (New York: Grove Press, 1967), p.63.

New print and digital media at the turn of the millennium, however, reveal a significant broadening in the way in which individuals in multiracial and multiethnic families make sense of their unions. Ranging from sociological compilations to confessional diaries, these narratives often radically revise the significance of emotion and intimacy in ways that can no longer always be mapped onto psychosexual desires for mastery or exoticism. If these new narratives suggest a movement beyond interracial romance as pathology, they also suggest a concerted movement beyond liberalism's narratives of colour-blindness, which would construct emotion and domesticity as spaces untouched by politics. Rather than presenting utopian views of rainbow marriages, in which love conquers all, these novels, memoirs, and blogs tend to draw attention to the ways in which differences of ethnicity, race, nationality, and culture affect, and are affected by, the growth of intimacy. Furthermore, in often focusing attention on structures of marriage, long-term partnership, childrearing, and family care, these new narratives move our attention away from the hypersexualisation of interracial romance and towards an understanding of extended family sociality. In doing so, they turn these conflicts into precisely their own source of narrative authority. The ability of intermarried white writers to speak as a vital part of Asian America need not always be understood as a voyeuristic usurpation of Asian voices, though they may still often function that way; their narrative presence might also be seen to emerge through the contradictions of their own changing social location.

Modern narratives of multiracial South Asian families mark concerted ambivalences over the ways in which marriage and family formation change, or fail to change, one's social identity. Does intermarriage obey biological and genetic models of familial descent, so that you can pass on racial or ethnic identity to your children but not inherit new identities back up from them? Or is multiraciality more plastic and pliable, bucking the logic of genetic descent, contagious without regard to biology or formative upbringing? We can find evidence that both models have influenced the way in which individuals understand intermarriages. For a perspective that emphasises rigidity, we might turn to the reflections of Ruth Prawer Jhabvala, a European migrant who resided in India for many years and whose authorial reputation has emerged through her portraits of middle-class Indian life. Jhabvala is an important forerunner of the new wave of late twentieth- and early twenty-first-century white writers who have used family life as a point of entry into new imaginaries of South Asia. In 'Myself in India', an essay published in the 1970s, Jhabvala wrote: 'My husband is Indian and so are my children. I am not, and less so every year'.[10] As Jhabvala imagines India as unable to assimilate her into its cultural body politic, or herself as unwilling to enact this identification, she marks out a vexed space for herself as a writer whose work has had a powerful effect on shaping representations of India for an Anglophone audience. However Jhabvala understands her narrative authority to write about India and Indians, she does not appear to draw this authority from intermarriage.

For a different perspective that instead understands identity as malleable and even possibly contagious via intermarriage, we might turn to the celebratory discourse of the Indian actor and food writer Madhur Jaffrey, who foregrounds her marriage to a white American in several of her cookbooks. In her narratives, Jaffrey understands her own culinary identity as expanded by the ethnicities and nationalities brought into her family through her intermarriage, her multiracial daughters, and the men of varying nationalities they have married. 'I see that we seem to be heading toward a softening of boundaries between all cuisines.... My own family, like so many others, is mixed. I, of course, am Indian. I am married to an American. My

---

[10] Ruth Prawer Jhabvala, 'Introduction: Myself in India', in *How I Became a Holy Mother and Other Stories* (Harmondsworth: Penguin Books, 1981), p.9.

children, through their marriages, have brought in Italian, Irish, English, and French blood to those nearest to me, my grandchildren. Two of my daughters studied in China and Taiwan and are complete Sinophiles, at least as far as food is concerned.... It is impossible not to pick up good ideas, good recipes and new ingredients as one travels'.[11] While Jaffrey is clearly not claiming that cooking, by itself, re-racialises embodied individuals, the ease with which her rhetoric moves from intermarriage to multiethnic family formation to knowledge acquired through travel suggests a view of social identity that is significantly more plastic than the view taken by Jhabvala. For Jaffrey, food and cooking offer a metaphor for a larger theory of cultural identity that is amenable to transformation through the domestic cosmopolitan practice of multiethnic families, not simply encoded through ancestral descent or racialised bodies.[12]

Exemplifying two ends of a spectrum, these autobiographical fragments hint at a larger, often unacknowledged, tension in the underlying theories of identity that enable such a field as Asian American studies. Why is it that a dominant category, such as 'American', is seen by academics to be porous, but a minority category, such as 'Asian American', is often treated with greater rigidity? In short, many scholars would be eager to argue that subjects from other countries who immigrate to America have a rightful purchase on the identity of 'American' and deplore pervasive mainstream practices of treating migrants (especially those from Asia and their descendants) as perennially foreign. Yet they might not be so eager to argue that white subjects can become a legitimate part of minority or minoritised communities. They might point to the fact that these categories are asymmetric—a nationality, especially one defined in terms of secular civic nationalism, is not equivalent to a category based on race and ethnicity, especially when subjects are visually marked as 'non-white' within a context of historical white privilege. Yet, as scholars have begun to reveal, even visual or physical markers can signify differently over time. As Viet Thanh Nguyen argues, the Irish did not *look* white to white Anglo-Saxon Protestants at the beginning of the twentieth century, even though many contemporary Americans would be hard pressed to differentiate these categories. The same might be said for Jewishness, which was once seen as incompatible with whiteness, but which is now often perceived as an integral part of white America. 'Race is not inherently visible through physical characteristics such as skin color, hair texture, and eye and nose shape, but...is instead something that we learn to see', Nguyen concludes.[13] Similar arguments that draw upon history, for example, would also encounter parallel problems. If we were to define minority communities through historical legacies of discrimination, we would similarly need to limit mainstream communities to particular histories in ways that deny their capacity for change. Indeed, many anxieties about admitting the porousness of Asian American identity are less philosophical than political in nature: they reflect legitimate fears of a hard-won public profile diminished by mainstream voices that then obscure, in the guise of bolstering, the imaginative work of individuals of Asian descent.

I would like to argue that there is a meaningful middle space between a rigid view and an absorptive view of Asian American identity: a prickly space where we find not a comfortable ground of being, but instead a borderland of active contestation where belonging within a new social group is often articulated through narratives of ambivalent belonging to a family in the

---

[11] Madhur Jaffrey, *World Vegetarian* (New York: Clarkson Potter Publishers, 1999), p.viii.

[12] For a more extended discussion of Jaffrey's approach to cosmopolitanism, see Shameem Black, 'Recipes for Cosmopolitanism: Cooking Across Borders in the South Asian Diaspora', in *Frontiers: A Journal of Women Studies*, Vol.31, no.1 (2010), pp.1–30.

[13] Viet Thanh Nguyen, *Race and Resistance: Literature and Politics in Asian America* (Oxford: Oxford University Press, 2002), p.170.

process of re-making itself. The story of how families are formed and unformed, in other words, is also a story of changing narrative authority both on the page and within the South Asian diaspora in America.

Intermarriage and Assimilation

'Intermarriage has been widely accepted as a key indication of assimilation', note Sean-Shong Hwang, Rogelio Saenz, and Benigno E. Aguirre.[14] But assimilation to what? Modern sociologists have now abandoned classic models of assimilation that tend to assume an inevitable and one-way process in which the minority seeks entry into the mainstream. Richard Alba and Victor Nee, in their important re-theorisation of American assimilation, reject these assumptions and instead advocate an understanding of assimilation that stresses its two-sided nature, arguing that assimilation changes the nature of the mainstream. They note the ways in which phenomena such as intermarriage can contribute to 'boundary blurring', which 'implies that the social profile of a boundary has become less distinct, and the clarity of the social distinction involved has become clouded'.[15]

Yet even Alba's and Nee's account, which consciously seeks to identify assimilation as dynamic and dialogic, tends to present this engagement in traditional terms of a minority group entering a mainstream, rather than the reverse. 'Important clues to assimilatory boundary change are found in the evidence...of narrowing social distances between new immigrant minorities and the European American majority. Such narrowings are a two-sided process: members of the minority group must seek entry into social contexts occupied by the majority group; and members of the majority must find their entry acceptable'.[16] While this model acknowledges a 'two-sided process', it assumes that desire runs in only one direction (from minority toward mainstream) and remains within a rhetoric of permission-seeking and consent-granting that replicates a monolithic power hierarchy. In this model, there appears to be little room to explore how white Americans might themselves seek entry into minority groups, and in doing so, trouble the boundaries of both mainstream and minority.

Intermarriage marks a prominent place where such a potentially two-way process seems especially important. The growing number of Asian American intermarriages is part of larger changing trends in United States' marriage patterns. Widely circumscribed through American anti-miscegenation state laws throughout the nineteenth and twentieth centuries, intermarriage only became fully legal across the entire United States after the landmark 1967 Supreme Court decision *Loving v Virginia*, which declared restrictions on interracial marriage to be unconstitutional. According to 'Marrying Out', the 2010 Pew Research Center report on American marriages, 14.6 percent of new marriages and 8 percent of all married couples in 2008 were interracial partnerships. In a seeming paradox, these rates were almost identical to the intermarriage rates for Asians in 1980, but reflect a doubling in the intermarriage rates for whites. This discrepancy reflects the rise in Asian immigration that increased the marriage pool not only for intermarriage with whites, but also for in-group marriage with other Asians.[17] Outmarriage rates for Indians, for example, declined slightly between 1980 and

---

[14] Sean-Shong Hwang, Rogelio Saenz and Benigno E. Aguirre, 'Structural and Assimilationist Explanations of Asian American Intermarriage', in *Journal of Marriage and Family*, Vol.59, no.3 (August 1997) p.758.
[15] Richard Alba and Victor Nee, *Remaking the American Mainstream: Assimilation and Contemporary Immigration* (Cambridge: Harvard University Press, 2003), p.60.
[16] *Ibid.*, p.286.
[17] Jeffrey S. Passel, Wendy Wang and Paul Taylor, 'Marrying Out', Pew Research Center (4 June 2010) [www.pewresearch.org/pubs/1616/american-marriage-interracial-interethnic, accessed 21 July 2011].

1990, but since the number of Indians in America increased vastly during this decade, the actual number of intermarriages rose dramatically.[18] As a result, Asian America is increasingly tied through marriage bonds to non-Asian American communities. These bonds have important consequences. As Peggy Pascoe puts it in her landmark study of American miscegenation law, 'because [marriage] stretches seamlessly from romance to respectability to responsibility, marriage has extraordinary power to naturalise some social relationships, and to stigmatise others as unnatural'.[19] This power extends from political questions about citizens' relationships with their state to literary concerns with the authority to tell particular kinds of stories.

The rising number of Asian American intermarriages raises new questions about how this changing landscape affects the work of cultural imagination. I turn now to a novel that grapples with this very predicament, Robbie Clipper Sethi's *The Bride Wore Red* (1996). A white American writer married to a Sikh Indian man, Sethi published her novel-in-stories in 1996 about a set of multiracial South Asian American families that feature interethnic and international marriage as a crucial component. Sethi's own narrative position, thus, biographically resembles that of her anchoring narrator, Sally, who begins and ends the novel-in-stories. While the stories are told from a wide variety of first person perspectives, which range across different middle-class iterations of gender and ethnicity, Sally's voice serves as the point of entry into the novel and foregrounds many of the questions that arise from Sethi's decision to write about South Asian family formation in the United States and India. In this sense, Sethi's Sally serves as a meta-authorial voice where the possibilities and limitations of assimilating into Indian familial and narrative structures are worked out. While multiethnic families are often seen as key blurrers of boundaries by sociologists, historians, and cultural scholars because they often produce multiethnic children, far less attention has been paid to the ways in which the identities of the married couple might be affected by their union. This is the cultural problematic that *The Bride Wore Red* invites us to consider.

For the space constraints of this essay, I locate *The Bride Wore Red* within the imaginative terrain of Asian America, since the novel was published by a US-based writer through American publishing institutions and strongly features the Punjabi diaspora in the United States. The novel foregrounds white Americans seeking entry into a minority American group, thus challenging the sociological assumption of assimilation as a movement from minority to majority. However, the novel might also be productively situated in light of a more conventional one-way assimilation into the dominant Indian state, since the novel is also interested in the possibilities (or impossibilities) of Indian expatriates and white American migrants making their way into the national imaginaries and lived geographies of South Asia. In this context, we might consider the way the modern Indian state has managed these processes at the turn of the millennium, ranging from the investment category of Non-Resident Indian to the recent rise of American white-collar workers seeking jobs in the subcontinent. Sethi's stories prefigure this form of reverse migration, which, while it continues to feature a minority passage into a majority culture, nonetheless challenges conventional cultural myths that construct Westernised spaces as desired destinations rather than as points of departure.

---

[18] Sharon M. Lee and Marilyn Fernandez, 'Trends in Asian American Racial/Ethnic Intermarriage: A Comparison of 1980 and 1990 Census Data', in *Sociological Perspectives*, Vol.41, no.2 (1998), p.328. Lee and Fernandez measured 1,125 exogamus Indian marriages in 1980 and 20,846 in 1990.

[19] Peggy Pascoe, *What Comes Naturally: Miscegenation Law and the Making of Race in America* (Oxford: Oxford University Press, 2009), p.2.

While well-reviewed in major mainstream American publications at the time of its appearance, when it was listed as a Barnes and Noble Discover Great New Writers choice, *The Bride Wore Red* has virtually disappeared from the cultural landscape of Asian America. Unlike the short stories of Jhumpa Lahiri, which resemble Sethi's in tone and scope, Sethi's fiction has not found a wide mainstream audience, nor has it extensively penetrated the scholarly or popular canons of Asian American literature. While part of this invisibility is simply the fate of the vast majority of literature, it may also attest to the ways in which Sethi's work troubles identitarian alignments between South Asian bodies and South Asian American fiction. Yet what is intriguing about Sethi's work is the way in which it both places itself within, and evicts itself from, the narrative authority of the South Asian diaspora in a transnational Indian-American cultural space. The novel can be read as a bid for the inclusion of white writers within South Asian cultural narratives, but it makes these claims, paradoxically, by exploring the reluctance of its white protagonists to fully embrace new roles and identities within their diasporic South Asian family structures.

Sethi's mixed-race marriages in *The Bride Wore Red* are predominantly Sikh Indian men who marry white American women. This particular form of family formation, in many crucial respects, reflects an atypical pattern of representation. According to sociological studies based on the 1980 United States census, Indian men are exceptional in being the only group among Asians where men were more likely than women to marry outside their group.[20] In the sample studied, based on marriages between 1975 and 1980, 17.22 percent of Indian men were married to white women, while only 7.55 percent of Indian women were married to white men.[21] This pattern was replicated in the 1990 census.[22] For all other Asian American groups, Asian women were more likely than Asian men to be part of an interracial marriage. This sociological finding correlates with the imaginative patterns in how Asian interracial dyads have been represented in American popular culture. In her important study of Asian American mixed-race narratives, Susan Koshy argues that:

> in the development of the white-Asian interracial romance over the twentieth century, narratives of the white man-Asian woman dyad emerged as the dominant form of the interracial romance, while the white woman-Asian man narrative became the recessive form. Stories of interracial desire centered on the white man-Asian woman dyad lent themselves more readily to establishing the assimilability of Asians, thus revealing the gender hierarchies underlying fictional representations of racialized sexuality.[23]

In Sethi's *The Bride Wore Red*, this 'recessive narrative' comes into play in ways that reverse the traditional direction and invite new questions about the assimilability of white Americans into South Asian culture. By featuring white women and Indian men, these stories invoke very different gender hierarchies that complicate the dominant narrative's reliance on binaries of privilege (white masculinity on one side, Asian femininity on the other) that have upheld traditional unidirectional models of assimilation.

---

[20] Hwang, Saenz, and Aguirre, 'Structural and Assimilationist Explanations', pp.765, 766.
[21] *Ibid.*, p.766.
[22] Lee and Fernandez, 'Trends in Asian American Racial/Ethnic Intermarriage', p.337.
[23] Susan Koshy, *Sexual Naturalization: Asian Americans and Miscegenation* (Stanford: Stanford University Press, 2004), p.132.

Familial Constraint, Narrative Authority

How might *The Bride Wore Red* be understood as a productive part of a South Asian American cultural imaginary? I turn again here to Jennifer Ho's account, which seeks to open up such a space within the field. Her defence of which non-Asian-authored texts to include within the Asian American canon—for Ho does not uncritically accept all writing featuring Asian or Asian American subjects as proper objects of attention—rests on two grounds: the first political, the second aesthetic. The works she valorises count 'as Asian American literature through [their] attention to social justice themes and [their] thoughtful, multi-dimensional, and careful depiction of Asian characters and Asian experiences'.[24] But what does 'thoughtful, multi-dimensional, and careful depiction' really entail? Much as I agree with Ho's defence of such border-crossing fiction, I also ask if we can specify more precisely what it is about particular works that makes them useful elements of an Asian American imaginary, rather than invoking a generalised aesthetic criteria that is uncontroversial in theory, yet highly contestable in practice.

I identify three key elements that novelists have effectively used to challenge omnipresent patterns of discursive domination.[25] First, these works tend to be based on a recognition that both selfhood and language are socially shaped, so that no singular account—including one's own—will ever be authoritative and complete. To recognise this social shaping, furthermore, is to acknowledge that what we do to know our own social identities is sometimes not radically different than what we do to learn about the social identities of others. For example, knowledge of oneself as 'Indian' is not limited to the immediate embodied experiences of one's daily life; it is also a knowledge that gains richness and meaning by studying history, reading literature, or following politics, activities that are obviously not restricted to individuals who identify as Indian. This structural similarity holds out the possibility (though not the certainty) that individuals may be able to claim a more intimate imaginative relationship to the experiences of others—not an identical experience, to be sure, but an important one. Second, I suggest that an ethics of cross-cultural representation requires re-imagining the self as a crucial part of imagining others. This interplay between thinking about oneself, and thinking about others, helps to push against the unconscious repetition of calcified forms of imaginative constraint (such as Orientalist stereotypes). Third, productive imaginative border crossing encourages the imagining self to admit its vulnerability, thus troubling the sense of mastery that writing about others (or claiming their identity) is said to afford. Encounters with otherness, paradoxically, often seem to require moments of failure as part of their ethical success.

The Bride Wore Red reflects an interest in all three of these elements. While in many respects its very title can be seen to replicate Orientalist tropes, the novel is also a self-consciously canny meditation on precisely such images. Sources of imaginative and familial constraint, throughout the novel, reveal themselves as paradoxical narrative motors that produce new forms of storytelling authority. The novel begins and ends with Sally's conscription into, and exit from, her Indian family, so that the generative power of narrative emerges as a function of the Indian family. Sally enters the text as the proverbial bride who wore red, a white American woman who steps off the plane in India with her fiancé for their Punjabi wedding in the 1970s. The story initially presents her desire as a form of feminist empowerment that mobilises traditional views of Asian men as effeminate (Sally describes her attraction to the diminutive size of her fiancé, who will never physically overpower her). Yet it

---

[24] Ho, 'The Place of Transgressive Texts', p.218.
[25] I theorise these elements in more depth in Shameem Black, *Fiction Across Borders: Imagining the Lives of Others in Late Twentieth-Century Novels* (New York: Columbia University Press, 2010), pp.35–45.

also complicates this desire for female liberation. First greeted by the tears of her future mother-in-law, Sally experiences India as a source of rejection, yet soon comes to find that this resistance to her presence is simultaneously an embrace: "'I don't think your mother wants me to marry you'", Sally says to her fiancé Deshi. "'She's insisting on it'", Deshi says, surprising her with his reply.[26] The moment when Deshi's family dresses Sally for marriage seems to her a marker of gendered confinement in which she surrenders her accustomed freedom and mastery over her body.

> After they have squeezed your breasts into a blouse so tight that you can hardly move your arms, so short it does not cover all your ribs, you step into a long cotton petticoat, and one of the sisters ties its drawstring top so close you fear for your circulation. Tucking one end into your waist, they wrap the six yards of vermilion silk around you so that you cannot walk without stepping on the spun-gold border. You cannot free your left arm. They bring out a bowl full of bangles soaked in milk and brush-burn your knuckles forcing them on (pp.12–13).

This relentless series of constriction, physical entrapment, and passivity on the part of the bride suggests the pain of passage of entry into her new South Asian family. Body parts are resculpted; new patterns of mobility are imposed. 'You stand awhile. You sit down. They get you up again. When they want you to move, they push. It's all so easy' (p.15). By making Sally participate in Punjabi wedding rituals, her Indian family exercises control over the terms of Sally's incorporation into South Asian culture and into the aspirational norms of their particular social class. Sally experiences the process as infantilising, comparing her wedding make-up to that of a child's dress-up game. Yet, while Sally sees this process as one of constraint and regression, her Indian relatives view it as a sign that they treat her as if she were Indian. Mataji, her mother-in-law's sister, reflects in a later story that 'my poor sister bought that Sally the best Benarsi sari she could find and a proper set of gold jewelry' (p.53). The wedding therefore serves as a cultural rebirth, a moment of challenge to Sally's autonomy as she is re-made and inscribed within Punjabi culture.

We might read this moment as a place where the novel thus performs an act of narrative self-authorisation, using the family to re-code a figure such as Sally as an appropriate and legitimate narrator of South Asian experiences. Indeed, the author photograph of Robbie Clipper Sethi on the back cover of the Picador USA paperback, where she is photographed in an ornate sari and jewellery, seems designed to signal the authority of Indianness-via-marriage to prospective readers: it follows in the tradition of making the body of the author the centrepiece for the legitimacy of her imaginative work. Yet Sally is both eager and, paradoxically, unwilling to enter into this new cultural script. She rejects the script of white mainstream culture: 'you've always thought yourself exotic, the one who didn't belong. When you told the boy next door that you were marrying an Indian, he laughed and said, *Sally, I always knew you'd end up with a foreigner; you never could stand the typical American boy*' (p.1), but she also resists what she sees as the norms of a traditional Indian family: '[Deshi] has defied [his mother] to risk this marriage between East and West. And isn't that what you wanted in a man all along?' (p.16). She is not the enthusiastic liberal subject all too eager to prove her lack of racism by embracing the norms of a new family structure; instead, she emerges as a narrative construct deeply ambivalent about the Indianness of her new life, and her stories track the failings and fault lines within her marriage. As the family structure

---

[26] Robbie Clipper Sethi, *The Bride Wore Red* (New York: Picador USA, 1996), p.9. Subsequent references will be cited parenthetically in the text.

conscripts Sally into Indianness, it also reaffirms her difference. This dynamic appears most vividly in 'The Housewarming', where a Sikh blessing celebration held on Halloween compels Sally to ask herself if she has been 'tricked or treated, cursed or blessed' (p.143) by her marriage. She ends the story unsure if she is experiencing the grace of full acceptance within her husband's family or spending her entire life in Halloween disguise without end. This self-reflective, vulnerable position forms a crucial part of her narrative claims.

This split perspective is further enacted at the level of form. Sally's stories are told in the second person, focalised through Sally's experiences and addressed to a 'you' that is simultaneously Sally and not Sally at the same time. Through the second person, Sally tells her story to herself, so that the story comes to serve the classic function of a soliloquy in which the speaker overhears her own intimate thoughts. At the same time, this 'you' also allows the narrative to conscript its audience into her subject position. Sally's voice thus emerges as the place where narrative authority makes its anxieties felt, as if there must be some *other* person telling this story. Sally does not claim the kind of full ownership over her story that the 'I' would confidently assert; instead, she lurks in a narrative no-man's land where she is simultaneously telling, yet not fully inhabiting, her story. This tentative location, where narrative authority is both claimed and denied, offers a microcosmic vision of the larger position she occupies within her diasporic South Asian family: she is at once the teller and yet not the teller of their complicated lives. As Sally comes to experience new possibilities of connection with South Asian cultural signifiers, she comes to inhabit her own 'I' more fully. Sally's 'I' appears only in 'The Pilgrimage' and 'A White Woman's Burden', the two stories that reflect her greatest moments of epiphanic identity with India (in one, she is moved by a religious pilgrimage; in the other, she is emboldened enough to want, for the first time, to bear a child with Deshi). Yet this first-person ownership is not a linear constant. Her second-person 'you' reappears in the deeply ambivalent story 'The Housewarming', and her sense of self fades in the final story, which reverts to the third person, where Sally—as she loses Deshi to a plane crash—has become a stranger distanced from herself, the daughter-in-law who now seeks to sever all connections with India in her life.

This pattern is amplified through the story of Gudrun (or Goodie), the second of the three white women in the novel who intermarry into Indian families. On the surface, Goodie reflects a kind of incorporation into her South Asian family that Sally does not: most conspicuously, whereas Sally does not wish to bear children (and only decides to do so late in life, when she loses her child to miscarriage), Goodie is pregnant at her wedding and goes on to bear four children, thus ensuring the myth of family continuity. Yet despite this structural implication, Goodie, in ways that resonate with Ruth Prawer Jhabvala's proclamation, appears to be less and less Indian the more children she bears. While she is given a first-person story called 'Gudrun's Saga', this story begins with the fragility of her incorporation into her South Asian family: 'If Hermie's parents ever found out that I'd been married before, they might starve themselves to death, the way they made a show of hunger striking when Hermie told them he was going to marry me', she begins (p.67). As the novel progresses, and Goodie's presence within it becomes more and more tenuous, her narrative authority lies in her repeated stories about how her children do not resemble her. 'Goodie tells this story every time the family has a function, her pink face reddening as she builds up to the punch line: "My children don't even look like me; everybody thinks they're adopted!"' (p.136). She inhabits a repetitive story of her alienation: being part of a South Asian family both authorises and delegitimates, so that her voice becomes circular and circumscribed: 'Goodie tells this story every time the family has a function'.

The narrative authority of white speakers, thus, emerges through modes of constraint and alienation rather than through assumptions of hegemonic mastery. This pattern continues even within the most optimistic moments of the novel, where Sally does, for brief periods of time, see herself as an integral part of the Indian world into which she has married. In 'The Pilgrimage' and 'A White Woman's Burden'—the titles of which both consciously foreground, rather than conceal, Orientalising tropes—Sally finds herself, despite the cool reserve with which she habitually treats her Indian in-laws, experiencing genuine feelings of connection and hope within a religious universe she does not fully inhabit. In both stories, Sally learns to become vulnerable to new landscapes, and in doing so, achieves a temporary moment of intimacy with her otherwise incompatible in-laws whose tastes, though also middle-class, appear provincial in her eyes. Looking at the Ganges in 'The Pilgrimage', she experiences an epiphanic moment in which she comes to experience the possibility of simultaneous union and dissonance between Western and Indian foundational touchstones:

'In the beginning God created the heaven and the earth', I said.
The Ganges stretched out silver on the valley floor below, so wide Hardwar looked like an anthill next to it.
'The Spirit of God moved upon the face of the waters'.
A woman at a bend in the path sat beside a huge brass jug. '*Pani*, sahib?'
We couldn't drink the water (p.45).

As Sally overlays the Biblical language of Genesis onto a sacred Hindu site, the narrative structure of the story suggests the possibility of genuine metaphorical marriage between Western and Indian religious anchors, in which the two intertwine just as the paragraphs fold around each other. It is most fully in this moment in India that she seems visibly moved by Biblical rhetoric: the more capable of responding to India's sacred sites she becomes, the more fully she also inhabits a Christian universe. Yet, at the same time, the novel refuses to erase real differences and points of alienation. The water in the Ganges may be that of a syncretic epiphany, but it is water neither Sally nor her husband can drink. Admitting this distance—Sally's original distance from India, Deshi's expatriate alienation, the class hierarchies exemplified by 'sahib'—becomes a productive failure, a refusal of the too-easy spiritual syncretism that has marked Western fascination with Indian religious discourse. This self-conscious acknowledgment heightens the power of the transformative touch between the silver Ganges and the waters of Genesis. It changes Sally's ability to perceive the India around her beyond the terms of lack or constraint that have marked her optic in 'The Bride Wore Red'. 'I opened my eyes. Same dark street, no Sitaram. Not even a pariah dog or a sacred cow. Still, there was something' (p.50). Playing upon classic tropes of awakening and enlightenment, this conclusion to the story hints at a change in Sally's perspective on India and her place in it. Calling attention to what is not there—the servant, the dog, and the cow, which mark differences of class, culture, and religion—Sally's monologue attempts to dissolve these differences without erasing them, including them formally in the story under the sign of their absence. She is able see with double vision, to acknowledge the way in which she is both insider and outsider in Indian cultural space. Intermarriage narratives thus emerge as stereoscopic rather than as unified visions that foreground the instability of their authorial location.

Sethi foregrounds this predicament of authority via constraint not only as a matter of family structure, but also as a response to tropes of Orientalist confinement. Here we might turn to the most metafictional story of the collection, 'Missing Persons', where Sethi combines the domestic realism of her other stories with an intrusive, elusive narrator who continually switches the genders of the ambiguously named protagonists Leslie and Surinder. In this story,

Sethi makes clear the intimacy between the politics and ethics of representation and interracial family formation. Beginning with the story of a white American middle-class woman named Leslie who falls in love with an Indian Sikh named Surinder, 'Missing Persons' abruptly abandons this beginning: 'But the tall dark stranger is so familiar from romance novels that Surinder threatens the originality of this story. If authorial intervention made him a woman, she might take the plot in a different direction' (p.176). This metafictional element explicitly raises the problem of narrative authority, how to tell this story without falling into patterns that tell us only about historically sedimented cultural images and reveal few fresh insights into the apparent objects of representation. The story moves back and forth between these two narratives, ostensibly as part of a continual search for unconventional narrative, which is (despite the author's best efforts) constantly corralled back into stereotype. The story identifies its only escape from familiar cultural scripts with a move outside the middle-class bourgeois family (both American and Indian) through a collaborative feminist ending set in India. Sethi presents this conclusion as the one unexpected, unscripted story, though it also resembles the kind of narrative that academics have, since the 1980s, habitually valorised as a challenge to hegemonic forms of social inscription (transnational sisterhood, expansive ideas of motherhood, refutations of America as a teleological destination for assimilation, and challenges to middle-class domestic norms). The layered quality of the story, which refuses to choose among its drafts, makes a virtue of a post-modernist valorisation of multiplicity common in the 1990s. The novel invites us to ask what we do with these 'failed stories', which are disowned by the narrator but nonetheless rendered visible within the final story, so that the story becomes a quest narrative for an alternative form of imaginative authority. What appears to be most liberating for representation, ironically, is the acknowledgment of constraint, both within the binds of Orientalist trope and the pressures of family formation.

In reflecting an awareness of preceding cultural narratives, the story seeks to enact a formal integration of post-modern technique and realist narrative that mimics and models the multiracial marriage of its content. Leaving the jagged edges of storytelling visible, making scars and sutures in the realist story part of its new workings, emerges as the most viable way in which *The Bride Wore Red* seeks to authorise itself as a piece of South Asian American literature. While the content of the final sisterhood story, in escape from heteronormative gendered middle-class constructs, appears to allow a fuller sense of integration between white and Indian families, the story maintains the ongoing importance of alienation within union by staging such dissonance within its form and genre. This practice allows *The Bride Wore Red* to articulate new modes of racial form, understood both literarily and sociologically.

It remains for Asian American literary studies to recognise how such narratives may be, to re-frame the title of Lavina Dingra Shankar and Rajini Srikanth's influential 1998 anthology of South Asian American cultural studies, both a part and apart of the Asian American imaginary. The paradigms of simultaneous inclusion and exclusion that have long characterised Asian Americans' situations as 'permanent aliens' in the United States, seen as foreign to the body politic despite material and ideational markers to the contrary, may also be a good way of describing the place of white individuals within South Asian American families, whose voices as new parts of Asian America are simultaneously enabled and constrained by the diasporic South Asian family structure. Here, Asian American discomfort with transgressive texts mirrors the discomfort that white writers like Sethi stage with their own narrative incursions into South Asian representational space. This tension, on both sides, is precisely what may render Sethi's portraits of the middle-class Punjabi diaspora valuable to South Asian American cultural studies. It works against the confident assumptions of social power that mark Orientalist imaginings, yet neither does it simply constitute a narcissistic voice that can only articulate its own inabilities and limitations. Though I have focused here on the voices of Sethi's white subjects, who most obviously share in the social privileges and embodied cultural spaces that Sethi herself inhabits, these are not the only central voices in her novel. Of the thirteen tales that structure the novel, five are told from the perspective of Punjabis, male and female, across three generations of migrants. While these narrators are all generally part of a middle-class and upper-middle-class structure, they also reflect differing modes of privilege within that class (some have lost power and money, now dependent on others for their survival, while others have ascended to positions of financial and social prominence). This oscillation back and forth enables the collection to meditate on the productive tensions within Sethi's authorial subject position while still taking genuine imaginative risks to tell these stories of white women's incorporation from completely different angles. These stories of intermarriage are sometimes central (as with a mother's dismay over her son's affair with a 'white-haired girl') and sometimes marginal, simply a small piece in a larger drama of belonging and stability within a Punjabi family structure.

This oscillation across voices resonates with the practice of improvisational, mixed, and decidedly 'inauthentic' identities that Vincent Cheng calls for in his important cultural study of identity, *Inauthentic*. Cheng sees the terrain of Asian America as a particularly promising place for the rise of such anti-essentialist identities because, as he claims, 'Asian American' has always been a 'mixed' category in numerous dimensions: it is composed of dozens of ethnicities, languages, and nationalities; marked by long histories of intermarriage and multiraciality; and positioned ambiguously in America's racial hierarchies between black and white.[27] Neither completely rigid, nor wholly plastic, these identities instead hold out the possibility to generate new spaces of narrative authority through dynamic engagement with their forms of constraint.

The family, as it emerges in Sethi's novel, is not a place where identity is seamlessly replicated, but a place where it is potentially transformed through productive modes of tension. Though Sally is often deeply at odds with her Indian family, she is even more lost without it. In the final story, when Deshi has died and Sally has decided to abandon all traces of India in her life, she emerges most clearly as the doctor who cannot heal herself. This moment of escape from her Indian family should, from her perspective, reflect a liberation, yet there is nothing triumphal about Sally's desolation once she has accomplished this end. Without her Indian family to struggle against and within, Sally no longer has a voice; it is at this point that her narrative, and Sethi's with it, must end.

Conclusion

Not all stories of intermarriage foreground this difficulty in the manner of Sethi's work. Moving us beyond the parameters of Asian America, an Australian Indian documentary made in 2001 by the filmmaker Safina Uberoi, *My Mother India*, articulates a different set of possibilities. The documentary tells the story of the filmmaker's parents, a white Australian woman and an Indian Sikh who build their lives together in India. Despite the clear ways in which Uberoi's white Australian mother Patricia is perceived as an oddity in her community, her long commitment both to her Indian family and to India itself ultimately articulates an assimilation narrative in which foreign whiteness and Indian identity are no longer seen to be incompatible. The film moves from images that emphasise comic foreign strangeness, such as Patricia's panties hanging on the laundry line, to shots that show her increasingly embedded within Indian family life. When the filmmaker marries, she tells us how her mother surprised

---

[27] Vincent J. Cheng, *Inauthentic: The Anxiety over Culture and Identity* (New Brunswick, NJ: Rutgers University Press, 2004), pp.143–8.

her by perfectly organising a traditional Sikh wedding. As with *The Bride Wore Red*, though in a different register, the trope of the wedding emerges as a prominent place to enact Patricia's inscription into the social fabric of Indian life. The documentary concludes with the narrator's confident voiceover pronouncement: 'My father is Indian, and my mother is too'.

Yet such assimilation into South Asian culture is not linear or unidirectional. Despite its optimistic ending, *My Mother India* also foregrounds how ruptures and breaks continue to haunt Patricia's relationship to India. During anti-Sikh riots in Delhi following the assassination of Indira Gandhi in 1984, for instance, Patricia—without consulting anyone, including her husband—sends her teenage son out of the country to live with relatives in Australia whom he has never met. Later, her youngest daughter follows suit. Yet, even as these episodes break the family apart, such moments of national violence also fracture the idea of an authentic 'Indianness' within the national imaginary. As anti-Sikh violence casts Sikhs as traitors to India, the divide between 'authentic Indian' and 'inauthentic foreigner' becomes increasingly difficult to sustain. The fracturing of the polity leads both to the fracturing of the interracial family *and*, paradoxically, to its deepened insistence that such fracturing is a testament to such families' roots within the Indian imaginary. Anti-Sikh violence may make Patricia fear that India is not the best place for her multiracial children, yet it paradoxically creates an experience of outsiderness that creates new forms of shared solidarity between a white migrant and her Sikh family. As Patricia and her husband remain in Delhi throughout the crisis, their alienation ironically leads to a replenished investment in India.

These stories of white women inscribed within the family worlds of South Asia and its diaspora thus ask us to re-calibrate our understanding of who might speak as 'Indian' and how. Rather than calling for a simple expansion of the canon of Asian American (or Asian Australian) literature through a process of inclusion—a process that, as the history of multiculturalism has shown us, leaves fundamental hierarchies intact—we might instead understand these new narrative voices as productive challenges to the underlying assumptions of literary studies. While fears of usurpation or Orientalism are often still sadly warranted, focusing exclusively on these phenomena may cause us to miss the important ways in which those seen as outsiders may have crucial stories to tell about the formation and function of minority or minoritised communities.

Index

Note: page numbers followed by 'n' refer to notes

Adiga, A.: *The White Tiger* 121, 130
adolescence: unconventional view 10–11
Adolescence Education Programme (AEP) 97–8, 98n
adolescent girls 102
adoption 27
adoptive siblings 27
adults and children: joint family system 66
agency: consumption 97
aging: India-US comparison 67; security policy 64
Agnes, F. 101n
Alba, R.: and Nee, V. 137
alienation 35; Hegelian schematic 26; philosophical concept 35; trope of 35
Allen, K.: and Walker, A. 81
Ambika 56, 57
ambivalence: sex 102
Anand (1971) 33
Anandabajar Patrika 64, 73
animal stories: generic 9
Anita 58
anti-Sikh violence 14
Art of Dying (Hariharan) 81, 82, 84
Asian Americans: identity 136; South Asian American fiction 132–46; studies 133, 136
Asian Indians 132n
assimilation: and intermarriage 137–9
assisted living 71
Australia 52, 53; remittances study 52–62
authorial subject position 145
authority: narrative 132–46
autobiographical fragments 136
ayahs 69

Bahri, D. 35–47
Bailey, R.: *Letting Children be Children* Report (2011) 93
Bajaj, K.: *Keep Off the Grass* 125
Bajwa, R.: *The Sari Shop* 129
Baldassar, L.: et al 55–6
Banta 57
Barbie dolls 97

Barker, M: and Duschinsky, R. 93
Behna ne bhai ki kalai se 28
Bengali language 63n
Bhagat, C.: *One Night @ the Call Centre* 125
Bhagwan 56
Bhattacharya, Purnima 69, 71–2
Bhattacharya, R. 2, 7–23
Biblical language: Genesis 143
Black, S. 6, 132–46
Black Skin, White Masks (1952) 134
Bombai ka Babu 28–30, 32
Bombay cinema 3, 23–34
Brahmin lineage 10
Brennan, S. 88
Bride Wore Red, The (Sethi) 6, 132, 138–46
Brindha 60
brother: *rakhi-* 41
brother-brother plots 26
brother-brother relationships 26
brother-sister relationships 26, 105–20
brotherhood 33
brothers and sisters: inheritance rights 105–6
Brumburg, J.J. 102–3
businesses: private 68

Cabraal, A.: and Singh, S. 4, 48–62
care 4–5; elder market 72; ethic in Indian fiction 77–89; family centered 65
caregiver: and care receiver 81
caring for children: Ruddick 80–1
caste *panchayats* 116
chaddi 92
Chalte Chalte (2003) 27
Chandra, V. 122
Chang, G. 12, 20
Chatterjee, I. 1
Chatterjee, Kalyani 70
Chatterjee, U. 125
Chattopadhyay, Gauri 69
chawl 27n
Cheng, V.: *Inauthentic* 145
Chief of the Herd (Mukerji) 14–15, 17, 18

INDEX

child-mother relationship 79
child-parent dyad 15
children: and adults 66; caring for 80–1; fiction 9; Hindu 17; and parents 16, 88; sexualisation 93–6
China: married women 50
Chitra 61
Christian Europe: ecclesiastical law 106
Christians 109; Parsis 109
Cinderella Ate my Daughter (Orenstein) 93
cinema: Bombay 3, 23–34
co-operation 15; possibilities 8
colonial India 118
colonial paternalism 19
Commonwealth literature 121
communalisation: politics 115
community 8
comprehensive sexuality education (CSE) 97
Confession, The (Vaidehi) 85, 86
conflict: inheritance 56
conjugality 1
consciousness: geographical 20
consent: women's 101n
consumer-led progressiveness 96
consumption: agency 97
contemporary India 8
continued migration: and diffusion 58
contract: intergenerational 77, 87, 89; metaphor 80
contractarianism: and ethic of care 77–89
coupledom: romantic 23–48
Coy, M.: and Garner, M. 93, 95
Crescent Moon (Tagore) 7
critical engagement: ethic of care 79
critical geography scholarship 106
critical legal scholars 112
cross-border connections 61
cross-fertilisation 20
cultural patterns 58
culture: Indian 78
Custom House, The (Hawthorne) 42

Dahlia 60–1
Das, G.: *A Fine Family* 123–5, 127
daughter-mother relationship 78
daughters: mothering 91; raising 91
Dayabhaga school 110n
death 81
deathbed intimacy 83
debt: and inheritance 56
democratic intent 12
Desai, K.: *The Inheritance of Loss* 129
Deshpande, S. 82–3; *The Binding Vine* 129
DesiLink Blogs 134
destruction: or hostility in natural world 19
Dhagamwar, V. 116
diffusion: and continued migration 58

discourse: natural history 9; old age security 64
displacement: extended family 23
diverse domination: key elements 140
Divine 8
donations: Indian causes 60–1
Duschinsky, R.: and Barker, M 93
dying 81, 82, 84
dysfunctional families 126

ecclesiastical law: Christian Europe 106
educated families 123
education: sexuality 97
Ehrenreich, B.: and Hochschild, A. 76
elder abode residents 69–70
elder care: market based 72
elder residences 68
elderly 44, 45; family-centered care 65
emotional bond: parent-child 16
emotional economy 3
Engels, F.: and Marx, K. 38
English-language fiction: family in 121–31
entrapment: physical 141
Etash 61
ethic of care: and contractarianism 77–89; critical engagement 79; Indian fiction 77–89
ethnicity: concept 132n
Europe: Christian 106
Eve-teasing 41
extended family: displacement 23

Falconer Al-Hindi, K.: and Moss, P. 112–13
familial economy 3
familial nominal 41
familial relations: multiple forms 7
family 2, 14; conventional understandings 5; definition 38–9
family-centered care: elderly 65
Fanon, F.: *Black Skin, White Masks* 134
father: relationship 18
fatherhood: and Hindu child 17
fear: free from 21
feminist mothering 90–104
feminist mothers 92, 97, 100
feminist scholarship 102
feminist voices 115
feminists: legal 113–20; minority identity 115–16
fiction: Indian English-language 121–31; South Asian American 132–46, *see also* Indian fiction
Fine Balance, A (Mistry) 125, 129–30
Fine Family, A (Das) 123–5, 127
Foucault, M. 95n
free from fear 21
freedom: struggle 17

INDEX

Freud, S. 83; *Wörterbuch der Deutschen Sprache* 37
friendship 24
frontier spirit 13

Ganges River 143
Garner, M.: and Coy, M. 93, 95
Gay-Neck (Mukerji) 10, 11, 16, 17, 21
gender: asymmetries 6; roles 2; transnational family 49
generational inversion 87
generations: second 54, 58–60, 61
generic animal stories 9
Genesis 143
geographical consciousness 20
geographical recentering 20
geography: critical 106
gerontolgical literature 77
Ghatak, R. 20–1
Ghond the Hunter (1928) 14, 21
Ghosh, S. 24n
Giddens, A. 38–9
gift-giving: personal 60
gifts and donations: for second generation 58–60
Gill, R. 94, 95, 103
Gilligan, C. 80
girls: adolescent 102; little and sexualised clothing 92–6
globalisation 36
God: symbiotic relationship 28
God of Small Things (Roy) 126

Hariharan, G.: *The Art of Dying* 81, 82, 84
Harsh 60
Hasan, Z. 115
Hawthorne, N. 42
heimlich: and *unheimlich* (Freud) 37
Hell-Heaven 42
Hemat 59
hero 11
Hindism 143
Hindu child: and fatherhood 17
Hindu Fables for Little Children (Mukerji) 15–16
Hindu Marriage Act (1955) 116
Hindu Succession Act (HSA 1956) 106, 108–12
Hindu women: property rights 109–12, 117
Ho, J.A. 133, 140
Hochschild, A.: and Ehrenreich, B. 76
homoeroticism 24n
Horn Book, The 9
hostility: in natural world 19
household systems 11

identity 15, 135; Asian American 136; minority 115–16; post-modern 118
immigrants: experience sequestration 37; story 38
incest 122
India: Constitution 10; Ministry of Human Resource Development 97; Succession Act (ISA 1925) 109
Indian causes: donations 60–1
Indian fiction 6, 121–31; ethic of care 77–89; old critical modes 122–3
inequalities: unspeakable 103
inheritance 55–7; conflict 56; and debt 56; rights for brothers and sisters 105–20
Inheritance of Loss (Desai) 129
inner self: conquest 13
institutions: private care 68
intergenerational contract 77, 87, 89
intergenerational family 73
intergenerational reciprocity 88
intergenerational uncertainty 63–76
intermarriage 132–46; and assimilation 137–9
International Organization for Migration (IOM) 51–2
Interpreter of Maladies (Lahiri) 36, 39, 40
interview sample 53
intimacy 32
inversion: generational 87
Ishaan 55–6

Jaffrey, M. 135–6
Jani, p. 130
Jaya 61
Jhabvala, R.P. 135
joint family 40, 65, 67; adults and children system 66
Jungle Beasts and Men (Mukerji) 13–14
jungle books 9–10
Juno 98–9
juvenile fiction 10

Kabhi Khushi Kabhie Gham (K3G) (2001) 33–4
Kakar, S. 78, 121
Kannabiran, K. 1
Keep off the Grass (Bajaj) 125
Kehily, M.J. 93, 95
Kenya 55
Khan, A. 64
kin networks: remittances 55
kinship: ideologies 5–6; practices 23; systems in pre-modern times 25
Kipling, R. 8n, 16, 17, 18
Kissing Outside the Lines (2011) 134
knowing: and knowledge 100

INDEX

knowledge 19, 100; legal 112–20; politics 99; production 112, 113
Kolkata: old age homes 69

Lahiri, J. 35, 37–8, 39, 127; *Interpreter of Maladies* 36, 39, 40; short stories 3, 35–47
Lamb, S. 4, 63–76, 88
law: and space scholarship 113
lawmakers 112
Lawrence, B. 115
legal feminists 113–20; post-structuralist 114
legal knowledge: construction 112–20
legal norms: enunciation 119
legal pluralism 118
legal reforms 111
legal scholars: critical 112
legislation: enforcement 117–20
Lena 61
lesbian 101–2
Letters from Java (Roy) 18
Letting Children be Children (Bailey) 93
Levitt, P.: et al 50; and Schiller, N.G. 51, 55
life 80; and religion 50; stories 51
liminal space 39
literature: Commonwealth 121; gerontological 77
little girls: sexualised clothing 92–6
lived-in spaces 119
loss: equation 47
Love, Sex, aur Dhokha (2010) 24
Lucid Moments (Deshpande) 82
Lye, C. 133

McRobbie, A. 95n
Mahabharata 18, 18n
mahaprasthan plan 18
Mahesh 59
maintenance 73
Majeed, J. 20
male preceptor figure 16
Malladi, A.: *Serving Crazy with Curry* 128
malling 92
Marine Drive rape case (2005) 100–1
marriage: metaphorical 142; US 137–8
married daughter: parental care prohibition 78, 78n
married women 50; China 50; India 50; migration 50
Marx, K.: and Engels, F. 38
maternal paradigm 79
maternalism: limits 82–4
Meera 94–5
Mehta, A. 126, 127
Mere Mehboob (1963) 26
metaphor of contract 80
metaphorical marriage 142
midnight vigil 14–17

migrants: remittances 54–5
migration 38, 51–2, 127; continued 58; gender 49; married women 50; multiple 57–8; transnational family 48
minority identity 115; feminists 115–16
Minow, M. 82
Mistry, R.: *A Fine Balance* 125, 128–9, 130
Mitakshara school 109–10, 110n
modern family 34
modernity: consumer-led progressiveness 96
Mohanram, R. 78
money: family 61–2; flows 52; India 52
money tree syndrome 55
moral obligation 81
moral panic 90
Moss, P.: and Falconer Al-Hindi, K. 112–13
mother-child relationship 79
mother-daughter relationship 78
mothering: conservative and progressive 96; daughters 91; feminist 90–104
mothers 21; dilemma 5; feminist 92, 97, 100
Mukerji, D.G. 2, 7–22; autobiography 12; *Chief of the Herd* 14–15, 17, 18; *Gay-Neck* 10, 11, 16, 17, 21; juvenile fiction 10; oeuvre 21; self designated role 20; socialisation 17; wandering protagonists 13; World War I 21
Mukherjee, B.: *Desirable Daughters* 128, 130
Mukherjee, J.G. 12
Mukherjee, M. 121
multi-spatial dimensions 105
multiple migrations 57–8
multiracial South Asian families 135
multiraciality 135
Munoz-Darde, V. 86–7
Murali 57–8
mutually independent intergenerational relationship 66
My Mother India (Uberoi) 145, 146

Nagarajan, V.: and Parashar, A. 5–6, 105–20
Namesake, The (Lahiri) 127
Narayan, R.K. 123
narrative authority 132–46
National Old Age Pension Scheme (NOAPS) 72, 73
natural history: rational discourse 9
natural world 19
Nee, V.: and Alba, R. 137
Need for the Legislation (2007) 73
Nehru, J. 19
Nguyen, T. 136
Niranjan 58
non-family members 41
non-government organisations (NGOs): non-profit 68
novels: Victorian 25

INDEX

nuclear family 59
nursing homes 71

old age: home loving 70
old age homes 68; Kolkata 69
old age security 63–76; discourses 64; models 75–6; state 72–5
Old Age Security Social and Income Security (OASIS) 73–4
old communal ideals 131
Orenstein, P. 93
Orientalist concerns 6
outmarriage 137–8
over-sexualisation 94

Palacios, R. 76
panic: moral 90
Parashar, A.: and Nagarajan, V. 5–6, 105–20
parent-child dyad 15
parental care (*seva*) 66; prohibition on married daughter 78, 78n
parenting: intertwined modes 15
parents and children 88; emotional bond 16
Parsis 109
Pascoe, P. 138
paternalism: colonial 19
people of nature 22
personal gift-giving 60
Pew Center: *Marrying Out* report (2010) 137
Phadke, S. 5, 90–104
phele daoya 70
physical entrapment 141
pioneer ideal 13
Piper, M. 102
pluralism: legal 118
politics: communalisation 115; of fun 100; knowledge 99
positive ontology concept 113n
post-colonial scholarship 114
post-modern identity 118
post-structuralism: legal feminist 114; theory 114
potential reversibility 89
Pratima 71
private businesses 68
private care institutions 68
Project OASIS 72
property: understandings 113
property rights: demands 118; Hindu women 109–12, 117
Protection of Children from Sexual Offences Act (2011) 101
punishments 116
Punjabi wedding rituals 141

race: concept 132n
Ragged Robin 93

raising daughters 91
Raja, I. 77–89
Rajan, S. 19
rakhi 27n
rakhi-brother 41
recentering: geographical 20
reciprocity 89; intergenerational 88
relations: familial 7
relationships: brother-brother 26; brother-sister 26, 105–20; father 18; mother-child 79; mother-daughter 78
religion 53; and life 50
religious personal laws (RPLs) 105–20; rights of siblings 106–8
remittances 4, 51–2; Australia study 52–62; changes in gifts 58–9; kin networks 55; migrants 54–5; representations 48–63; second generation 54, 61
Resh, E. 102
residence: elder 68; right 110
respect for elders 64
reversibility: potential 89
rhizome metaphor 113
rights: inheritance 105–6; property 109–12, 117, 118; residence 110; siblings 106–8; women's fundamental 116
risk: and sexuality in urban India 90–104
rites of passage 10–13
romance 34; interracial 134; sibling relationship 24
Romance of Siblinghood in Bombay Cinema, The essay (Vanita) 3
romantic coupledom 23–48
Roy, S. 18
Ruddick, S. 79, 80–1
Russian Princes 12

Sarkar, N. 63
Schiller, N.G.: and Levitt, P. 51, 55
scholars: critical legal 112
scholarship: feminist 102; post-colonial 114
second generation 59; gifts and donations for 58–60; giving 59; remittances 54, 61
self-authorisation 141
self-control 16
self-interest 89
self-realisation: and self-sacrifice 21
self-transformations 7–23
sequins 94
Sethi, R.C. 132, 141; *The Bride Wore Red* 6, 132, 138–46
seva (parental care) 66
Sevenhuijsen, S. 79
sex: ambivalence 102; socialisation role 5
sexual risk 90
sexualisation: children 93–6; little girls' clothing 92–6

INDEX

sexuality 90–104; and risk in urban India 90–104
sexuality education: comprehensive (CSE) 97
Shangvi, S.D.: *The Lost Flamingoes of Bombay* 127
shares of sons and daughter: succession rules 108
Sharrad, P. 6, 121–31
short stories (Lahiri) 3
sibling-driven plots 26
siblinghood 24–5, 28, 29; good versus bad 33
siblings: adoptive 27; modern valuations 26; relationship romance 24; rights 106–8; songs 28
sickbed 83
Silvey, R. 114
Singh, S.: and Cabraal, A. 4, 48–62
sister-brother relationships 26, 105–20
sisters: and brothers 105–6
Sobti, K.: *Listen, Girl* 80, 87–8, 89
social contract theory 79–80, 81, 89
social field approach 51
social security 72n
socialisation 2, 17; sex role 5
sociological research 1
Solan, M. 36
songs: sibling 28
soul-mate: true 25
South Asian American fiction 132–46
South Asian families: multiracial 135
Space between Us (Umrigar) 129
space scholarship: and law 113
spatial dimensions 119
spatial practices 106
spiritualism 126
Sreenivas, M. 118
state: old age security 72–5; women's fundamental rights 116
Stone Center for Developmental Services and Studies (Wellesley College) 80
structures: family 128
succession rules: shares of sons/daughters shares 108
symbiotic relationship: God 28

Tagore, R. 17–18, 20
Tawaif (1985) 27
team spirit 17
technology 33
tentative location 142
Tharoor, S.: *Riot* 128
Third and Final Continent (Lahiri) 35, 38
Times of India 64
transnational family: Australia study 48–62
transnationalism: cultural patterns 58
true soul-mate 25

Uberoi, S. 145–6
Umrigar, T.: *The Space Between Us* 129
Unaccustomed Earth (Lahiri) 39
uncertainty: intergenerational 63–76
unheimlich: and *heimlich* (Freud) 37
United Nations (UN): Universal Declaration of Human Rights (UDHR) 72, 72n
United States of America (USA) 36; marriage 137–8; Supplemental Security Income (SSI) 74
unspeakable inequalities 103
urban India: sexuality and risk 90–104

values: family 127
Vani 94
Vanita, R. 23–34; *The Romance of Siblinghood in Bombay Cinema* 3
Vatuk, S. 88–9
Veer, P. van der 13n
Vendor of Sweets, The (Narayan) 123
Victorian novels 25
vigil: midnight 14–17
violence: anti-Sikh 14
voices: feminist 115

Waiting Room (Mehta) 126
Walker, A.: and Allen, K. 81
wandering 18; protagonists (Mukerji) 13
Wellesley College: Stone Center for Developmental Services and Studies 80
Westcott, M. 86
White Tiger, The (Adiga) 121, 130
white women 6
Wolf, N. 102, 103
women: consent 101n; fundamental rights 116; Hindu 109–12, 117; married 50; white 6
Woodward, K. 83
World Bank 76
World War I 21
Wörterbuch der Deutschen Sprache (Freud) 37

Yu, T. 133

zamindari clan 130
Zelizer, V.A. 52

www.routledge.com/9780415507592

Related titles from Routledge

Migration, Family and the Welfare State

Integrating Migrants and Refugees in Scandinavia

Edited by Karen Fog Olwig, Birgitte Romme Larsen and Mikkel Rytter

This book explores understandings and practices of integration in the Scandinavian welfare societies of Denmark, Norway and Sweden through a comprehensive range of detailed ethnographic studies. The three Scandinavian countries have had parallel histories as welfare societies receiving increasing numbers of migrants and refugees after World War II, and yet they have reacted in dissimilar ways to the presence of foreigners. The book analyses the impact of these differences and similarities on immigrants, refugees and their descendants across three intersecting themes: integration as a welfare state project; integration as political discourse and practice; and integration as immigrants' and refugees' quest for improvement and belonging.

This book was originally published as a special issue of the *Journal of Ethnic and Migration Studies*.

June 2012: 246 x 174: 192pp
Hb: 978-0-415-50759-2
£80 / $125

For more information and to order a copy visit
www.routledge.com/9780415507592

Available from all good bookshops